T0357665

"Kudos to Jimmie Hawkins, who has done it again. *[Bro-]ken and Unbowed*, that offered a necessary history of [move-]ments of resistance and liberation, this book provid[es]evolution of African American culture and identit[y ...] sis of a historian of religion and the commitment to understanding shifts in African American identity of a justice practitioner, Hawkins reminds us not only how identity has shifted but also why it matters. Further, while many talk about what Black people think, this book explodes the mythology of an essentialist monolithic view of Black thought and explores the various contextual contingencies that shape Black reality throughout several generations. I highly recommend this book to all who wish to understand the changing complexities of Black identity and the significance of its responsiveness to the concerns of each historical moment."

—Rodney S. Sadler Jr., Associate Professor of Bible and Director of the Center of Social Justice and Reconciliation, Union Presbyterian Seminary

"*The Shaping of Black Identities* meets people through a lens of lived experiences of Black Americans and their generational pursuit for a better life. It helped me to see my own biological family differently through the eras that shaped and impacted their lives. In my efforts to navigate identity of self, culture, and God throughout ministry, I find this book helpful in acknowledging who I am, who I serve, and how I serve them."

—Cecelia D. Armstrong, co-moderator of the 226th General Assembly of the Presbyterian Church (U.S.A.) and associate pastor of St. James Presbyterian Church

"What does it mean to be Black in America? Hawkins's analysis of 'Black generational uniqueness' is a weaving of history, sociology, pop culture, and the spirits of each generation from 1900 to present. From the cultural and historical moments to the movements and slogans that define generations, *The Shaping of Black Identities* is a necessary read for those both inside and outside the Black experience. For us outsiders, Hawkins provides a necessary grounding and understanding of each generation at precisely the time when anti-Black sentiment and racial tensions are high. Highly recommended for those interested in the liberation and freedom of all people."

—Patrick B. Reyes, dean at Auburn Theological Seminary and author of *The Purpose Gap: Empowering Communities of Color to Find Meaning and Thrive*

The Shaping of Black Identities

The Shaping of Black Identities

*Redefining the Generations
through the Legacy of Race and Culture*

Jimmie R. Hawkins

WJK WESTMINSTER
JOHN KNOX PRESS
LOUISVILLE • KENTUCKY

First edition
Published by Westminster John Knox Press
Louisville, Kentucky

25 26 27 28 29 30 31 32 33 34—10 9 8 7 6 5 4 3 2 1

Book design by Sharon Adams
Cover design by Stephen Brayda
Cover art by Lavett Ballard. Used by permission.

Library of Congress Cataloging-in-Publication Data

Names: Hawkins, Jimmie R., author.
Title: The shaping of black identities : redefining the generations through
  the legacy of race and culture / Jimmie R. Hawkins.
Description: First edition. | Louisville, Kentucky : Westminster John Knox
  Press, 2025. | Includes bibliographical references and index. | Summary:
  "An examination of Black life, culture, and the struggle for racial
  justice in the United States that describes six generations of Blacks
  and speaks to the active, liberative, and distinct historical attempt to
  define the self"-- Provided by publisher.
Identifiers: LCCN 2024052578 (print) | LCCN 2024052579 (ebook) | ISBN
  9780664269197 (paperback) | ISBN 9781646984169 (ebook)
Subjects: LCSH: African Americans--Race identity. | African
  Americans--Social conditions--History. | African Americans--Civil
  rights--History. | Social change--United States. | Generations.
Classification: LCC E185.625 .H3875 2025 (print) | LCC E185.625 (ebook) |
  DDC 305.896/073--dc23/eng/20241223
LC record available at https://lccn.loc.gov/2024052578
LC ebook record available at https://lccn.loc.gov/2024052579

Most Westminster John Knox Press books are available at special quantity discounts when purchased in bulk by corporations, organizations, and special-interest groups. For more information, please e-mail SpecialSales@wjkbooks.com.

Contents

Acknowledgments

This book is dedicated to my family. My wife, Sheinita; daughter, Kaela; and son, James, have been extremely supportive and understanding during the writing of this book. The encouragement of our extended family, including my sisters, Vanessa, Bonita, Karen, and Tina, has been so impactful. My brothers, Neal and Edward, are always a part of my life. Our mother, Elsie Lee, is the bedrock of the family and has helped make everything I do possible. Sheinita's mother and sisters, Mary, Deidre, Denise, Diane, and J.P., have made our family circle more intimate.

I want to thank my colleagues at the Office of Public Witness and the Presbyterian Ministry at the United Nations for their friendship and support and constant commitment to justice. As always, I want to remember professors of the past who have inspired me by their scholarship, mentorship, and faithfulness to justice and advocacy. The Drs. Earl E. Thorpe, Gayraud Wilmore, and, more recently, Brian Blount, have contributed to academic excellence for people of faith and all Americans.

I acknowledge that God, the creator of heaven and earth, enables each one of us to know ourselves as those created in the image and likeness of God, a God who gives us identity and purpose and who calls us to care and respect one another.

Introduction

Defining a generation can be challenging, and years don't always exactly correlate with people's experiences. In fact, it's so hard that the Census has given only one generation exact dates: the baby boomers, born between 1946 and 1964. Various researchers have defined millennials as being born anywhere from 1978 to 2004. Neil Howe and William Strauss, who are known for being the first to name a generation "millennial," include those born between 1982 and 2000 (later they amended it to 2004). *Time* used the years 1980 and 2000 to define the generation, as did the Obama administration in a report the White House issued in 2014. For this project, I defined a millennial as anyone born between 1980 and 2000, roughly anyone between the ages of eighteen and thirty-seven in 2018, though most of my interviewees line up with the Pew Research Center's new definition of a millennial as being born between 1981 and 1996. I was born in 1981, one of the earliest millennials. Sometimes I am grouped under generation X, or more commonly a micro-generation called the xennials, often identified as being born between 1977 and 1983. This microgeneration grew up in an analog world and came of age in a digital one.[1]

—Reniqua Allen, *It Was All A Dream*

This book is about Black identity. It is about how identity is formed and shaped by internal and external forces. It is about collective memory and the stories told to each succeeding generation about the lives of the preceding generations. It is about ancestors and the veneration they are due. It is founded in the categorization of generations of African Americans who lived in the twentieth and twenty-first centuries and the impact living in America has had on Black people. Most of all, it is about belonging.

1

For all people, identity is vital to developing a healthy psyche, and it provides a sense of belonging. Americans have been assigned subsets of identity profiles by a series of markers based on regional, biological, or racial connections. Nothing has impacted an individual's sense of identity as much as racial identity. Race has been one of the greatest demarcation lines for every racial and ethnic demographic. It serves as a tribal connector and generates commonalities in groupthink and communal aspirations. *Scholars have long concluded that race plays a determining role in the formation of self-awareness.* African Americans were divided into caste rankings based on how light or dark they were. In the 1800s Eastern and Southern European immigrants faced racial qualifiers that limited citizenship to "free white persons." Liebler and Zacher's 2016 study analyzed the impact that history, geographic region, and race have on a person's identity. They stated, "A person's race can impact their interaction experiences, interests, opportunities, health, and wealth, among other things. . . . The race history of a place is connected with the current identity claims of people who live there."[2] According to a 2019 Pew Research study, 52 percent of Black adults stated that their race played a significant role in how they defined themselves. Being Black was central to their ethnic identity and helped them express how they felt about their lives, while only 15 percent of whites responded in a similar manner. Eighty-one percent felt a sense of connection to a wider Black community, with 36 percent replying that they felt "very connected." This intuitive connection motivated 60 percent of respondents to identify that their participation in philanthropic service derived from a desire to help others overcome their common adversity.[3]

For Black people, the search for meaning is pivotal and ongoing. Black identity is rooted in the existential experience of being Black in America. For Blacks, racial identity is intimately connected to American identity, with a constant pull from each for dominance. It is a struggle that for many remains unresolved, despite the adoption of African American as an identity brand, though many prefer to be labeled as Black. Historians and sociologists often discuss the uniqueness of identity cohesion despite, and in many ways because of, the race-conscious nature of a society that constantly reminds Black people they are considered to be "outside of the norm." Native Americans, Hispanics, Asians, and other people of color live under similar societal pressures. Blacks, with the exception of indigenous Americans, are the only people who did not migrate to this land. Instead, they were kidnapped and violently trafficked for the purpose of commerce. Many are offended by those who ardently proclaim that America is a land of immigrants.[4]

Unlike other racial-ethnic demographic groups, Blacks are the only Americans whose heritage resides more in the color of their skin than in a connection to a foreign land or tribe. Few have an emotional attachment to the continent of African nations, as few rituals, beliefs, or customs survived the cultural extermination of slavery. The vast majority have no family memory of the tribes from whence their ancestors originated. For most, their story starts and ends in America, and they openly reject an African legacy. According to professor Howard W. French, the combination of American politics, popular culture, and miseducation prevented the development of a close relationship between African Americans and African people. Blacks were "denatured," separated from an association with Africans emotionally or mentally:

> For a very long time in the twentieth century, during the Jim Crow years in particular, African-Americans were encouraged to shun the idea of a connection to Africa, to think poorly of Africa—to celebrate traits in themselves, which supposedly distanced themselves from Africa, in other words, to think of themselves as more cultured, more Christian, more White, more civilized than Africans and therefore to look at "Africanness" as a matter of shame or a kind of taint that needed to be avoided.[5]

Not only is there a disconnect with Africans but also with other Americans. Separatist inclinations exist between African Americans and whites concerning politics, society, and thoughts about life in general. A 2020 survey reported that Blacks were much more focused on issues of racial justice. While more optimistic about the future, they were more engaged in social justice issues than whites and complained that racial justice did not get the level of attention needed to implement change. They defined whiteness as a privilege, and 80 percent stressed that Americans needed to become more informed on the history of white supremacy and racial injustice.[6] Seventy-one percent of Blacks described U.S. race relations as "generally bad" while 50 percent did not believe that Blacks would ever be treated equally to whites. Only 7 percent of whites agreed. Seventy-three percent of Blacks blamed Donald Trump for a worsening in race relations while only 49 percent of whites blamed Trump.[7] Scholar Anna Brown's 2019 research found that 78 percent of Blacks believed that the country had not made enough racial progress in granting Blacks equal rights while only 37 percent of whites agreed. Blacks were far more likely to have reported instances of discrimination. Fifty-nine percent of Black respondents viewed slavery as having a lasting negative impact, and 84 percent thought that race was a major factor in limiting opportunity.

Whites (54 percent) disagreed that being Black was a disadvantage or that their whiteness provided advantages. Whites attributed family instability and a lack of parental role models as prevailing causes for the inability of Blacks to advance. Political parties registered a huge racial disparity. White Republicans were far less likely to align with Blacks on issues of race. Whites as a whole reported that they were less likely to talk about racial issues with those outside of their racial grouping.[8] There were evaluative differences when listing the most significant lifetime events. Blacks were the only demographic for which any historic event matched the significance of the terrorist attacks of September 11, 2001, as 60 percent listed Barack Obama's election as one of the top ten historic events of their lifetime. Among whites, Obama's election was a distant second (36 percent) compared to the 80 percent who prioritized September 11. Blacks ranked the Civil Rights Movement in third place behind the election of Obama and 9/11, while it did not rank in the top ten most significant events for whites.[9]

This book is about Black life, identity, and culture. It creates a new listing of six generations emerging out of an examination of the Black experience in the twentieth and twenty-first centuries. It follows the organizational outline developed by Pew Research Center in its outlining of Americans who lived between 1900 and 2020. It covers the twentieth century and the first two decades of the twenty-first century, from 1900 to 2020. Six sections outline the generations and the perspectives adopted by those who lived the experience of that generation. It contains an analysis of the various cultural climates that have influenced Black life and culture. There is detailed information on the formative years of each generation to help readers understand general attitudes and perceptions and how they are influenced by the cultural, political, economic, and racial environment of the nation. It is the only book that names and characterizes all six generations from an African American worldview.

The most widely accepted identity charting by generation has been via the categories introduced by Pew Research Center. Pew's registry details generations throughout the twentieth century to the first two decades of the twenty-first century, stretching from 1900 until 2020. They are listed below along with their 2020 Black population.

- Greatest Generation (1900–1924): 2,200,000
- Silent Generation (1925–45) (population is included in the Baby Boomers total)
- Baby Boomers (1946–64): 8,300,000
- Generation X (1965–80): 8,900,000
- Millennials (1981–96): 11,000,000
- Generation Z (1997–2020): 11,600,000[10]

While Pew's generations are widely accepted, it is a tremendous undertaking to lump groupings of disparate people together and come up with universally accurate descriptions when the only consideration is period in time. There exist distinctions between perspectives even when persons are of the same age and geographical region. There is a need for reexamination in distinguishing generational uniqueness by creating a more diverse range of categories. Pew admitted as much in 2023 when it revised the way it would offer descriptions of categorized groups. It determined, "Even when we have historical data, we will attempt to control for other factors beyond age in making generational comparisons. . . . [V]iews have been influenced by external forces that uniquely shaped them during their formative years. These forces may have been social changes, economic circumstances, technological advances or political movements."[11]

There have been several efforts to expand Pew's chart in order to add greater specificity within generational groupings. Duke Research studied the ways in which local history impacted identity formation and determined that a person's identity can't be understood outside of societal influences. University sociologist Mary Elizabeth Hughes surmised that, due to different periods and regions, Baby Boomers not only differ from all other generations but from each other. She stated, "Who are the boomers? The boomers are a lot of people. Ironically, we fall into talking about them as if they are a cohesive group. But they are the most heterogeneous generation so far." She surveyed their characteristics and found the disparities so great that she divided them into two categories. Those born between 1946 and 1955 were labeled "early boomers"; those born between 1956 and 1964 were called "late boomers."[12] Beverly Mahone, in a *HuffPost* article titled "When Will African American Baby Boomers Be Counted?" called for racial specificity as it relates to healthcare:

> As an African American Baby Boomer and journalist, I am always amazed at the studies that come out involving members of my generation. Rarely do I read any health studies or statistics exclusively for older Black adults. . . . The overwhelming majority of those studies cater to older white adults. But the cold, hard truth is we get the same diseases, and we should be studied individually for possible trends in health conditions. . . . It's as if African American baby boomers don't exist, or our issues aren't important enough to be studied at-large."[13]

Investigation into Black generational uniqueness has been undertaken by researchers to assign Black identity labels. Undergraduate students at Rice University produced the "Kinder Houston Area Survey." It determined:

> Different generations of African-Americans grew up in worlds with measurably different opportunities, and their experiences may have had a lasting impact on their worldviews. The *Silent Generation* (born 1928–1945) endured the full effects of the Jim Crow laws. *Baby Boomers* (1946–1964) were the children of the Civil Rights Movement.

Generation X (1965–1980) came of age during the Fair Housing Act and the Black Power Movement. *Millennials* (1981–2000) benefited greatly from these major successes, despite the continuing realities of racism and discrimination.[14]

Denise G. Yull's 2014 paper on the impact of "race and space" in public education proposed that Black children needed an educational program influenced by the circumstances of their environment. She developed four generational groups that included Elders/Silent Generation (1930–49), Black Power/Baby Boomer Generation (1950–69), Generation X/Hip Hop (1970–87), and Generation Y/Millennial (1988–95).[15]

Ellis Cose, in *The End of Anger: A New Generation's Take on Race and Rage*, maintained that race must be considered in any investigative efforts to discern generational uniqueness. His study researched Blacks and whites according to their proximity to the Civil Rights Movement. He analyzed their judgments, ways they engaged with each other, and resulting perceptions. He summarized, "How Blacks and whites view each other has a lot to do with the era that spawned them. . . . The civil rights revolution fundamentally transformed Black-white relations and every generation since then has seen a further shift in that relationship. . . . Generations matter deeply, because experiences, and hence expectations, differ profoundly depending on the era in which one came of age."[16] He analyzed more than five hundred questionnaires and two hundred interviews and created three generations. Blacks were listed as "Generation 1: Fighters," "Generation 2: Dreamers," and "Generation 3: Believers." Whites were labeled as "Generation 1: Hostiles," "Generation 2: Neutrals," and "Generation 3: Allies." Generation 1 (born before 1944) introduced a new age in America as they disrupted the hold of Jim Crow on Black life. They broke down the walls of discrimination but were deeply scarred and therefore unable to trust whites. Generation 2 (1945–69), children of "the Dream," took advantage of available opportunities but still experienced lingering prejudice. Generation 3 (1970–95) was described as the one most unlike the other two. They were more hopeful and acknowledged that while racism existed, it could be overcome by hard work and perseverance.[17]

Bakari Kitwana's *The Hip-Hop Generation* examined how the post-civil rights era generation was the first to live without the stigma of Jim Crow segregation. While it was influenced by the previous generation, it also rejected many of its standards and looked inward for meaning. He contended that hip-hop culture manufactured the worldview of individuals who lived within its sphere of influence. "Collectively, hip-hop-generation writers, artists, filmmakers, activists, and scholars like these laid the foundation for understanding our generation's worldview." He noted that, ironically, the same power structures that hip-hop raged against for causing the plights of urban youth ultimately control hip-hop.[18] *It's Bigger Than Hip Hop,* by M. K. Asante Jr., focused on the generation following the Civil Rights Movement and dissected the influence of hip-hop. He documented, through a series of interviews, the contention that hip-hop was not the panacea it marketed itself to be.

> The term "post-hip-hop" describes a period of time—right now— of great transition for a new generation in search of a deeper, more encompassing understanding of themselves in a context outside of the corporate hip-hop monopoly. While hip-hop may be a part of this new understanding, it will neither dominate nor dictate it, just as one can observe the civil rights generation's ethos within the hip-hop generation, yet the two remain autonomously connected.[19]

Nelson George, in *Buppies, B-Boys, Baps, and Bohos,* explored the generation born after the Civil Rights Movement and created four distinct categories of Black young adults.

> There is the Buppie, ambitious and acquisitive, determined to savor the fruits of integration by any means necessary; the B-Boys, molded by hip hop aesthetics and the tragedies of underclass life; the Black American Princess or Prince a/k/a Bap, who, whether by family heritage or personal will, enjoys an expectation of mainstream success and acceptance that borders on arrogance; and the Bohos, a thoughtful, self-conscious figure like *A Different World's* Cree Summer or *Living Color's* Vernon Reid whose range of interest and taste challenges both Black and white stereotypes of African American behavior.[20]

Reniqua Allen has written extensively on "Black Millennials" and has a number of informative articles on the age group. Her book, *It Was All a Dream,* examined the struggles of young Blacks between the years 1981 and 1996. They initially believed in the promise of America but became disillusioned by societal barriers placed before them. Regardless, they refused to give in to despair.[21]

Utilizing Pew's timeframes, this book reworks Pew's initial six classifications into six African American generational listings. It presents a stratificational framing of Black people by creating six categories from the twentieth century to the start of the twenty-first. Over 120 years of generational descriptions are provided exploring how Black people born within historical time frames responded to life in America. Each contains the African American experience within segments between 1900 and 2020.

The generational categories are:

- *New Negro Generation* (1900–1924)
- *Motown Generation* (1925–45)
- *Black Power Generation* (1946–64)
- *Hip-Hop Generation* (1965–80)
- *#BlackLivesMatter Generation* (1981–96)
- *Obama Generation* (1997–2020)

Each generational charting explores the societal factors that played a role in the development of a collective spiritual, emotional, and psychological world-view as generations developed an identity shaped by their collective life experience. Each generation differed not only from white Americans who lived in their time period but also from previous Black generations. The *New Negro Generation* (1900–1924) were the children of enslaved men and women with high illiteracy rates and few institutional resources. They knew oppression and hunger during the Great Depression and responded by vacating the South. Members of the New Negro Generation are fewest in number and are over one hundred years of age. The *Motown Generation* (1925–45) were byproducts of the Great Migration, with parents born in the South and children born in the North. The *Black Power Generation* (1946–64, aged 56–74 years) grew up in the aftermath of a world war and the resulting prosperity. They were the children of veterans and benefited from limited application of the New Deal toward people of color. The *Hip-Hop Generation* (1965–80) lived during the Civil Rights Movement, the urban insurrections, the Great Society, the New Frontier, and Affirmative Action. The *#BlackLivesMatter Generation* (1981–96) witnessed openings in business, education, and entertainment. The *Obama Generation* (1997–2020) grew up believing, "Yes We Can!" They marched in protest of racial injustice and helped vote into office the first female vice president. This generation has the youngest members, with a scarcity of information available.

The development of each generation is studied within an examination of the political climate in which they lived. The generations responded to the harsh realities of life by blending attitudes and strategies into a communal response to advance the cause of racial equity. Tactics involved political confrontations, entrepreneurship, societal acceptance, and personal improvement. An examination of contextual American society for each generation reveals important information on factors that influenced each generation. The microscope shall be focused on the political landscape, with specific viewing of the role presidents have had on Black life. The expansion, or destabilization, of Black rights can be measured by the policy positions of an administration and the personal opinions of the one holding the office. Blacks understand that the *president* can have unparalleled impact on American society, especially on race relations. A 2020 *Smithsonian* article reported that presidents have immense impact on racial progress. "For better and for worse, the presidency, and its stewards over more than 200 years of history, plays a unique role in the racial relations of the country. The president has a tremendous ability to defend the civil liberties of the most vulnerable citizens and help heal racial divisions. Alternatively, the president can exacerbate racial tensions and enflame violence."[22]

While not widely reported, Blacks have been immersed in presidential politics in each epoch of American history. For generations, Blacks were legally and societally prohibited from holding office and even voting; nevertheless, they lobbied, advocated, and confronted those in office. During each presidential administration, Blacks lobbied, harassed, and confronted the president of their day, attempting to probe consciences and solicit protection of Black rights. No president escaped reproach as anti-slavery advocates made their case. Beginning with George Washington, presidents received letters, telegraphs, and personal visits.[23] Woodrow Wilson did not hide his endorsement of white supremacy and had to contend with William Monroe Trotter, Ida B. Wells-Barnett, W. E. B. Du Bois, and Marcus Garvey. Franklin D. Roosevelt's "Black Cabinet" pushed him to support anti-lynching legislation, or at the very least to condemn lynching. Eleanor Roosevelt's record on civil rights and alignment with the goals of Blacks was far and beyond the efforts of any president, including her husband. Walter White, head of the NAACP, met with each president between Calvin Coolidge and Harry Truman. Truman grew in his racial sensitivity after the blinding of a Black soldier awakened an officer's empathy. Eisenhower was akin to Lincoln when his desire to preserve the Union forced him to take decisive action on behalf of Black people. John F. Kennedy was beloved in the Black community as African Americans gained access to his administration. Lyndon B. Johnson's legacy was rescued by his advocacy for civil rights even as his deceit concerning the Vietnam War marred his presidential reputation. Bill Clinton is a beloved white president, as he bonded with Black folk on both personal and presidential levels. Barack Obama will be forever esteemed by Black America for providing hope, inspiration, and dream fulfillment through the image of a young Black boy gingerly touching his hair.

Each generation has often been disappointed by the lack of political courage and has judged presidents harshly for their inaction. In 1948, historian Arthur Schlesinger Sr. asked a group of fifty-five historians to rank presidents from George Washington to Franklin D. Roosevelt, utilizing personal opinion as a tool to evaluate office performance. Not one of the historians was Black. His son, Arthur Schlesinger Jr., did a similar study in 1996 utilizing the same five categories of rank: "Great, Near Great, Average, Below Average, and Failure." Arthur Jr. had one Black historian out of a group of thirty-two. African

American professors Hanes Walton Jr. and Robert Smith surveyed forty-four Black political scientists and historians on their evaluations of presidents. They arrived at differing rankings than either Schlesinger. Presidents were placed in categories ranging from "white supremacist," "racist," "racially neutral," "racially ambivalent," and "anti-racist." George Bush, Dwight Eisenhower, and Gerald Ford, for example, were labeled as "racially ambivalent" and Ronald Reagan as "racist."[24] In 2017, Walton and Tillery created an Editorial Opinion Score (EOS) from 9,406 African American newspaper editorials drawn from 43 papers published between 1900 and 2016. Nineteen presidents were ranked according to "presidential greatness." Lyndon Johnson was ranked number 1. Surprisingly, Obama was number 5 in the "overall EOS" and number 7 under "civil rights."[25]

This book is intended for all who want to understand Black identity and the generations that produced a legacy of accomplishment through struggle. It is for those who want to understand how Black identity has been shaped by internal and external factors and the response of an oppressed people. Each generation's story is a collective narrative that is still being written. We are all on a journey together, and we all want to better understand one another as well as to be understood. We all wish to truly know ourselves as individuals and as a part of a group of people united in history and desires. To be human is to be able to articulate one's hopes and dreams. By having a sense of personal and communal identity, we are able to connect with others. Knowing the details of the Black experience familiarizes us with the American experience and the connections we all have.

African American Generations

1900–2020

1

New Negro Generation (Greatest Generation)

1900–1924

The mind of the Negro seems suddenly to have slipped from under the tyranny of social intimidation and to be shaking off the psychology of imitation and implied inferiority. By shedding the old chrysalis of the Negro problem, we are achieving something like a spiritual emancipation. Until recently, lacking self-understanding, we have been almost as much of a problem to ourselves as we still are to others. But the decade that found us with a problem has left us with only a task. The multitude perhaps feels as yet only a strange relief and a new vague urge, but the thinking few know that in the reaction the vital inner grip of prejudice has been broken. With this renewed self-respect and self-dependence, the life of the Negro community is bound to enter a new dynamic phase, the buoyancy from within compensating for whatever pressure there may be of conditions from without. The migrant masses, shifting from countryside to city, hurdle several generations of experience at a leap, but more important, the same thing happens spiritually in the life-attitudes and self-expression of the Young Negro, in his poetry, his art, his education and his new outlook, with the additional advantage, of course, of the poise and greater certainty of knowing what it is all about. From this comes the promise and warrant of a new leadership.[1]
  —Alain Locke, "Alain Locke on 'The New Negro' (1925)"

This new generation presented to America a New Negro. Changed forever by living between two world wars, they endured an economic depression and created the greatest artistic renaissance in world history. They were talented, outspoken, brash, radiant, persistent, and driven to change the world. This generation was born and nurtured in an environment of Black empowerment striving to overcome extreme racial oppression.

The story of Africans in America is a paradoxical narrative of pushback and achievement despite the onslaught of racist discrimination and violent persecution. Blacks faced a rising tide of discriminatory actions that sought to limit their ability to rise above their assigned status, one of servitude and inferiority. American society consistently maintained a sympathetic embrace of white supremacy. Long-lasting psychological damage has been done to the American psyche by the embrace of Negro inferiority.[2]

Alain Locke coined the term the "New Negro" and was an outspoken critic of the suppression of Blacks in American society. He was one of the most influential individuals of his time and was a major influencer undergirding the Harlem Renaissance. In the introduction to his anthology *The New Negro*, he put forth the concept of a new self-awareness on the part of African Americans. He identified Harlem as the center of Black life and the hub for artistic and cultural expression. He announced that Blacks were correcting false and stereotypical images portrayed by the white community, and he called for Blacks to reinvent themselves according to their own estimation. No longer should one define oneself as a victim of oppression but rather as a person of worth with a healthy identity. He called on Black people to accept the wholeness of Black life, warts and all.

> The younger generation is vibrant with a new psychology; the new spirit is awake in the masses. . . . The mind of the Negro seems suddenly to have slipped from under the tyranny of social intimidation and to be shaking off the psychology of imitation and implied inferiority. . . . We are achieving something like a spiritual emancipation . . . renewed self-respect and self-dependence, the life of the Negro community is bound to enter a new dynamic phase.[3]

To contend with the repercussions of slavery it took determined intentionality to implement the political, economic, and social foundations that nurtured the New Negro Generation. James Weldon Johnson commented, "If I could have my wish, the Negro would retain his racial identity, with unhampered freedom to develop his own qualities—the best of those qualities American civilization is much in need of."[4]

In order to properly understand this generation, one must examine Black life in the nineteenth century and the previous generation, which could be properly labeled the "Liberation Generation" and consists of the parents and grandparents of the New Negro Generation. Their life's purpose was to overcome the deficiencies that existed throughout American society. Slavery had lasting impacts that inflicted societal burdens including illiteracy, immense poverty, disenfranchisement, and a caste system that locked Blacks at the bottom of society's barrel. Once separated from slavery's shackles, the Liberation

Generation labored to create a world unlike any that Blacks had experienced in the American landscape. This generation experienced a life of contrasting realities as tragedy and progress each competed to triumph over the other. Motivated by a desire to self-elevate, they created their own opportunities as each generation embraced a cohesive racial identity. In the face of opposing and, at times, conflicting ideologies from different leaders, Blacks did not wait for a messiah to appear and lead them. They took matters into their own hands. An unspoken yet shared covenant prompted racial alignment against the forces arrayed against them. They designed contextual strategies to challenge racist domination as they sought to limit mental and emotional subjugation.

There were obstacles impeding progress, but, nevertheless, there was progress. Despite the odds, their surreal reality prompted new modes of resistance. Baratunde Thurston shared information on his family's ancestor. "My great-grandfather was named Benjamin Lonesome, and he was born in 1879 in Caroline County, Virginia. According to my mother, he was part Native American, born a slave, and taught himself to read. According to his obituary, he moved to Washington, DC, in 1896 and started working for the Highway Division of the DC government in 1900. He died at the age of ninety-six."[5] Hattie Brown was told the story of her enslaved ancestors by her grandmother, Luvenia, who was born enslaved in 1848. Luvenia's father's name was Luke Smith and he was a thorn in the side of his owner, as he constantly ran away. When he was discovered, he would receive a whipping, but that didn't stop him. When Union troops were stationed in New Bern, North Carolina, at Fort Totten, he escaped with his wife and two children. She became a midwife and knew how to use plants for a variety of healing methods. Hattie recounted, "Toward the end, she often talked about being lonely. Nobody still around had been through what she had been through. She told these stories again and again. She drilled them into us. She knew that, from time to time, hard times would come upon us, and, sure enough, she was right. She wanted us to know what she had been through. She meant us never to forget."[6]

In the years between 1865 and 1900, in both the North and South, children experienced racial denigration enforced by law. Southerners limited economic opportunities for Blacks under the crushing debts of sharecropping and northerners withheld skilled labor positions. Blacks were locked into second-class citizenship with inferior resources and diminished dignity. White supremacy became the nation's political and social policy and impacted every aspect of Black life. Both wealthy and impoverished whites took every opportunity to remind Blacks of their secondary status. Impoverished whites looked down on them as inferior to feel better about their own lot in life. Following the Civil War defeat, the South initiated a malicious public relations campaign that portrayed Blacks as lazy, unambitious, unintelligent, barbaric, imbecilic, and criminal. Historical distortions redacted a treasonous rebellion to protect the institution of slavery, distorting it into a story of southern resistance to northern tyranny and demonizing Black people. A nationwide mounting of statues and memorials to southern white men honored traitors as having fought to defend their homes and families from northern political and economic dominance. Throughout the twentieth century, derogatory cartoon-like caricatures appeared in newspapers, magazines, and on the radio. They featured racist stereotypes and depictions of Black men as a threat to white society and to white women as dangerous rapists. False scientific theories purported white racial superiority and fed justifications for European colonialism and American imperialism around the world.

Children of this generation grew up in a society wherein southern states mirrored one another and passed repressive restrictions. Their earliest memories included drinking water from "colored" water fountains, sitting at the back of buses, and living in segregated housing. They were sequestered into dilapidated neighborhoods were birthed in Negro hospitals, and urinated in separate toilets. Despite progressive Reconstruction-era state constitutions, school segregation was introduced in North Carolina, Florida, South Carolina, Oklahoma, Mississippi, Missouri, Texas, and New Mexico. White teachers could not teach at Black schools. The education offered to Black children did not compare to the educational opportunities offered to white children. School officials intentionally kept resources to a minimum out of racial animosity, prejudice, and self-interest. Black children received limited education to prevent their achieving professional or societal status equal to whites. Efforts were made to program them to serve as domestics in servitude to white families and as low-paying farm and factory laborers. Recreation options such as fishing, boating, and bathing facilities were limited by segregation. Black and white baseball teams could not play within two blocks of each other.

Blacks of this generation were refused entry into public parks, beaches, golf courses, tennis courts, and swimming pools despite the fact that most were paid for with their tax dollars.[7] In Georgia, Black barbers were prohibited from styling the hair of white women. Bars, parks, and mental institutions were segregated. Segregation existed in life as well as in death via burial in segregated cemeteries. Rental apartments prevented the sharing of living quarters under the threat of imprisonment. In Louisiana institutions for the blind, for whom race did not matter, people were separated by race anyway. In South Carolina white children could not be adopted by Black families. Oklahoma had the largest number of Black towns and an equally high number of repressive ordinances. Interracial marriages were outlawed in Wyoming, Florida, Mississippi, Maryland, Arizona, Georgia, and Missouri.[8] New Negro Generation member Russell A. Harvey, 105 years old in 2020, remembered life in North-west Philadelphia. Growing up he loved to visit the Colonial Movie House. He reminisced about having to pay the same as white customers despite the fact that seating was racially segregated. "I would go, even though we had to sit in the balcony."[9]

By the first decade of the twentieth century (1900–1910), America was in the midst of a transformation from an agrarian to an industrial society as northern factories replaced southern farms as the country's economic bed-rock. Transportation was widely available as railroads and automobiles offered quicker and more comfortable movement. Communication extended to all as telegraphs and newspapers spread information from one coast to the other. Ninety percent of all Blacks lived in the South, with 60 percent laboring on farms as tenant farmers or sharecroppers. Women were largely employed as domestic workers as cooks, housekeepers, laundresses, and caregivers for white children. Ten percent of workers were in shops and factories; a minuscule 2 percent were white-collar workers such as educators, doctors, and ministers. Forty-four percent of Black adults could not read or write.[10] Black life expec-tancy was a mere thirty-three years while whites lived to an average of forty-five years. A Black centenarian from the South reflected, "The times I wanted to forget, but now realize I never will and shouldn't, are the farming days. We were up at dawn and worked until dusk. From the time you were able to carry a cucumber bucket, you were a part of the work force on the farm my mother sharecropped. There were eight children, and we were the only way she was able to make any profit on this farm."[11]

This generation matured in a world that was often a hostile, angry, and violent place, even for children. They grew up in the shadow of impending violence intended to teach them to fear white people. An Oklahoma State University study, "Evaluating the Oral Narratives of Minority Centenarians: A Case Study in Social Justice" (2018), reported on conversations with four Black centenarians. They reminisced on what it was like growing up Black in the beginning of the twentieth century. The conversations ranged from liv-ing in Jim Crow segregation to the Tulsa massacre.[12] *Black Enterprise* told the story of runner and author Ida Keeling as she recounted the horrors of life in America. It was a place where violence could befall any person of color and there was little one could do to prevent it. She remembered vividly the story of the young boy who was bouncing a ball against a wall with a sign prohibiting the behavior. The boy couldn't read. A policeman shot the boy and both his parents when they tried to prevent his murder.[13] Relations between the two races never completely healed as racial denigration and animosity left lifelong scars. Their mistrust of whites endured as they maintain a watchful eye on for-mer adversaries and are saddened, but not surprised, at today's racial hostility because they vividly remember the days of their youth. Daisy Turner, the daughter of slaves, was typical when it came to relations with whites. She was being interviewed at the age of one hundred and she asked the interviewer, "Are you a prejudiced woman?" The interviewer, named Beck, replied in the negative and later commented, "I expected to fall out of favor with her. She was suspicious of people." Turner's grandson, David Rogers, commented that she "used to have pots and pans on the door so if you opened it, she could tell you were coming in."[14]

THE PRESIDENTS

Those born within this generation experienced four presidential administrations: Theodore Roosevelt (1901–9, twenty-sixth president), William Howard Taft (1909–13, twenty-seventh president), Woodrow Wilson (1913–21, twenty-eighth president), and Warren G. Harding (1921–23, twenty-ninth president). The first three were born before the end of slavery (in 1856, 1857, and 1858), and Harding was born the year it ended, in 1865. All grew up in a society immersed in white supremacy and struggled to overcome popular conceptions of Black inferiority. They were not successful. Taft and Harding were one-termers and viewed as ineffective presidents while Roosevelt (1905) and Wilson (1920) each won Nobel Peace Prizes, neither for actions taken on behalf of people of color, especially Blacks.

Theodore Roosevelt (1901–9), the twenty-sixth president, was born in 1858 into a wealthy family. He struggled with infirmity and illness as a child and was emotionally impacted by the death of his mother and his wife on the same day in the family home. His wife of four years died giving birth to their daughter while, in another room of the house, his mother died of typhoid fever.[15] He idolized his father and spent his adult life attempting to live in his father's image. To overcome his extreme grief and earlier constant sickness, asthma in particular, he created a persona of extreme bravado. He was reluctant to second-guess himself in public, and once he made a decision, he stuck to it despite the consequences. He could be extremely impulsive and at times privately regretted quick decisions, such as a promise to not run for a second term as president. He is generally perceived as a progressive president who was concerned about the common man. He was successful in passing antitrust regulations that limited the unconstrained power of corporations, which caused the elite to view him as a class traitor. He projected American might overseas and won a Nobel Peace Prize for negotiating an end to the Russo-Japanese War in 1905. He gave birth to the conservation movement and preserved millions of acres of land as the inheritance of the American people.

Despite being the party of Lincoln, Republican presidents were less loyal to Black constituents and slowly eliminated from their platforms any mention of Black rights. They were hesitant to ostracize southern politicians and their voters. While recognizing the willingness of southern politicians to obstruct the passage of legislation, they failed to recognize the growing influence of the Black vote. Black voters were developing into major players in elections, especially presidential campaigns. Northern Blacks were beginning to flex political muscle in ways not witnessed since Reconstruction. Having grown up in a period of political hopefulness, this generation directed tremendous attention and effort toward developing relationships with the White House. They learned the significance of voting in improving their lot and the widespread implications of political power and influence. They were voting as a bloc and in each election were moving ever closer to being able to influence an election's outcome.[16]

At the beginning of his time in the White House, Roosevelt was extremely popular with Black Americans for his stated declaration to judge each person on their personal merit. Having nurtured a lifelong sense that he had to continuously prove himself, he measured others by the same yardstick and advocated that ability should open doors of opportunity. As early as 1901 he shared his thoughts on his convictions on meritocracy. "I have not been able to think out any solution of the terrible problem offered by the presence of the Negro on this continent, but of one thing I am sure, and that is that . . . the only wise and honorable and Christian thing to do is to treat each black man and each white man strictly on his merits as a man, giving him no more and no less than he shows himself worthy to have."[17] Edmund Morris, in *Theodore Rex*, wrote of the president's ideology about Blacks:

> Negroes could rise to the social heights, at least on an individual basis. Collective equality was clearly out of the question, given their "natural limitations" in the evolutionary scheme of things. But a Black man who advanced faster than his fellows should be rewarded with every privilege that democracy could bestow. . . . For those Blacks who did not, Roosevelt had little political sympathy. The Georgia blood of his unreconstructed mother persuaded him that the 15th Amendment had been "a mistake," and that, in nine cases out of ten, disenfranchisement was justified. Blacks were better suited for service than suffrage; on the whole, they were "altogether inferior to the whites." Yet, Roosevelt believed (as most Americans did not) that this inferiority was temporary. . . . Negro advancement must "necessarily be painful"–but equality would come, as Black Americans, generation by generation, acquired the civilized characteristics of whites.[18]

African Americans had made remarkable advances for a recently liberated people. They labored relentlessly to create a world where the injustices of the past were rectified by founding institutions of self-help. In thrty-five years, a landless, illiterate, impoverished, and politically disenfranchised people transformed into a free people making much out of little. A survival instinct caused Blacks to band together to create neighborhoods and towns filled with churches, businesses, self-help societies, and schools that produced teachers, lawyers, and doctors. By 1900, there were 1,700 Black physicians, 212 dentists, 728 lawyers, 310 journalists, and several thousand college, secondary, and elementary school teachers.

This was the first generation of Blacks to experience a small but developing middle class with neighbors who were professionally trained. E. Franklin Frazier wrote of Durham, North Carolina:

> Durham offers none of the color and creative life we find among Negroes in New York City. It's a city of fine homes, exquisite churches, and middle-class respectability. It is not the place where men write and dream; but a place where black men calculate and work. No longer can men say that the Negro is lazy and shiftless and a consumer. He is going to work. He has a middle class. . . . But the Negro is at last developing a middle class, and his main center is in Durham. . . . Through his effort and success, the Negro is becoming an integral part of the business life of America and is sharing particularly in the economic development of the New South, which is perhaps the outstanding economic consequence of the World War on America.[19]

Born in 1913, Dorcas E. Carter grew up in New Bern, North Carolina. She gave an interview in 2001 about a disastrous fire that consumed the homes of three thousand African Americans in 1922. She thought nostalgically on what her community lost in the fire.

> My community had beautiful homes that looked just like the historic New Bern homes right now. All of George Street was so pretty, and prosperous. The people always dressed so modest, so cultured. You could see the men escorting the ladies, lifting them up to the curb, all dressed with their canes and derbies. They owned their own homes, and they were self-made people. We had butchers and merchants, tailors, brick masons, carpenters, a blacksmith, a shoemaker, a barbershop. We had morticians, doctors, lawyers. It was a very dedicated, family neighborhood, until the fire came and destroyed it.[20]

There were color differentiations within the Black middle class. Among Blacks, a multicolored people divided themselves along light and dark venues; light complexion increased opportunity and denoted superior ability and intellect. Rather than embracing an appreciation for their natural beauty, Black beauty standards were measured by whiteness in skin tone, straightness of hair texture, and Caucasian facial features. The Black middle class congregated along racial lines, as those with light skin scampered to the top of the pecking order while those with darker skin struggled to catch the crumbs that fell from the table. Elite societies sought admission into the white world by mimicking their customs and mannerisms. Critics such as E. Franklin Frazier harshly criticized the Black middle class as selfish separatists. But not all agreed, as other Black scholars refuted his analysis and contended that it was much more complex a relationship. Willard B. Gatewood, in "Aristocrats of Color," wrote:

> Aristocrats of color exhibited a self-conscious elitism that bred attitudes and behavior marked by ambivalence if not contradiction. On some occasions this elitism led to condescension and even contempt toward those below them on the social scale; they viewed the social pretensions of upstart nobodies from the middle class as a triumph of vulgarity and the behavior of the submerged masses as a major source of anti-Negro prejudice. On other occasions the same elitism manifested itself in a sense of mission and a strong commitment to advance the common interests of the race. Aristocrats figured prominently in numerous civic, social uplift, and civil rights causes and attempted to utilize their access to the white power structure to temper the more blatant forms of white prejudice, and they also continually preached "the lesson of respectability and refinement" and offered themselves as exemplary models. . . . Rather than being either traitors to their race or mere imitators of middle-class whites, as their critics often claimed, they can more appropriately be described as a culturally and often racially composite people capable of blending black culture with the white culture they knew so well.[21]

The first institution firmly established after enslavement ended was the church, which served a variety of purposes. While a minority retained membership in white denominations, the Black majority joined denominations founded as symbols of religious freedom and social independence. The African Methodist Episcopal Church (AME), African Methodist Episcopal Zion Church (AMEZ), the Colored Methodist Episcopal Church (CME), and the Black Baptists created entities controlled entirely by Blacks. The institutionalization of faith went beyond religious empowerment, as schools, vigilance committees, and entrepreneur endeavors blossomed from ecclesial ranks. Black ministers were social, political, and economic leaders throughout the Black community and exercised authority beyond it.[22]

Political organizations lobbied for civil rights and an end to racial violence and sought to address issues directly. Political organizations emerged first in the North and spread to the South. Between 1893 and 1909, empowerment organizations created business and social enhancement, including the

National Afro-American League (1890), National Afro-American Council (1893), National Federation of Afro-American Women (1896), National Association of Colored Women (1896), American Negro Academy (1897), Women's Convention of the National Baptist Convention (1900), National Negro Business League (1900), Niagara Movement (1905), National Association for the Advancement of Colored People (1909), the National Urban League (1910), Association for the Study of Negro Life and History (1915); and the Universal Negro Improvement Association (1916).[23]

The quest for an education motivated this generation to pursue its most sought-after prize. There were nationwide campaigns to provide proper schooling for Black children. Parents were unwavering in its undertaking. Larcenia Floyd and her twelve siblings were inspired by their illiterate, sharecropping parents to finish school. Each of the twelve who survived earned a high school diploma in North Carolina.[24] Between 1912 and 1932, Julius Rosenwald partnered with the Black community to construct 4,977 schools, 217 homes for teachers, and 163 machine shops for students at the cost of $4.4 million. By his death in 1932, one-third of Black students were educated in Rosenwald schools in fifteen states. North Carolina had 813 schools. The African American community that wanted to build a school had to take the initiative. Remarkably, Blacks raised matching funds totaling over $4.7 million for the education of their children.[25] Alethea Williams-King described the herculean effort put forth by Blacks in her community of Blount's Creek, North Carolina. She commented, "The Rosenwald Fund required that each community commit so much to building the school. In other words, the Rosenwald Fund just provided seed money. That's all. They did not provide the bulk of the funds that it actually took to build the school." She cherished the memory of teachers who were strict but loving. "These teachers understood that they had to prepare these children for a world that would not treat them the way they did, a hostile world that they had to grow up in, because that was the nature of segregation during that time." There were six schools in Beaufort County, where she lived. Hers was made from wood and rose to a height of three stories. It was called the "three teacher school" because teachers were required to teach three or four grades during a semester.[26]

By the beginning of the twentieth century, Black colleges and universities had been established. Lincoln, Howard, Hampton, Tuskegee, Fisk, and others were training grounds educating a viable middle class. By 1900, there were seventy-eight Black educational institutions that educated Black students with over two thousand graduates. Hampton Institute (1868), Fisk University (1865), Berea College (1855), Atlanta University (1865), and Howard University (1867) were schools of pride. Many struggled from underfunding, yet those who graduated became leaders determined to expand opportunities for the masses. Black women played a dominant role in founding academic institutions to educate Black girls at Palmer Institute, North Carolina; the National Training School for Women in Washington, DC; and the Daytona Normal and Industrial School in Florida. Law and medical school graduates trained others and provided invaluable support to a people devoid of resources. Founded in 1876, Meharry Medical College (Tennessee) and Howard's medical school trained a new class of physicians to serve their communities. There was a school of architecture established at Tuskegee Institute in 1892 and Howard University in 1950.[27]

This generation was the first to have leaders who were college educated at both minority and majority institutions. W. E. B. Du Bois, Monroe Trotter, and Alain Locke were Harvard graduates; Mary McLeod Bethune and Booker T. Washington were HBCU (Historically Black Colleges and Universities) graduates. The first doctorate degrees were awarded to people including W. E. B. Du Bois (1895, Harvard, history), Charles Henry Turner (1907, University of Chicago, entomology), Carter G. Woodson (1912, Harvard, history), and others. The first female PhD recipients were Eva B. Dykes (Radcliffe College, English literature), Sadie T. Mossell Alexander (University of Pennsylvania, law), and Georgiana R. Simpson (University of Chicago, German philosophy); all graduated in 1921. Blacks served as editors of the Harvard and Yale Law Reviews in 1921.[28] Fraternal organizations included Alpha Kappa Alpha Sorority, Kappa Alpha Psi and Omega Psi Phi Fraternity, Delta Sigma Theta Sorority, Phi Beta Sigma Sorority, Iota Phi Theta Fraternity, Zeta Phi Beta Sorority, and Sigma Gamma Rho Sorority. Since that time numerous others have joined their ranks with the same mission and goals, which is community uplift through individual molding of character: National Sorority of Phi Delta Kappa, Inc. (1923), Gamma Phi Delta Sorority, Inc. (1942), Zeta Delta Phi (1962), Sigma Phi Rho (1978), Delta Psi Chi (1985), and Nu Gamma Alpha (1962). Since their creation, chapters have been established in Asia, the Caribbean, Europe, and Africa.[29]

This generation witnessed Black leaders as national figures who displayed a wide array of talents, strategies, and ideologies. They demanded equality, utilizing ideologies that complemented and contrasted each other. For more than half a century Frederick Douglass was the most influential leader of the Black race. With his death in February of 1895, Black America lost one leader as others sought ascendance to the throne.[30] W. E. B. Du Bois (1868–1963) was a proponent of academic training and organized, militant resistance. He was the most outstanding intellect, Black or white, in the nation and can be credited with creating a "Negro intelligentsia." Never lacking in self-confidence, he unashamedly stated, "I think I may say without boasting that in the period from 1910 to 1930 I was a main factor in revolutionizing the attitude of the American Negro toward caste. My stinging hammer blows made Negroes aware of themselves, confident of their possibilities and determined self-assertion." In 1903, he penned one of the most influential books on race in American history, *The Souls of Black Folk*.[31] Marcus Garvey (1887–1940) called for Black Nationalism, racial independence, and pride. He was born in Jamaica and created the first and largest movement led by and for Blacks in the United States in the twentieth century. The Universal Negro Improvement Association (UNIA) grew to 700 branches in 38 states and 200 branches worldwide. His movement controlled the Negro Factories Corporation, which in turn controlled grocery stores, restaurants, a printing plant, a steam laundry, and the Black Star Line Steamship. Garvey stressed self-reliance and pride in one's African lineage. Hundreds of thousands of followers loyally gave their support to the UNIA.[32] He stressed racial equality. "I am the equal of any white man. I want you to feel the same way. We have come now to the turning point of the Negro where we have changed from the old cringing weakling and transformed into full grown men demanding our portion as men."[33]

Then Booker T. Washington (1862–1915) ascended as the preeminent race spokesperson (1895), elevating the Tuskegee Institute as the premier institution of higher learning. He promoted economic subservience and social accommodation at the cost of Black pride and self-determination. His accommodationist policy appealed to whites who treated him as a favored son and financially supported his endeavors. His ability to direct white philanthropy kept most Black critics at bay. But not all, as he was severely criticized by the more radical leadership of W. E. B. Du Bois, Ida B. Wells Barnett, and William Monroe Trotter. Du Bois mockingly renamed Washington's speech "The Atlanta Cotton Exposition," calling it the "Atlanta Compromise."[34] In it he limited the quest for Black advancement to the service sectors of farming and domestic work, which was in opposition to Du Bois's agenda of creating a Black professional class.

President Roosevelt found appealing Booker T. Washington's ideological position that Blacks should stay out of politics and focus on economic and moral uplift. Washington became a trusted presidential advisor for Black appointments to higher office. Like white supporters of winning presidential candidates, they received highly valued presidential political appointments. Most of the Black appointees chosen by Roosevelt and by Taft were nominated by Washington.[35] During his administration, Roosevelt made the highest federal judicial and executive appointments of Blacks up to that moment in the country's history: Recorder of Deeds for the District of Columbia, Register of the Treasury, Navy Auditor, and several other appointments.[36] Robert H. Terrell was promoted to a Justice of the Peace in Washington, DC. Charles W. Anderson was the New York Collector of Internal Revenue, and William H.

Lewis was Assistant Attorney General. Despite southern opposition, Roosevelt refused to rescind the appointment of William D. Crum as the Collectorship of the port at Charleston, South Carolina, and performed a similar action for a postmistress, Minnie Cox, in Indianola, Mississippi.[37] It would not be until the end of the Second World War that such high-ranking positions in the federal government would be again held by Blacks.[38] Yet while he loudly publicized his appointments, he appointed fewer Blacks to political positions than his predecessors.[39] Historian Lerone Bennett Jr. was critical of those who received positions. He charged that most were self-serving and did little to help their community. He wrote,

> Black politicians produced during the early 20s and 30s were, by and large, men whose interests were centered on self rather than the community. . . . Black politicians of this era adopted attitudes of separation from Black community issues, these matters should be left to Black civic groups, because "politics is politics and civic leadership is civic leadership." Thus, Black politicians soft peddled "race issues" that might antagonize important elements in the white electorate.[40]

After only two months in office, the newly elected president invited Booker T. Washington to have dinner at the White House. He later wrote to a friend that he did not "know a white man in the South who is as good a man as Booker T. Washington." Blacks responded with praise for both Washington and the president, who was referred to as "our president."[41] The rest of America was not so kind. The white press and public were apoplectic and exploded in outrage. Newspaper headlines read: "Roosevelt Dines a Darkey," "A Rank Negrophilist," "Our Coon-Flavored President," and "Roosevelt Proposes to Coddle the Sons of Ham." The *Memphis Scimitar* printed, "The most damnable outrage which has ever been perpetrated by any citizen of the United States was committed yesterday by the President, when he invited a n***** to dine with him at the White House."[42] He suffered tremendous political damage due to his invitation to Washington, which left a wound that never healed. After the tumultuous uproar over Washington's dining in the White House, he never made that mistake again.

Despite early enchantment, Roosevelt's relationship with the Black community was unstable and filled with inconsistencies. After his Rough Riders were rescued by Black troops, he praised their courage. "We found them to be an excellent breed of Yankees. I am sure that I speak the sentiments of officers and men in the assemblage when I say that between you and the other cavalry regiments there exists a tie which we trust will never be broken. . . . I don't think that any Rough Rider will ever forget the tie that binds us to the Ninth and Tenth Cavalry."[43] A year later, he seemingly rescinded his earlier sentiments when he criticized the same troops with accusations that he had to keep them from retreating with a pistol.[44] Despite his public vow to treat a person based on personal merit, he carried many of the prejudices so dominant in the times in which he lived. He was against interracial dating and marriage and proclaimed that "race purity must be maintained." He held an extremely low perception of the personal dignity of Blacks, never taking into consideration the impact of societal and political discrimination as the primary cause for a struggling people. He believed that Blacks were inferior to whites in every regard, especially in intellect.[45] By his second term he was openly hostile to civil rights and Black enfranchisement. Roosevelt's upstart political party, the Progressive Party, contained white supremacist ideology in its platform as he endorsed the tyranny of home rule for white Southerners depite the South's racist suppression of Black people. Rather than challenge Southern legislators, he assured Southern whites that he would not disrupt the status quo. He praised Southern traditions and blamed lynching on the predatory sexual behavior of Black men. A reoccurring criticism he directed at the Black community was the charge of collective guilt for crimes committed by members of the race. He accused Blacks of refusing to disclose the identities of rapists in their community and stated that they were guilty as accomplices for withholding information. "The colored man who fails to condemn crime in another colored man . . . is the worst enemy of his own people, as well as an enemy to all the people."[46]

During Roosevelt's time in office, two civil rights organizations were founded to promote racial pride and the elimination of white supremacy. In 1905, William Monroe Trotter and W. E. B. Du Bois met with more than two dozen African Americans in Niagara, Canada, to establish the Niagara Movement. The original purpose was to diminish the influence of Booker T. Washington, but it incorporated a more extensive program. Its Declaration of Principles stated, "We refuse to allow the impression to remain that the Negro-American assents to inferiority, is submissive under oppression and apologetic before insults." It uncompromisingly demanded racial justice in the fields of criminal justice, employment, religion, housing, healthcare, and education. As the first Black civil rights organization formed in the twentieth century, it soon had 34 state chapters with 170 members by 1906.[47] It met annually until 1908, when a Springfield, Illinois, race massacre murdered eight Black citizens, exiled two thousand, and burned forty homes to the ground. The following year the leaders of Niagara met in New York City and established the National Association for the Advancement of Colored People (NAACP) to combat racial violence. Unlike its predecessor, it was integrated, with Black and white founders. African American founders included W. E. B. Du Bois, Ida Wells-Barnett, William Monroe Trotter, Archibald Grimke, and Mary Church

Terrell. Whites included Mary White Ovington, Henry Moskowitz, William English Walling, and Oswald Garrison Villard. In 1910 it established an office, named a president, and appointed a board of directors. Du Bois was named the director of publications and research, where he founded the influential magazine *The Crisis*.[48]

William Howard Taft (1909–13), the twenty-seventh president, is remembered more for the ire of his mentor and predecessor Theodore Roosevelt than for any presidential achievements. He meandered through his presidency stress eating and playing golf to relieve anxiety. He was of huge girth and once had to be pried out of the White House bathtub. (It was subsequently replaced with one that could hold three men.) He was the only American to serve both as president and Chief Justice of the Supreme Court. This one-term president's "dollar diplomacy" was sold as a means to exchange "dollars for bullets" and also served as a way of influencing foreign governments in Latin America and Asia.[49] Despite his ruined reputation as an incompetent chief executive, he did have several notable accomplishments. His administration filed eighty antitrust suits, created the parcel postal system and the Department of Labor, and established the Interstate Commerce Commission.[50] The wife of the president, Helen Herron Taft, planted the first Japanese cherry trees in the nation's capital alongside the wife of the Japanese ambassador.

Unwilling to make the same mistake his mentor and predecessor President Roosevelt made by inviting Booker T. Washington into the White House, Taft was reluctant to engage directly with Black Americans. He advised Blacks to trust southerners and to submit to the "guardianship of the South."[51] In a 1909 speech, he reputed an "ignorant, irresponsible element" (Blacks) and applauded whites for refusing to be dominated by such. He assured them that the federal government had no intention of interfering in the affairs of southern states and did not have the authority to stop lynching.[52] He also endorsed Washington's ideological program of accommodation. While visiting Tuskegee he commended industrial education and praised Black leaders who "evidently do not believe in attempting the unattainable . . . I am not one of those who believe it is well to educate the mass of Negroes with academic or university education."[53] He stated publicly that Blacks were to play no role in politics and supported racist theories of his day. In 1906 he wrote in support of Jim Crow laws that disenfranchised southern Blacks. He harshly judged Blacks as lacking the sophistication to be capable voters. "When a class of persons is so ignorant and so subject to oppression and misleading that they are merely political children, not having the mental stature of manhood, then it can hardly be said that their voice in the government secures any benefit for them." Taft was tepid in his appointments and rejected any to which southern whites objected, as they did during most administrations.[54] Despite hesitations, he did elevate Robert H. Terrell to a federal judgeship in Washington, DC, making him DC's first Black judge.

On April 3, 1911, President Taft was visited by Texas Congressman John Garner. He had sponsored legislation to permanently remove all Blacks from military service by repealing the 1866 act that created six segregated units reserved exclusively for Black troops. His goal was to eliminate any Black presence, as it was a rather safe assumption that no officer wanted Blacks injected into their ranks. Garner also requested that Taft remove the all-Black Ninth Cavalry from San Antonio, Texas. He complained that the unit had actively protested segregated seating on local streetcars and posed a threat to "law and order." Taft transferred the Ninth Cavalry to Rio Grande City, Texas, but was forced to rescind the order after protests from local white citizens. He had complicated an already delicate situation as the residents of San Antonio resisted moving the troops back to their region. Taft resolved the tension by reassigning the Ninth to Fort Russell, Wyoming. It made no difference to him that the Black soldiers had served admirably, providing security to whites who resented their very presence.[55]

Despite the fact that he sought to stay as far away from Black engagement as possible, the Black community was determined to engage with the president. During the second year of his presidency, August 13, 1910, the president received a letter from 150 Black ministers who urged him to use the resources of the federal government to intervene after the 1910 massacre in Slocum, Texas. They wrote, "An impartial enforcement of law and unprejudiced treatment of citizens, regardless of ancestry, would leave little excuse for a meeting like this. . . . It is the hope of the colored Ministers . . . as well as the hope of the colored people throughout America, that you may use the powers of your great Office to suppress lynching, murder and other forms of lawlessness in this country."[56]

The political savvy of the Black community was flowering into a sophisticated political machine. After careful deliberation, Black newspapers, for the first time, published articles in opposition to the Republican Party as they vigorously opposed Taft's reelection. There was a contingent of Blacks who disagreed and campaigned that the incumbent was the best and only option for Black people. They correctly assessed that Roosevelt couldn't win and that Woodrow Wilson would be no friend to the Black community, therefore Taft was the only logical choice. In an attempt to pacify those in opposition to his reelection, the president held out a fig leaf. In a 1912 speech given at Georgia Industrial School, he confessed, "I am fully alive to the heart pangs that a Colored man endures when suffering from the contemptuous insults of the white men not at all his equal either in point of intelligence or devotion to duty. I know the sense of injustice that has oftentimes burned itself into his breast when he realizes that his rights have been trampled upon and his claims to fair treatment rejected solely because of the color of his skin." His bid for reelection was futile, as he lost both the Black vote and the election and came in a distant third.[57]

The 1912 presidential election of Democrat Woodrow Wilson (1913–21, twenty-eighth president) was momentous, as he guided the United States through WWI and helped establish the League of Nations, even though Congress never voted to officially join. His most memorable phrase was in his 1917 address to Congress: "We shall fight for the things we have always carried nearest our hearts—for democracy, for the right of those who submit to authority to have a voice in their own governments. . . . The world must be made safe for democracy."[58] He made the world safe for democracy abroad but not for Blacks in his own country. His campaign was welcomed by Blacks, including W. E. B. Du Bois, hoping that he would be a racial moderate. His stump promises were music to the ears of many. "I want to assure them that should I become President of the United States they may count upon me for absolute fair dealing, for everything by which I could assist in advancing the interests of their race in the United States."[59] They forgot that while president of Princeton University, he had refused to accept any Black applicants as students. Soon after Wilson's election, hopes were dashed. One of his first actions was to support a bill outlawing interracial marriage in the District of Columbia. He installed segregationist practices in federal offices where they had never existed before. Not only did he segregate workers, but he also demoted those holding positions. He ordered that all applications include a photograph, which ensured the exclusion of Black hires. He refused to honor requests for meetings with Black leaders and refused to accept invitations to conferences convened by Black organizations. He told "darkey stories" in cabinet meetings using what he imagined were Negro dialects.[60] He justified his actions by saying, "The purpose of these measures was to reduce the friction. It is as far as possible from being a movement against the Negroes. I sincerely believe it to be in their interest. . . . Segregation was caused by friction between the colored and white clerks, and not done to injure or humiliate the colored clerks, but to avoid friction."[61] He responded to criticism by stating that his hands were tied when it came to racial discrimination.

This was not the nineteenth century, and a twentieth-century Negro confronted the president, who faced a Black community that had many human and institutional resources. Black businesses lent economic support as insurance companies, banks, grocers, retailers, undertakers, barbers, and beauticians provided services to Black people who were denied services by white businesses. Businessman Benjamin J. Davis commented to his Atlanta colleagues, "The white man does nothing with us that he can with a white man.

He builds businesses for the employment of white boys and girls; we must build businesses for the employment of Black boys and girls. We must have more producers of wealth."[62] With a focus on racial solidarity and Black capitalism, business organizations promoted racial cooperation for the development of the community. Business interests varied from "mom and pop" stores, retail shops, newspapers, theaters, hotels, banks, insurance companies, mills, juke joints, barbershops and salons, and funeral homes. Some of the most financially profitable were insurance companies: North Carolina Mutual (1898) and Atlanta Life (1905). Madam C. J. Walker made millions selling hair care products. According to Lerone Bennett Jr., at the beginning of the twentieth century there were "four Black-owned banks and sixty-four drugstores. The professional class (grew) to more than 47,000. There were 21,267 teachers, 15,528 ministers, 1,734 doctors, 212 dentists, 310 journalists, 728 lawyers, 2,000 actors and showmen, 236 artists, 247 photographers and one Black congressman (George H. White)."[63] By 1910, one out of every four Black farmers owned his land, and farmers had amassed more than 15 million acres of arable farmland. In that same time frame, Black communities created 275 Black-owned newspapers by 1910; ten years later that number had doubled. Black resistance manifested itself through editorials, news stories, journals, and peaceful protests around the country. The West Coast's *California Eagle*, the Midwest's *Chicago Defender*, and the eastern *Baltimore Afro-American* were important sources of information and networking.[64] By 1913, there were "40,000 Black churches, 35,000 black teachers, 17,495 ministers, 5,606 musicians, 3,553 physicians, surgeons, and dentists, 3,433 trained nurses, 798 lawyers, judges, and justices, and 1,700,000 Black students in public schools."[65]

This generation was filled with men and women who effectively lobbied the highest levels of government. They acted boldly and accused the administration of conspiring against African Americans to deny them their rights of citzenship. They were not intimidated by political segregationists and presented their demands in the face of those who did everything they could to deny them their rights. W. E. B. Du Bois initially supported Wilson but turned against him as Wilson emerged as a segregationist. He railed against the president and ruthlessly described him as unfit from birth to comprehend racial injustice. He emotionally criticized the president, "There was the greatest flood of discriminatory bills both in Congress and among the states that has probably ever been introduced since the Civil War. . . . We do not believe Woodrow Wilson admires Negroes."[66] William Monroe Trotter was even more damning and infuriated Wilson after an angry confrontation at the White House. Wilson revealed his racial insensitivity when he said, "Segregation is not humiliating, but a benefit and ought to so be regarded by you gentlemen." After hearing the president inartfully justify his actions, Trotter pushed back and reminded the president of his progressive campaign promises. It was to no avail. As Wilson angrily ushered them out, he made the startling announcement that if Blacks were unhappy with his actions, they could vote for someone else in the next election.[67] An already perturbed president was incensed when Trotter held a press conference on the grounds of the White House and revealed the details of the confrontation.[68] Black leaders continued to criticize the actions of the Wilson administration. They publicly protested the 1915 invasion of Haiti, resulting in the murder of hundreds of its citizens. And the president's viewing and endorsement of the racist film *Birth of a Nation* evoked widespread criticism from the Black community.[69]

In 1913 and 1920, Black women led protest marches against racial violence. Black activist leaders included Osceola Adams, Vashti Turley Murphy, and Bertha Pitts Campbell of the National Association of Colored Women. White suffragists organized a march in the nation's capital for March 3, 1913, but didn't plan on the twenty-two women of Delta Sigma Theta Sorority who, along with Ida B. Wells, attended. When they appeared, they were told to go to the back of the line of five thousand white women. Ida Wells and others walked in the midst of the crowd. The Deltas returned to march in DC in 1918 in a large march led by Bertha Campbell.[70] In 1920, New York City was stunned by the presence of ten thousand "silent marchers" who walked in opposition to racial violence, especially lynching. This was the largest march of its kind against racial violence. Elise Johnson McDougald wrote about Black women, "It is not surprising that only the most determined women forge ahead to results other than mere survival. . . . We find the Negro woman, figuratively struck in the face daily by contempt from the world about her. Within her soul, she knows little of peace and happiness. But through it all, she is courageously standing erect, developing within herself the moral strength to rise above and conquer false attitudes."[71]

During Wilson's administration, between 1910 and 1920, a perfect storm led to the beginning of the greatest migration in American history as Blacks deserted their homeland in the South for northern prospects. This movement had both formal and informal motivators. The major factors were the severity of southern oppression counterbalanced by northern economic incentives. Conditions that pushed them from the South included Jim Crow laws, lynching, disfranchisement, educational inequity, racial segregation, second-class status, environmental disasters, and racial violence. Isabel Wilkerson, in *The Warmth of Other Suns*, wrote,

> From the early years of the twentieth century to well past its middle age, nearly every Black family in the American South, which meant nearly every Black family in America, had a decision to make. . . . It

was during the First World War that a silent pilgrimage took its first steps within the borders of this country. . . . Historians would come to call it the Great Migration. . . . Over the course of six decades, some six million Black Southerners left the land of their forefathers and fanned out across the country for an uncertain existence in nearly every other corner of America. The Great Migration would become a turning point in history. It would transform urban America and recast the social and political order of every city it touched. It would force the South to search its soul and finally to lay aside a feudal caste system. It grew out of the unmet promises made after the Civil War and, through the sheer weight of it, helped push the country toward the civil rights revolutions of the 1960s.[72]

Like their white counterparts, Blacks answered the call of duty as 370,000 fought in World War I. Du Bois encouraged Blacks to participate in the war effort as a means to press for civil rights. Commissioned officers numbered 1,400, and 200,000 soldiers were deployed to service in Europe, with 40,000 experiencing combat. Under French command, Black troops received the respect they were fighting for back home.[73] Wilson's administration assigned Black soldiers to noncombat units and publicly claimed that they were too cowardly to fight effectively. The Navy limited their service to roles as mess-boys, and the Marines refused to enlist any who desired to serve. After being treated with respect by the French, they responded by fighting fiercely for French liberation. Some 171 troops were awarded the highest military honors from the French. Private Henry Johnson and Needham Roberts were the first two Black soldiers to win the French Croix de Guerre. No Black soldier was awarded a single Medal of Honor from their home country, the United States.[74]

President Warren Gamaliel Harding (1921–23) is widely considered one of the worst men to be president. He was nominated as a compromise candidate after nine attempts at a nomination failed. His administration is linked to corruption, graft, stupidity, and incompetence. The president issued a "call to normalcy," a term he coined when he mispronounced *normality*. After listening to his inauguration speech, newspaper columnist H. L. Mencken wrote in his column, "No other such a dreadful nitwit is to be found in the pages of American history."[75] His administration is remembered for corruption and graft more than anything else. His interior secretary, Albert Fall, was the first member of any presidential cabinet to be incarcerated. His Attorney General, Harry Daugherty, barely escaped the same fate. The previous Attorney General, Jes Smith, was found with his head in a wastebasket and a bullet in his temple. The Secretary of the Navy, Edward Denby, resigned his position after public exposure of his criminal activity. Charlie Forbes, Veterans Bureau, was confronted by the president, who was witnessed choking him while stammering, "You yellow rat! You double-crossing bastard!" Forbes was sentenced to two years in prison and fined $10,000. The Veterans Bureau's general counsel, Charles Cramer, guilty of graft, during an investigation of Forbes, locked himself in his bathroom and killed himself. Harding exclaimed to a friend, "My God, this is a hell of a job! I have no trouble with my enemies. I can take care of my enemies alright. But my damn friends, my GD friends. . . . They are the ones that keep me walking the floor nights!"[76]

Harding was reluctant in his approach to Black voters. During the 1920 presidential election he was visited by two groups of Blacks representing their religious constituents. The Baptists stopped by his home in the morning and the Methodists in the afternoon. Monroe Trotter was in their midst, and he inquired for an end to segregation in the federal government. To Trotter's surprise, the candidate stated,

> If the United States cannot prevent segregation in his own service, we are not in any sense a democracy. . . . If I have anything to do with it, there shall be good American obedience to the law. Brutal, unlawful violence, whether it proceeds from those that break the law or from those that take the law into their own hands, can only be dealt with in one way by true Americans. Fear not. Here upon this beloved soil you shall have that justice that every man and woman of us knows would have been prayed for by Abraham Lincoln. Your people, by their restraint, their patience, their wisdom, integrity, labor and belief in God have earned it, and America will bestow it.

A month later in Oklahoma, he backtracked from his prior position and refused to support the "Force Bill" in support of Black rights.

> Somebody asked me what I would do about the racial question. I cannot answer that for you. That is too serious a problem for some of us to solve who do not know it as you do in your daily lives. But I would not be fit to be president of the United States if I did not tell you in the South precisely the same I would say in the North. I want you to know that I believe in equality before the law. That is one of the guarantees of the American constitution. You cannot give one right to a white man and the same right to a black man, but, while I stand for that particular principle, I want you in Oklahoma to know that does not mean the white man and the black man must be made to experience the enjoyment of their rights in each other's company.

Trotter sent him a telegram reminding him of his earlier statements and asked if he was erasing his earlier position, as Black voters were concerned.[77]

Harding was a backward-looking man evaluating American life as lived in a small town. He lacked the ability to analyze the social changes the country was undergoing, especially as they related to Blacks. The state of Ohio's seventh son to be president failed to identify the political demands of Blacks and their growing activism.[78] He gave the appearance of possessing a progressive racial stance when he stated during his acceptance of the nomination, "Negro citizens of America should be guaranteed the full enjoyment of all their rights."[79] He boldly declared on southern terrain, "I want to see the time come when Black men will regard themselves as full participants in the benefits and duties of American citizens. We cannot go on, as we have gone on for more than half a century, with one great section of our population . . . set off from real contribution to solving national issues, because of a division of race lines."[80] Whites in the audience were stunned while Blacks applauded enthusiastically.

There was little effort behind his words. Even in the midst of spreading racial violence across the country, the president did little. There was the ever-present reign of domestic terror rampaging throughout the entire country. This epoch was filled with domestic terrorism manifested through continuous racial violence. It was a time of deadly racial massacres as whites attacked and murdered Blacks without regard to guilt or innocence. Harding maintained the racist policies of his predecessor and refused to render support to any civil rights legislation or policies. When elected president, he allowed the segregation of federal offices instigated by Wilson to continue unhindered. Just years prior to his election, racial massacres erupted, with the 1919 "Red Summer" of violence being particularly deadly. The Ku Klux Klan had reestablished itself with a much wider geographic reach from Maine to California. He would not allow the Justice Department to act against lynchings or the KKK. He gave the issue of racial justice little attention. Lynching was a weapon of terror utilized between 1900 and 1910 in which 754 victims were tortured and murdered; only 92 were white. In 1910, when Black boxer Jack Johnson beat white boxer Jim Jeffries in Reno, Nevada, between eleven and twenty-six Blacks were murdered and hundreds were seriously injured, by individuals and by mobs. In 1917–19, a murderous rampage of lynchings, fires, and massacres thundered across the nation. The Ku Klux Klan was revived, and Black soldiers in uniform had a target on their backs. By 1918, over 2,400 Blacks were lynched, tortured, mutilated, burned alive, castrated, dismembered, dragged, hanged, or shot to death. Advertisements of these lynchings drew crowds from two thousand to fifteen thousand. Trophies in the form of fingers, teeth, pieces of heart and liver, bones, ashes, clothes, sexual organs, and ropes were smuggled away as keepsakes. A macabre postcard read, "This is the barbecue we had last night!" There were no repercussions as white mobs posed for pictures with the corpses. Their intent was to maintain white supremacy by terrorizing African Americans to keep them from getting out of line. Every Black household understood the penalty for standing up for oneself and family—violence and death.[81] In the South, terrorism targeted individuals daily but evolved to destroy entire communities. From 1917 to 1923, thousands of homes and business were destroyed, and land was seized. Black communities suffered murder and widespread property destruction in Chicago, Tulsa, Omaha, East St. Louis, Chester, and Youngstown.[82] Violence beyond description erupted in Wilmington, North Carolina (1898); Atlanta, Georgia (1906); Springfield, Illinois (1908); East St. Louis, Illinois (1917); Tulsa, Oklahoma (1921); and Rosewood, Florida (1923).[83] In 1919, the "Red Summer" described ongoing destruction of life and property as twenty-six areas, including Longview, Texas; Chicago, Illinois; Knoxville, Tennessee; Omaha, Nebraska; and Elaine, Arkansas, were rampaged by racial violence initiated by white mobs who randomly murdered innocent men, women, and children. In July of 1917, East St. Louis was the site of one of the worst episodes of racial violence to date as false rumors spread that a Black man had shot a white Missourian. Whites drove through Black neighborhoods and shot randomly at any Black face they could aim a gun toward. Homes, churches, and businesses were burned as the police stood by and at times participated. The end result was the death of more than one hundred Blacks and thirty-nine whites.

Blacks lived in the midst of daily violence from a variety of sources. Urban Americans of all races experienced expansions in domestic altercations and murder. Between 1900 and 1925, the nation's homicide rate nearly doubled in Baltimore. It tripled in New Orleans and Chicago and quadrupled in Cleveland. White public perception blamed the rise in crime on Negroes and immigrants. According to scholar Jeffrey S. Adler, "The urban violence of the 1920s, however, was another matter and included an explosion in robberies and robbery-homicides. A new breed of criminal seemed more calculating and more predatory, as holdup men and bank robbers, armed with Thompson submachine guns and fast getaway cars, invaded business districts, targeted respectable citizens, and evaded law enforcers."[84] Antiquated policing led to prosecution rates in the twentieth percentiles. Under the extreme pressure of urban living, violence increased within the Black community. Chicago saw an increase in domestic violence and intimate murders. One study reported on family murders within the Black, German, and Italian migrant communities and the differing causes. Both white and Black women murdered family members, but white women were far more likely to murder their children. When white women murdered, over half of the victims were children. Black women murdered their children only 2.3 percent of the time. Black women killed mostly Black men (95.4 percent), and between 1911 and 1920, 100 percent of those killed were men. Almost none of the Black women attempted suicide afterward while under half (44 percent) of white women did. For Black families, the causation was disagreement over gender roles complicated by the stresses of poverty; dilapidated housing; and discrimination in employment, housing, and education. Poverty incinerated the masculinity of men, and both genders struggled with their inability to provide for the family. Most of the killings were by spouses and girlfriends in response to domestic violence. Adler surmised, "The combination of strong women and emotionally besieged men proved to be explosive. Such circumstances also account for the absence of suicide or attempted suicide by African-American husband killers. . . . Most African-American husband killers felt justified in their actions."[85]

America has always demonstrated an obsession with skin color. Detrimental lessons of caste and class distinctions have been passed along socioeconomic lines as well as from one race to another. Each racial demographic adopted the white community's color hierarchy. America's preoccupation with skin color was evident during the administration of President Harding. Ironically, Harding's family was targeted for abuse over the suspicion that they were Black. There was little doubt in the minds of those familiar with the family of their biracial composition. His mother was a midwife, an occupation held widely by Black women. Throughout their school years the Harding children were called the N-word because of their bronze complexions. According to historian Nathan Miller, "The boy grew up amid gossip that haunted him all the way to the White House, that the Hardings had African American blood. At school, Warren and the other Harding children were taunted as 'n*****s.'"[86] When he proposed to the daughter of the town's banker, Florence "Floss" Kling De Wolfe, his potential father-in-law absolutely refused to allow Harding to marry his daughter. In a public confrontation on a city street, he accused him of being Black. William Estabrook Chancellor, 1920 Republican opposition candidate, disliked Harding and hated Black people. He undertook an investigation of Harding's race. He labeled Harding's father as a mulatto, describing the thickness of his lips and skin like chocolate. During his campaign, rumors flooded the country. Several papers, including the *Chicago Tribune* and the *Washington Post*, supported his suspicions. An October leaflet declared,

> Warren Gamaliel Harding is not a white man; He is not a Creole; He is not a mulatto; he is a mestizo, as his physical feature show. I might cite the names of scores of persons who have always considered Warren Gamaliel Harding a colored man and who resent his present masquerade as a white candidate upon the ticket of a hitherto honorable and dignified party. . . . Of hundreds of persons interviewed all those who knew him as a rural schoolboy and as a college student,

everyone without exception says that Warren Gamaliel Harding was always considered a colored boy and nicknamed accordingly.[87]

On August 2, 1923, Harding died suddenly after only three years in office. The aftermath revealed massive corruption in his cabinet. Du Bois exclaimed in frustration, "May God write us down as asses, if ever again we are found putting our trust in either the Republican or the Democratic Parties."[88] There was generated an aura of sophistication, class, and fashion that did not elude Black America.[89] By the end of Harding's term, northern Black voters began to actualize the transition from voting predominantly for Republicans and were moving to the Democratic Party.

SUMMARY OF THE NEW NEGRO GENERATION

The New Negro Generation (1900–1924) is the most advanced in age of any of the six generations. In 2020, most of its members were centenarians, between 120 and 96 years of age. According to the New England Centenarian Study, certain characteristics can be concluded about all centenarians. Fifty percent of men in this category have longevity in their family, with 17 percent of their siblings being likely to reach one hundred years of age. Their children also have a remarkable chance of living until the age of one hundred. Most had children after the age of thirty-five, were thin, and were not frequent smokers.[90] According to the 1980 census, about 75–83 percent of centenarians are white while 14–21 percent are Black; between 2 and 6 percent are Hispanic. In 2016, there were 9,476 African Americans one hundred years old or older (1,783 men and 7,693 women). They comprised 12 percent of all centenarians. Between 1980 and 2018, centenarians had the highest growth rate of any age demographic in the United States. In 1980, there were 32,194 total centenarians; by 2018 the number almost tripled to 93,927 adults aged one hundred years old or older. In 2017, some 12 percent were African American, totaling 9,986 comprised of 8,053 women and 1,933 men.[91] They constituted 0.2 percent of those sixty-five years or older. Those aged eighty-five and older are expected to expand twofold from 6.5 million in 2018 to 14.4 million by 2030, a 123 percent increase.[92] There was a decrease in mortality differences as between 9 and 27 percent of Black centenarians were over 105 years while 4–10 percent of whites are of similar age. Around 50 percent live alone or in a single-family unit; women are more likely to live in a setting with a group. Only 14 to 33 percent of Blacks live in a group setting. The vast majority are widowed women. Blacks are more impoverished than whites, with 40 percent being poor. Women are more educated than men, upwards of 60 percent of whom have an eighth-grade education or below.[93]

The Georgia Centenarian Study disclosed several health disparities between whites and New Negro Generation members for a small number of diseases. Blacks suffer more from diabetes and hypertension while whites suffer more from osteoporosis. Whites experience better physical and cognitive functioning than African Americans. African Americans have more of a history with smoking and obesity.[94] There have been informal discussions on the rate of aging between the races. Within the Black community, phrases such as "Black don't crack" hint at a belief that Blacks age better than whites and live longer. Robert Douglas Young, in his gerontology thesis at Georgia State University, explored the long-standing myth linking race with longevity and the thought that African Americans had a propensity for living longer and in better health. He noted that in 2006, the oldest living persons in nine of the eleven former Confederate States of America and Washington, DC, were Black. Three of the oldest four were African American. He deduced that if a white person and a Black person both lived to be eighty years of age, the latter tended to eventually outlive the former.[95] A 2019 study by Rutgers New Jersey Medical School found that the darker melanin in Black faces prevents damaging ultraviolet rays from causing aging and wrinkling. Dr. Boris Paskhover revealed that the facial bones in Blacks are denser and don't break down as easily over time. The *Journal of the American Geriatrics Society* published a report that also concluded that there was a decrease in the Black mortality rate for centenarians. "A possible phenomenon called the Black-white mortality crossover. . . . Although mortality was higher for Blacks than for whites at younger ages. . . . There remained the possibility that, after some older age, mortality for Blacks became lower than for whites."[96]

The Black experience has been a constant battle to dismantle the assault of racial inferiority for both the individual and the community. Blacks were uniquely impacted by prejudicial obstacles placed in their path that informed their views on the nation, and even themselves. This generation was told to fight back and to give as good as they received from fathers who had experienced war and mothers who modeled how to survive. They were taught to be fighters and resisters to oppression. Thurgood Marshall's father told him, "If someone calls you a 'N*****' take it up right then and there."[97] Langston Hughes wrote in the 1945 *Negro Digest* of her refusal to pay a different price for a meal than what her white friend paid. Rather than subject herself to unfair treatment, she put the tray down in front of the racist cashier and walked out.[98]

The New Negro Generation love their family and enjoy visits. They are especially devoted to grand and great grandchildren. Black people stay connected with their extended families, and this provides a sense of love and care. They come from large families, as infant mortality was high and the extra hands were needed to work on the farm. Families with no less than seven or eight siblings were the norm. Oftentimes, brothers and sisters were responsible for young siblings, especially the females. Emily Boone grew up in a family with twelve children in San Diego and had wonderful memories of family life together. She came from a musical family. The children would sing while her father strummed the guitar. She reflected, "When the other kids were playing, I loved to stay inside with Mother (learning to crochet)."[99] In 2020, Hester Ford was 116 years of age. She grew up on a farm, married at fourteen, purchased a farm, and raised a family. When she died, she had 12 children, 68 grandchildren, 125 great-grandchildren and 120 great-great-grandchildren.[100] The South Carolina native lived in Charlotte, North Carolina, with her daughter, who took her for a walk each day, something that she looked forward to.[101]

Despite living in a time of constant threat, hostility was offset by the love and nurture of parents who protected and provided for their needs. Children were educated by elders who wanted them to emerge from domestic terrorism as mentally healthy human beings. Parents pursued the primary goal of the alleviation of racist discrimination and worked to create paths of opportunity for their children. Parents were on constant guard that their children did not adopt a subservient consciousness despite the degrading perceptions propagated in society. They learned lessons from parents who were deceitfully submissive in the presence of whites but taught their children resistance. Black children were well aware that they lived in a world where they were devalued. Actress and singer Lena Horne, who died in 2010 at the age of ninety-two, was uncompromising in her racial identity. She refused to be pigeonholed in minor roles as a maid and was a vocal advocate against racism. The *New York Times* listed this quote in her obituary: "My identity is very clear to me now. I am a black woman. I'm free. I no longer have to be a 'credit.' I don't have to be a symbol to anybody; I don't have to be a first to anybody. I don't have to be an imitation of a white woman that Hollywood sort of hoped I'd become. I'm me, and I'm like nobody else."[102]

New Negro Generation members were strengthened by a philosophy of tough love, hard work, and quiet endurance. They grew up hearing that these were hard times and only the strong survive; at the time, this was a motif of Black life. They did not have time to feel sorry for themselves because the world did not care. Life is hard and complaining does you no good. Dr. Walter Reynolds's children had three proverbs drilled into their minds: "Life is tough, but you have to be tougher. Keep a positive attitude even though things get hard. There will always be opportunities for you to excel."[103] Edna L. Middleton, 102, lived a full and rich life, unafraid of hard work. During World War II she worked in in the Charleston Naval Shipyard as a riveter, a job normally associated with men and Rosie the Riveter.[104] Bishop Henry Beard Delany was the first elected Black bishop of the Episcopal Church, U.S.A. He and his wife, Nanny James Logan, instilled in their children a sense of regal pride that they were not better than anyone else and that no one else was better than they were. Their daughters, Sarah and Bessie, wrote a book titled *Having Our Say*. In it they wrote, "In 1918 Papa became the first elected Negro bishop of the Episcopal Church, U.S.A. That's a long way for a man who was born a slave on a Georgia plantation. But if you had known Papa, you wouldn't be surprised. He was always improving himself, and he and Mama taught us to reach high."[105] The Senior Historian at the National World War II Museum in New Orleans, Rob Citino, stated that the U.S. military had "racist characterizations" of African American soldiers during the war. "We went to war with Hitler, the world's most horrible racist, and we did so with a segregated army because, despite guarantees of equal treatment, this was still Jim Crow America. African Americans were still subject to all kinds of limitations and discrimination based on the color of their skin. I think they were fighting for the promise of America rather than the reality of America."[106] At the age of 110, Lawrence Brooks shared his pride in serving during World War II. He revealed conflicting memories of his time in the military. He gained much from the training and self-discipline the army instilled in him but was saddened and hurt by the way he was treated. He served in an army fighting against evil overseas, but the institution lacked the ability to see the evil it inflicted on its own Black citizens. "I was treated so much better in Australia than I was by my own white people. I wondered about that. That's what worried me so much."[107]

They internalized the values of thriftiness. Elders repeated to them that if they were to acquire anything, they would have to earn it on their own. Parents taught them to value every dollar earned and to save as much as possible. This generation believes in saving money and acquiring property, primarily land, and once you get it, you keep it in the family. Investments in land acquisition were for the purpose of obtaining economic security. They were determined to bequeath property to their children and to provide an economic foundation. Clifton L. Taulbert said, "In the agrarian South, land ownership more than any other factor decided who had status; the more land a person owned, the more he was worth."[108] The Great Depression and the lack of everything during that time has remained a vital lesson to be prepared. Their fathers were farm laborers who struggled as migrant workers, sharecroppers, and tenant farmers. Their mothers had to work as hard as their fathers; one-third of Black women performed the same backbreaking work on the farm. Few received wages equal to white farmers, and they rarely broke even by the year's end. Those off the farm were unskilled laborers in the service industry and held the lowest-paying jobs in low-wage factories.[109] A rare few of their neighbors owned their farms while whites were far more likely to own the land they worked. Their parents either rented or leased the home they lived in. According to the 1900 Census, 90 percent of this generation spent their childhood on a southern farm in a home their family did not own. Only one-fifth owned their homes compared to white home ownership, which was twice that total. They worked deliberately to purchase land and establish themselves as vibrant parts of their community with a stake in life.

This generation greatly values education and encouraged their children and grandchildren to acquire it. They were taught to get an education and taught the same to their children as a pathway to success. They sent their children to college in record numbers. They are willing to help financially as long as their money is not being wasted. Children started life with little or insufficient access to education. Few attended schools, and those who did were taught in inadequate buildings amid a scarcity of books. This lack birthed something inside of them determined to overcome. After the right to vote, education was a priority for Black parents who wanted their children to have everything they were denied, especially literacy. A 2018 Oklahoma State University study stated, "One centenarian was so deeply affected by her impoverished childhood that she vowed her children would receive an education and always have nice clothing to wear. She remembered being isolated and lonely during her childhood due to the lack of resources her family had. Another centenarian came from a family of educators and taught in a segregated school system, eventually working his way up to principal."[110]

Audrey James was one of the first Black students to enroll in the University of Nevada, Las Vegas. She was the only Black student in her literature class. While teaching first grade at an elementary school, she took classes in the evening and each summer until she graduated with a Bachelor of Science degree in elementary education in 1965. She continued her studies, and in 1971 she was awarded a Master of Education degree. She inspired two of her nieces to also attend UNLV, where they both earned degrees in education. They fondly remember her motivational words: "To believe in the almighty God. With that kind of faith, you can succeed. You can overcome the barriers. And, of course, you need to go to school. That's the main thing. Stay in school. Because it helps you to live a better life, all the way around."[111] Dr. Walter Reynolds was the first African American to graduate from the University of Oregon Medical School. His father insisted that his children seek an education, as his own was prohibited after the fifth grade. His oldest son earned a master's degree from the University of Washington and motivated his brother to be just as ambitious. Reynolds enrolled his children in all-white elementary, middle, and high schools.[112] One hundred-year-old John Morton-Finney of Kentucky had earned eleven academic degrees by 1989. He joined the army and served in the Philippines. He worked as a teacher and lawyer and learned six languages. He defended his love of acquiring education: "I always kept in mind how (his parents) were denied, by law and by custom, the right to read or write."[113]

Despite their advanced age, many are extremely optimistic, with a fine sense of humor. They expressed feelings of being blessed to see another day and are grateful to be alive after enduring the worst hardships of life. Susannah Mushatt Jones of New York City loves to start each day with a breakfast of bacon, grits, and scrambled eggs. She is described as feisty and adores wearing lacy lingerie. She justifies her behavior by saying, "You can never get too old to wear fancy stuff."[114] Her niece, Lavilla Watson, describes her as having "a tremendous work ethic and enjoys life." Ninety-four-year-old Martha Tucker finally got to enjoy a joy denied to her when she got married: wearing a wedding dress. When she wed in Jim Crow Birmingham, Alabama, she was refused entry into the retail store and could only hunt through a box in the basement for secondhand attire. Arriving at the boutique, she was so excited that she tried on two dresses and a garter. Despite the fact that it occurred seventy years after her wedding and forty-five years after the death of her husband, she exclaimed, "I always said before I left this world that I was going to get in a wedding dress. And I'm glad I did. . . . My dream has come true."[115]

In 2020, Louisiana resident Lawrence Brooks was the oldest World War II veteran at 111 years old. He was born September 12, 1909, and served in the 91st Engineer Battalion in New Guinea and the Philippines. On the National WWII Museum's YouTube channel, he laughingly recounted the time when he was aboard a C-47 military plane carrying barbed wire from Australia to New Guinea. After discarding the barbed wire in the ocean, he moved closer to the front of the plane. His plans were to stay close to the pilot and copilot, the only two crew members with parachutes. He remembered saying, "If they go out there and jump, I'm gonna grab one of them."[116] Maggie Katie Brown Kidd celebrated her 114th birthday on December 8, 2018. She revealed that she was not opposed to dating.[117] Alison Velez Lane remarked of her 102-year-old friend, Edna Middleton, "Edna was so full of life and loved life. She was never mean and was a sweet spirit. She was a hero who lived for decades."[118] Ethel Jones, 102, was described by Rochelle Sherlock, the Coordinator of the Senior Coalition of Vallejo, California, as one of the most positive people she had ever encountered:

Somehow this remarkable woman managed to be grateful for all that she had been given. She did not resent or distrust others, nor did she become embittered by her circumstances. Rather, she lived in appreciation and cultivated a heart of loving and kindness. Ethel's countenance radiated with joy, and she whole-heartedly embraced others. She loved to sing and volunteered into her nineties at the senior center in the Tenderloin District of San Francisco. I was immediately struck by how open and kind Ethel was when I first met her. I felt as if I had met an angel on this earth. Ethel can teach us far more than how to add years to our lives. She exemplifies how to add life to our years.[119]

World War II veteran Lawrence Brooks (110) shared, "I had some good times, and I had some bad times. I just tried to put all the good ones and the bad ones together and tried to forget about all of them." His key to a good life is to "serve God and be nice to people."[120]

This generation believes in values, manners, and politeness. They are saddened by the rudeness of modern society and don't understand children who are allowed to be rude. A good smack of the hand solves a lot of parental headaches. They grew up in the winding years of Victorian America with its stringent rules about family values. Sex outside of marriage and children born outside of wedlock could bring shame on a family and led to communal isolation, affecting business and status. Aileen Reed, 103, attending a 2013 reception honoring centenarians, was asked her thoughts on the youth of that year in comparison to the youth when she was alive. "The youth today are wild and have no guidance. More prayer is needed."[121]

There was a distinct separation between the norms for men and women. And while its hold had diminished over time, Victorian virtues had significant influence on this generation, especially for Black women who sought to overcome racist stereotypes concerning their character. In the article "Black Ideal of Womanhood," the characteristics of Black female teachers were described: "The Black Victorian schoolteacher exemplified the interplay of two cultures—European-American and African-American. . . . A teacher was expected to combine intellect and high morality with a leading personality, physical grace, and perfect beauty to represent an ideal of Black Womanhood. . . . She was also essential to the 'up lift' of the entire Black community."[122] Their appearance is of great importance and dates back to the days of slavery when the only time they could shine without repercussions was when getting ready for church on Sunday. They wore their best as a sign that their souls were not defeated and as a way of honoring God. They never go out liberally dressed and believe in dressing up for church and even for going to the grocery store. They believe a woman should never go out without a head covering, and this generation is famous for wearing beautifully elaborate hats. *Time* magazine elaborated on the importance of hats for Black women who grew up in this generation:

> Morally unassailable, she was virtuous and modest. Her personality was amiable—or "sweet" to use black parlance—she was also altruistic and pious. In appear-ance she was well groomed and presentable at all times. Her hair was carefully arranged and her costume was immaculate and appropriate for the occasion. In public she wore the traditional Victorian attire: A floor-length dress, with fitted bodice, a full skirt, and long sleeves often trimmed with a ruffle or lace. For formal wear, she would likely don a low-cut gown, which might reveal a considerable por-tion of her "neck." The ever present hanky with tatted or crocheted trim displayed her delicate taste and her ability at fine needlework. In all these attributes, Black Victoria upheld the expectations of "true womanhood" which were shared by the larger society. She was a "lady."[123]

Ninety-six-year-old actor Cicely Tyson gave an interview to *Elle* in 2020 and commented on how important the church was to her earlier life experience. "We spent our time in church from Sunday morning to Saturday night. . . . We perform(ed) in church all the time, myself, my sister, my brother. I played the organ, I played the piano, I sang in the choir. The church was really where, subconsciously, I was sopping up all of this, whatever I use now, to perform."[124]

Hester Ford was 115 years old when she died in 2021 in Charlotte, North Carolina. She lived through sharecropping, the 1918 flu epidemic, the Great Depression, World Wars I and II, Jim Crow segregation, the Civil Rights Movement, the election of President Barack Obama, Donald Trump's first term, and COVID-19. In an NPR interview, her great-granddaughter, Tanisha Patterson-Powe, described her as being extremely disciplined and focused on her faith in God. Her daily prayer was done repeatedly through the day at certain times of the day as a regular part of her faith journey.[125] The Grio reported that the oldest living person in the world was an African American woman, Jeralean Talley (115 years), born May 23, 1899. Mrs. Talley shared her secret to long life as her faith in God. "It's coming from above. That's the best advice I can give you. It's not in my hands or your hands." She reported that each person should "do unto others as you would have them do unto you, that's my way of living."[126] Born in 1916, Captain Eugene W. Gore was given his own ship with a white crew, something unheard of in his day. He was at first nervous to be over a white crew, but his faith in God helped him to believe that he could do it. "You know, God works in mysterious ways, his wonders to perform. I don't care how bad a group you get in, there's somebody in there that sympathizes with Black people . . . a Black man as a captain in 1953, '54, that was a high position."[127]

For them, faith in God is of primary importance. Many believe that God has a purpose for their life. They are at peace with their God, themselves, and others. In 2020, Ida Keeling was 104 years old and a record-holding runner who didn't start running until the age of sixty-seven. She is the first centenarian woman to complete a one-hundred-meter run, holds two records in the sixty (95–99 age group) and one-hundred-meter dashes (100–104 age group). Her daughter, Cheryl "Shelley" Keeling, said about her mother's legacy, "What I love about what Mother did is she didn't just inspire young people, who said, 'I want to be like her.' She inspired other older adults, centenarians, to get out and do it. She would say, 'Just get out there! Take what you have and get out there. Don't get stuck on what you don't have and what you've lost. Get out there and use what you have to do whatever you can do and whatever you can accomplish.'"[128]

This generation pursues a life dedicated to social justice. Many give back to the community by acts of philanthropy and by acts of service to others. Kindness is an attribute that many try to demonstrate to others. They live so that their lives reflect their faith in how they treat others. In 2021, ninety-four-year-old Martha Tucker was described by her granddaughter as "a giver" and a lifelong advocate for voting rights, working polls since 1963. She was dedicated to doing her part and last worked at a poll in the 2020 election. While they acknowledge change in the nation, they are dedicated to keeping alive the stories of those whose lives were taken and their families that were devastated. Injustice made them determined to speak out and to never forget nor be paralyzed by slow societal change. Many express frustrations with the slow pace of advancement but don't accept excuses from either whites or Blacks for failure to take advantage of opportunities. In 2020, a 106-year-old resident of Orange County, California, Warren Bussey, openly shared his opinions on the younger generation. He served in a segregated military during World War II and expressed the optimism that the country had changed significantly. He was excited about the election of Barack Obama as president and wanted to live long enough to see another Black person elected to the presidency. He accused younger Blacks of putting forth a lot of talk but said that they lacked the actions needed to realize their dreams. "They do a lot of talk, and that's all."[129] He wanted them to invest in their futures by purchasing a home. He encouraged living a life where hard work produced results and the adage that if you want something you have to work for it. "I would like to see more blacks buying homes, open up businesses. But it doesn't look too good. . . . Hope that my people will wake up."[130]

In summary, this generation has much to teach Americans about living a life of value and contribution. With the exception of the slavery era, they endured the most severe period of racial injustice in American history. Yet their outlook on life is inspirational to those who encounter them because of their belief that life can be better. We can be better.

2

Motown Generation (Silent Generation)

1925–45

When I was a kid, Motown was a myth, a role model, a stack of records on the Motorola hi-fi in the living room. To white folks Motown may have been symbolized by Diana Ross, but in my house, Motown was Eddie Kendricks and David Ruffin and Gladys Knight and my personal favorites, Edwin Staff and Short "Function at the Junction" Long. Like so many '60s happening, Motown seemed more socially significant than it was intended to be. Along with Sidney Poitier and Bill Cosby, Berry Gordy's record label was viewed as the cutting edge of integration in the entertainment industry. Every Copacabana date by Marvin Gaye, NBC T.C.B. special starring the Temptations and the Supremes and Look magazine feature on Gordy's family empire in Detroit was another step forward for first Negroes, then Blacks. While white critics bashed the company for Las Vegasization of rhythm & blues, Gordy's desire to be accepted by American mainstream institutions, even tacky ones like Vegas, seemed natural to the civil rights generation, though not to their Black power kids.[1]
—Nelson George, *Buppies, B-Boys, Baps, and Bohos*

New Negro Generation parents raised the Motown Generation and applied the lessons of life they learned from their parents. The Motown Generation was impacted by events that were unique and not experienced by any previous generation: the Roaring Twenties, Harlem Renaissance, Great Depression, and World War II. The third decade of the twentieth century, the Roaring Twenties (1920 to 1929), saw herculean productivity in commerce and the doubling of national wealth. A "consumer society" purchased clothing, home appliances, radios and especially automobiles.[2] An ironic result of Prohibition (1920–33), the outlawing of alcohol production and consumption, was an increase in criminal activity and the development of a professional criminal class. Extralegal activities provided easy money through bootlegging and rum running. Underlying many of the significant events was the fact that for the first time more Americans lived in cities than on farms. At a time when half of southern Blacks in urban centers were unemployed, white society was not looking to advance the Black cause due to their desire that Blacks remain in menial jobs with low pay.

This generation was symbolized by the music of Motown as an agent of cultural change in America. The achievements of the previous generation in the area of artistic creativity inspired the Motown Generation. This generation lived through an artistic revolution with lasting influences on a variety of creative expressions. Newly migrated Southerners brought with them the musical sounds and culinary tastes of southern life that matured in a northern environment. Art was created without apology for its Afrocentric themes. Blacks became their own measurement of excellence for the promotion of Black pride and to highlight Black history. Black culture celebrated itself as a vibrant and significant contribution to American genius. It found prominence in ways not witnessed during any previous period of the country's history. African American artistry contributed to everything from music, dance, basketry, pottery, quilting, blacksmithing, boatbuilding, carpentry, woodcarving, ironworking, and graveyard decorations. In architecture, the shotgun house design that originated in New Orleans spread nationwide.[3] Black artists utilized almost every genre of art, from sculpture, literature, music, and dance, to give the world a front-row seat to Black distinction. Members of this generation read essays, poems, and books and listened to live music produced by Black hands for digestion by Black minds. Whites who had no idea about the Negro origins of elements of Black culture that were adopted nationwide.[4]

Music has always been fundamental to the Black experience, and Motown's impact extended beyond music as it helped to normalize the Black experience. Children snapped fingers on Saturday nights to blues and jazz played at the uptown clubs and joyfully swayed to spirituals in church on Sunday morning. This generation propelled Black music to the forefront of American culture with songs written by Black lyricists, vocalized by Black singers, and played by Black bands. Black music was redefined beyond "race music" that was limited to a Black audience; it set the musical standard for excellence. This made Black music, and therein, Black people, acceptable. NAACP chairman Julian Bond declared that "Motown shaped the culture and did all the things that made the 1960s what they were. So, if you don't understand Motown and the influence it had on a generation of black and white young people, then you can't understand the United States, you can't understand America."[5] Motown singers displayed authentic, positive images of Blackness that displaced prejudicial stereotypes of minstrelsy. Motown artists elevated Black music as a manifesto for social change through crossover appeal to all audiences. Motown's influence was subtle yet impactful as segregationist modes were challenged by integrated dancing venues. Motown Records founder Berry Gordy commented, "I felt that I wanted to do music for all people, and it turned out that people began feeling it and Black people, white people, Jews, gentiles, cops and robbers, all loved Motown. I know that there are more similarities in the world in people than differences and my goal in Motown was to bring those similarities out in music and love, togetherness and trust."[6] According to Christina Pomoni in "The Social Impact of Motown Music in American Culture,"

> Motown associated music with the Black civil rights struggle by being the first record label owned by an African-American. Under the leadership of Berry Gordy Jr., who aspired to bridge the gap of racial discrimination by producing music that could appeal to all people, regardless of the color of their skin, Motown became a vehicle of black pride and self-expression. Besides, the broad appeal of Motown integrated the political and cultural aspects of the broader socio-political environment and associated music and the right of black communities to social equality.[7]

The BBC reported,

> On 12 January 1959, the music sensation that changed America— and the world beyond it—was set in motion. . . . Motown was powerfully significant as a Black-owned corporation employing multi-racial staff within its label teams; in an era when America was undeniably divided, and the mainstream was an exclusionary zone. . . . Hitsville produced music as a vital, unifying life force. [Founder Berry Gordy reflected,] "I wanted songs for the whites, Blacks, the Jews, Gentiles . . . I wanted everybody to enjoy my music. . . . It was a beautiful feeling, when we were so full of hate and anger and everybody was so full of unrest, that we saw people actually join together, get out of their cars and dance to a song that meant we should rejoice. . . . The Motown sound was a very big influence in the civil rights movement. It was not that we marched or paraded; we just promoted it through love. . . . [D]espite the hostility and racism we faced, we knew we were bringing joy to people. The audiences were segregated. The venues had a rope down the middle of the audience separating blacks from whites, but soon the rope was gone and black kids and white kids were dancing together to the same music. It created a bond that echoed throughout the world."[8]

Even in the midst of a music revolution, this generation grew up in an unimaginably desperate period for Black families, as almost every area of life was rife with considerable obstacles. In 1927, the Great Mississippi Flood destroyed lives. President Calvin Coolidge appointed his secretary of commerce, Herbert Hoover, to oversee the recovery effort. Hoover failed to be a fair arbitrator in the distribution of assistance as he bartered with southern legislators in hopes of one day occupying the White House. Authorities saved white communities by intentionally flooding Black homes located along the riverbanks by lowering the protective levees, displacing several thousand Black families. In order to receive federal rations, Black residents were commandeered by local and National Guard men for restoration work. A brutal addition to the forced labor were the crimes perpetrated in the form of lynching, torture, and rape.[9]

White supremacy undergirded every political platform well into the 1930s. Political disenfranchisement included poll taxes, white-only voting primaries, literary requirements, and grandfather clauses. Black people were barred from previously held offices and could no longer serve as sheriffs, justices of the peace, jurors, county commissioners, or school board members. They were used to unending moments of crisis. They were able to maintain remarkable calmness in the face of calamity. They grew up during a time when life was constantly in crisis due to events like the 1929 stock market crash, the Great Depression, and World War II.

Domestic terrorism played a major role in the massive migration to northern and western regions of the country. There were other factors as well: an 1898 boll weevil infestation destroyed cotton crops and decreased farm employment for over a decade. The 1927 Great Mississippi Flood wiped away a multitude of Black homes, with few possessing the resources needed to rebuild. Enticements that pulled them to the North and West included higher wages, somewhat better schools, and a less harsh social environment. World War I (1914–18) increased the demand for labor, as European migration drastically decreased due to people volunteering in their own countries.[10] In that first decade, 170,000 Blacks left the South. The vast majority of self-deportees were young and male. Between 1910 and 1920, 454,000 departed by car and train. Between 1920 and 1930, 749,000 relocated.[11] New York gained over 260,000 new residents and Chicago more than 230,000. Southern states were hit hard by a loss of laborers. Between 1920 and 1930, a whopping 45 percent of Black males between the ages of 15 and 34 escaped Georgia for a better life.[12]

Migration slowed slightly during the Great Depression, but by the end of the 1920s, 1.5 million had migrated.[13] They ventured to every region where work was found and a new way of life might be possible. By 1917, job opportunities in steel producing mills, meat packing houses, automobile factories, and construction sites were abundant. For the first time many were granted the right to vote, earn legitimate salaries, and send their children to better equipped schools. Importantly, they escaped the constant threat of racial violence.[14] Black newspapers urged migration. The *Chicago Defender* was most persistent in pushing the southern exodus. It published as a headline on January 6, 1917, "Millions to Leave South," and stated plainly that it was "Better to die of frostbite than at the hands of a mob in the South."[15] The paper printed northern train schedules and strongly worded editorials urging migration. Northern industrialists actively recruited Blacks to come to the new Promised Land. Charles S. Johnson described the cities which attracted the migrants:

> And there was New York City with its polite personal service and its Harlem—the Mecca of the Negroes the country over . . . Detroit, the automobile center, with its sophistication of skill and fancy wages reflecting the daring economic policies of Henry Ford . . . Philadelphia, with its comfortable old traditions; and the innumerable little industrial towns where fabulous wages were paid. White and Black these cities lured, but the Blacks they lured with a demoniac appeal.[16]

Segregated yet vibrant neighborhoods were created in Baltimore, Dallas, Durham, Louisville, Norfolk, Oklahoma City, Richmond, Roanoke, and St. Louis.

Northern housing segregation was as widespread as it was in the South; redlining was practiced, mortgage loans were denied, and investment loans to create businesses were nonexistent. Regardless, for many, compared to life in the South, this was as close to paradise as they had ever experienced. Black life in the North was not regulated by white domination. Urban Blacks were more educated and were not dependent on whites for every aspect of their livelihood. A Black bourgeoisie consisting of generations of free-born families had established aristocratic societies assuming upper-class status. It was a world that contained Black lawyers, entrepreneurs, teachers, journalists, artisans, and funeral home operators and other professionals. Although segregated, Black neighborhoods provided a variety of resources, employment, and material supplies. Survival was based on a reliance on each other and, to the satisfaction of the new migrants, there was very little personal contact with white society.[17] Black voting strength in northern cities first influenced, and then decided, the outcome of elections in Chicago, New York, Cleveland, Cincinnati, and Philadelphia.[18]

There were negative consequences for the migrated community. With the desire for a better life, there were also the ramifications of relocating to a region whose culture you were unfamiliar with. While the suffering in the South has ample publicity, the North was not the perfect Promised Land some anticipated. In the North there was rampant racial discrimination, limited housing units, employment harassment, and a lack of equality in education. Blacks were assigned to the lowest status jobs with unequal pay. A "job ceiling" prevented promotion and limited one's ability to expand within one's profession. The undesirable jobs were often labeled "Negro jobs."

Amazingly, in spite of these horrors, this generation grew up in the midst of an artistic explosion. Centered in Harlem, New York, the Harlem Renaissance produced some of the most significant works of creativity in the history of America. It broadcast the feelings, thoughts, dreams, frustrations, and desires of a "New Negro." It was born out of a commitment to reinterpret the story of a people who no longer sought permission nor inspiration from white society. White cultural standards would no longer be the foundation on which Black art would be constructed. Alain LeRoy Locke (1885–1954), Harvard graduate and the first Black Oxford Rhodes scholar, coined the term *the New Negro* and was the definitive figure in calling forth works of Black imagination. He challenged Black artists to reclaim their African heritage, utilizing racial identity as a source of creativity. He wrote, "If in our lifetime the Negro should not be able to celebrate his full initiation into American democracy, he can at least . . . celebrate the attainment of a significant and satisfying new phase of group development, and with it a spiritual Coming of Age."[19] The book *Harlem Renaissance* observed of the Renaissance, "The search for visual images—hewn from memory, experience, and history—that convey a Black American identity is the achievement of the Harlem Renaissance artists. In many ways the images of these artists created a watershed: before the 1920s Black painters such as Henry O. Tanner and Edward Bannister and the sculptor Edmonia Lewis rarely portrayed the day-to-day realities of Black life. . . . The Black community, when it appeared in American art, was most often represented in the works of White American artists. . . . [T]hese images contrast sharply with the simplicity and directness of the images of Harlem Renaissance artists. Their work has the look of something new, something raw and deliberate, a tradition freshly crafted and conceived. If they contributed anything, they contributed the sense that for the first time the Black artist could take control of the images of Black America."[20] Harlem became the cultural center of the Black universe and challenged ideas about racial inferiority that were prevalent at the time. In a segregated America, whites invaded Harlem for entertainment, and after hours white sophisticates mingled with the Harlem Blacks. Louis Armstrong, Duke Ellington, Josephine Baker, Paul Robeson, Paul Laurence Dunbar, James Weldon Johnson, Claude McKay, Langston Hughes, and Zora Neale Hurston demonstrated to the world that Black artistry was second to none. The impressionable Zora Neale Hurston said it best: "Sometimes, I feel discriminated against, but it does not make me angry. It merely astonishes me. How can any deny themselves the pleasure of my company? It's beyond me."[21]

Literature exploded with a tidal wave of Afrocentric expression. One of the first outputs was Charles Johnson's publication of his novel, *There Is Confusion*, that introduced the arrival of Black literature as a genre. Langston Hughes, author of *The Negro Artist* and *The Racial Mountain*, echoed Locke in his call for the creation of a uniquely Negro voice, original and distinctive, with an identity centered on Blackness. Within a decade, sixteen writers had published more than fifty volumes of poetry and fiction.[22] A few included Paul Laurence Dunbar, Anna Julia Cooper, W. E. B. Du Bois, Pauline Hopkins, Charles W. Chesnutt, Augusta Savage, James Weldon Johnson, Langston Hughes, Claude McKay, Jean Toomer, Zora Neale Hurston, and Aaron Douglas.[23]

Renaissance music influenced American culture in greater measures than any other genre. Jazz music was especially impactful, as New Orleans jazz found a worldwide audience. Jelly Roll Morton created audio sensations like nothing anyone had ever experienced before. Composers Bob Cole, Will Marion Cook, James Reese Europe, J. Rosamond Johnson, and Duke Ellington transcribed on paper musical creations that rivaled the classics. The Excelsior Brass Band, Olympia Brass Band, and Tuxedo Band played for listeners eager for new musical expressions. From New York to California, artists were thrilled as late-night partiers such as King Oliver, Sidney Bechet, Kid Ory, and Louis Armstrong spawned a new era in recording and live performances.[24] Singers Ma Rainey ("Mother of the Blues"), Bessie Smith, and Josephine Baker sang the blues with soulful harmonies that impacted white and Black musicians. Jelly Roll Morton played the piano in a way that led the soul to dance all night long. Music inspired dance. The Buck, Pigeon Wing, Jig, Cake-Walk, Ring Dance, Buzzard Lope, Water Dances, Juba, Black Bottom, Big Apple, Charleston, Ballin' the Jack, Shimmy, the Mooche, Lindy Hop, Jitterbug, Shag, Suzi-Q, Tap, Camel Walk, Truckin', and the Twist added new styles of speed and flexibility to dancing.

University art departments on the campuses of Fisk and Howard graduated new and upcoming artists. Between two world wars, a small film industry materialized to produce two hundred "race movies" that targeted Black audiences. With all-Black casts, they presented Black people in non-stereotypical roles as doctors, policemen, cowboys, judges, gangsters, and soldiers living normal family lives. Director and producer Oscar Micheaux attacked stereotypical images and racially degrading media.[25]

THE PRESIDENTS

The presidents of this period were Calvin Coolidge (1923–29, thirtieth president), Herbert Hoover (1929–33, thirty-first president), and Franklin D. Roosevelt (1933–45, thirty-second president).

President John Calvin Coolidge Jr. (1923–29), the thirtieth president, began his presidency with little fanfare and ended it in much the same manner. He was ushered into office by the sudden death of President Warren G. Harding, for whom he served as vice president. After deciding not to run for reelection, he left office in January of 1929. He died on January 5, 1933. When writer Dorothy Parker was informed of his death, she asked, "How can they tell?"[26]

Calvin Coolidge generated a great deal of excitement when running as Warren G. Harding's vice-presidential candidate, as he publicly uttered some of the strongest affirmations of Black rights ever stated by a candidate:

> There is especially due to the colored race a more general recognition of their constitutional rights. Tempted with disloyalty they remained loyal, serving in the military forces with distinction, obedient to the draft to the extent of hundreds of thousands, investing $1 out of every five they possessed in Liberty Bonds, surely they hold the double title of citizenship, by birth and by conquest, to be relieved from all imposition, to be defended from lynching and to be freely granted equal opportunities.[27]

The Black press responded with excitement at the president's condemnation of lynching, the strongest thus far by any candidate or president. In his first address to Congress, he excited Blacks who heard the speech. He made remarkably progressive statements in support of Black rights: He stated in his First Annual Message to Congress on the State of the Union, December 6, 1923, "Numbered among our population are some 12,000,000 colored people. Under our Constitution their rights are just as sacred as those of any other citizen. It is both a public and a private duty to protect those rights."[28]

Early in his presidency, he had meetings in the White House with a number of Black leaders, including the fiery William Monroe Trotter. Tuskegee Institute's president, Robert Russa Moton, communicated regularly with the new president. He requested money for Howard University's medical hospital and for assistance to Blacks migrating from the South.

But President Coolidge offered no leadership for Black America. He soon reversed course from his earlier progressive statements and did little to advance the Black cause during his presidency. The newly elected president concluded a congressional speech with the startling announcement that it was not the purview of the federal government to interfere in matters of race in local communities. He supported the definition of political parties as "lily-white" to the exclusion of Blacks and appointed two Southern whites to his cabinet who endorsed white supremacy. A proponent of eugenics, he stressed that races should remain pure.[29] In his first Congressional address, he supported anti-immigrant sentiments claiming that non-Americans have no place in the country. His inaction was evident in that he had very few Black federal appointments other than a few loyalists of the late Booker T. Washington. The trend that began during the administration of Theodore Roosevelt, when Blacks reconsidered their loyalty to the Republican Party, was amplified during the Coolidge administration. Blacks openly questioned being faithful to a Republican Party that had nothing to offer, not even pretense.[30]

Coolidge gave only lip service to addressing the violence inflicted upon the Black population. He voiced support for anti-lynching legislation but never lobbied Congress, nor did he voice public endorsement for the passage of any bills. Racial violence served the dual purpose of upholding white supremacy while preventing Black elevation. Domestic terrorism by the KKK resurfaced with a particular vehemence. By 1929, the number of lynchings multiplied as competition for jobs intensified. Journalist Hilton Butler exclaimed, "Dust had been blown from the shotgun, the whip, and the noose, and Ku Klux Klan practices were being resumed in the certainty that dead men not only tell no tales but create vacancies."[31] Black people faced constant threats from race massacres. Incidents in the cities of Atlanta, New Orleans, Memphis, Wilmington, and the Phoenix Riot in South Carolina were vicious and deadly. Whenever there was a perceived threat of Black advancement, death ensued. A line drawn from 1890 through the years following World Wars I and II to the Civil Rights Movement documents the violent hysteria that resulted in the deaths of hundreds, wounding of thousands, and millions of dollars in property destruction.[32] Lynching continued to be a blood sport advertised as a bizarre family event. Newspapers printed advertisements that announced special trains to transport spectators to lynchings. Printed postcards displayed victims surrounded by participants who collected body parts as souvenirs. Between 1882 and 1900, there was an average of 150.4 lynchings per year. For seventy years, between 1882 to the 1950s, there were 4,739 victims murdered by vigilante mobs. The number could rise as high as six thousand if one takes into consideration unreported events, those murdered in race massacres, and interracial murders. Between 1901 and 1910, there was an average of 84.6 lynchings annually, with 82 percent occurring in the southern states of Mississippi (581), Georgia (530), Texas (493), and Louisiana (391). Adult males comprised 95 percent of all victims; of those, 72 percent were Black.[33]

Herbert Hoover (1929–33, thirty-first president) was a highly regarded, newly elected president in 1929. Four years later, he was vilified as one of the worst as the world was in the grips of a Great Depression. His reputation as an expert crisis manager and humanitarian was in tatters. He failed miserably to analyze the complexities of the country's problems as the Great Depression, the stock market crash, and Adolf Hitler's rise to power in Germany all met at his presidential crossroad.[34]

Unfortunately, Black life was about to get a lot worse. The Great Depression, 1929 to 1939, was caused by the 1929 stock market crash that resulted in economic devastation throughout the 1930s. Although its origin was in the United States, almost every country in the world was impacted. During this crisis, unemployment reached 15 million, and almost half of all lending institutions closed.[35] Northern jobs ended, and the South was battered economically even before the crash of the stock market in 1929. Blacks in both the North and South were hit the hardest. By 1932 one-half were unemployed. In the migration cities of Detroit, Chicago, Philadelphia, and New York, one in every three Black families depended on public assistance. There was even worse job loss in Atlanta (65 percent unemployment) and Norfolk (80 percent). Family life in the South was a living nightmare. Widespread economic loss compounded with extreme poverty, confining many with few options other than sharecropping. The Depression hit Blacks particularly hard. Sheila Kingsberry-Burt remembered an oppressive labor environment where lack was compounded by exploitation.

> It was a life that you could never get ahead in. There was no getting ahead. You got a crop, and the resources for the crop were provided by the farm owner. You worked his farm and your crop. When the harvest time came, you ended up with whatever your crop earned, minus the costs of cultivating the crop, minus whatever you had gotten from him to sustain you until the harvest time. . . . They never had enough. When your money ran out from the sale of that year, you go right back to getting the credit from the farmer till the next year. Always in debt. Always owing.[36]

Hoover's efforts to relieve the Depression failed as one-quarter of the nation's workforce lost their jobs. It was not that he didn't respond; it was that his actions made things worse. He rejected government economic intervention as a means to promote job growth. He believed that industrial productivity had to be derived solely from business innovation and entrepreneurship. The result was a nation that spiraled into economic limbo.[37] The lives of millions were impacted as homes and jobs vanished. Homeless refugee camps were labeled Hoovervilles. He not only failed to provide leadership and inspiration, but he also cut emergency benefits providing both food and shelter. His rationale was that it would threaten American capitalism. He insisted that people could not be released from poverty by the use of public funds.

Contrary to societal trends wherein low economic productivity increased criminal activity, the Depression put to an end crime's previous upsurge. By the 1930s there was a rapid decrease in crime across the country, not due to effective policing or judicatory action but because there was less criminal activity.

Between 1933 and 1940, homicide rates plummeted by 35 percent. There was a 20 percent reduction in Black murders and a 48 percent decrease for whites. Regardless of the falling crime rates, hysteria swept the nation as the fear of being robbed, or even worse, murdered, prevailed. Accusations targeted the Black community, as did prosecutions, resulting in the nation's first "war on crime." Law enforcement was enlarged through increases in the federal law force and the creation of the federal prison system and the FBI. Selective prosecutions were based on race and class, but mostly race. Black arrest rates for murder increased by 25 percent while white arrests fell by 8 percentage points. Black arrests for robbery rose by 23 percent and dropped for whites by 42 percent. Between 1926 and 1940, total incarceration rates rose by 67 percent, with Black rates increasing by one-third. By 1930 the rate of Black executions reversed. Whereas before, 60 percent of executed prisoners were white, by 1930, 60 percent of executed prisoners were Black. Scholar Jeffrey S. Adler disclosed,

> Responses to the early 1920s crime wave enabled government officials to enhance federal law enforcement authority, construct the federal prison system, and build the FBI into a major crime-fighting and sur-veillance institution. State and local legislators invoked the war on crime to launch the "big-house" era of prisons, reduce the power of judges and juries, fend off criticism of police brutality, and shore up a shaky racial hierarchy. Racially focused police dragnets became commonplace, and prosecutors, under the guise of crime fighting, expanded their discretion and sharply increased convictions of defen-dants, a growing proportion of whom were African American. Thus, while violent crime fell during the 1930s, prison populations rose, and the proportion of African American inmates swelled. Capital punish-ment followed a similar trajectory, ballooning during the early 1930s and increasingly aimed at African Americans.[38]

Hoover was a leading supporter of increased law enforcement for a fear-ful nation and was consistently noncommittal in addressing injustices in the criminal justice system. He refused to address the apparent injustice of the convictions of the nine Scottsboro boys for rape. He was even more notice-ably silent in his failure to address any of the fifty lynchings that occurred during his time in office. To compound matters, he nominated Judge John J. Parker for the federal court, a man reviled for his racially prejudicial state-ments about Blacks. He was rejected only after a successful congressional lob-bying campaign by the NAACP compelled the Senate to vote down Parker's confirmation.

Every institution was affected by racism, with education being highly impacted. Local support for Black education dissipated under the premise that education ruined Blacks for their status as hired workers and would generate dissatisfaction. Black parents desperately wanted their children to go to school, but often their children needed to work to help the family survive. Sheila Kingsberry-Burt remembered the burden of child labor and how it evaporated any hope of an education. "The truth is, you missed almost as much time out of school as you did going to school because you had to stay out and work the farm." Lucille Bridges, the mother of Ruby Bridges, one of four children who integrated the all-white school system in New Orleans, commented, "When I was a child, white and Black would pick cotton together. The bus would come pick up the white kids, but I couldn't go to school. I would watch them go with tears in my eyes. I prayed if I ever got married, I wanted my kids to go to school."[39]

Education was already a particularly unequal institution, as Black students suffered all-around shortages. Segregated schools for Black students had larger class sizes, lower teacher salaries, and fewer resources while funds were directed toward white schools. This was even more damaging considering that education opportunities were intentionally limited. Whites were highly unresponsive and hostile to demands for education opportunities for Black children. The average educational experience consisted of attendance at an elementary school. In 1930, Black children attended school for only fifteen to twenty weeks a year. In 1932, there were no high schools to serve Black children in 230 counties. There were only sixteen Black high schools in the states of Florida, Louisiana, Mississippi, and South Carolina. North Carolina stood alone; 20 percent of Black children in the state had access to a high school education. A report by the American Council on Education reported that schools that served Black children in the Deep South could barely be defined as schools. The report on Dine Hollow, Alabama, read:

> A typical rural Negro school is at Dine Hollow. It is in a dilapidated building, once whitewashed, standing in a rocky field unfit for cultivation. Dust-covered weeds spread a carpet all around, except for an uneven, bare area on one side that looks like a ball field. Behind the school is a small building with a broken, sagging door. As we approach, a nervous, middle-aged woman comes to the door of the school. She greets us in a discouraged voice marked by a speech impediment. Escorted inside, we observe that the broken benches are crowded to three times their normal capacity. Only a few battered books are in sight, and we look in vain for maps or charts. We learn that four grades are assembled here.[40]

Blacks paid what historian James Anderson termed a "Black tax" or double tax. They paid their local and state taxes that funded white schools, and they provided funding for local Black schools, which were tremendously under-funded.[41] Carter Godwin Woodson, in *The Mis-Education of the Negro* (1933), voiced pessimism about the education afforded children of color. He questioned its detrimental impact on young minds. He charged that America's education system did not qualify as a quality education to help Blacks overcome cycles of poverty and racial discrimination. Rather, it reinforced inferiority and second-class status.[42]

Black progress continued as Blacks seized every available opportunity. Despite the racial discrimination that limited their employment opportunities, select entrepreneurs achieved millionaire status. Annie Minerva Turnbo-Malone, Madame C. J. Walker, and Anthony Overton made millions in the manufacturing and sale of hair care products and cosmetics created for an African American clientele. By 1934, some 134 Black banks were founded, including the first one started by a woman, St. Luke Penny Saving Bank, in Richmond, Virginia.[43] Black empowerment organizations offered resources and commercial networking opportunities, including The National Association of Wage Earners, National Negro Business League, National Urban League, and the Universal Negro Improvement Association.

There were some advances in the education of Black children. Throughout the 1930s, the literacy rate for Blacks increased to over 80 percent, only 10 percentage points below the white rate. This was a remarkable achievement, as forty years earlier, 60 percent were illiterate. Georgia saw an increase in literacy from 30 percent to 74 percent, with similar numbers in Louisiana. In the 1930s Black teachers were underpaid, undertrained, and overworked, with minimal resources. By 1940 the educational levels of Black teachers had improved remarkably. Thirteen states reported that 35.1 percent had a college degree, with Oklahoma (65.8 percent) and West Virginia (60.1 percent) among the highest. The southern states of Alabama (18.6 percent) and Mississippi (9.1 percent) had the lowest.[44] The 117 Historical Black Colleges and Universities (HBCU) contributed greatly, as eighty-one private institutions paired with thirty-six public schools to educate students. Denominations founded seventy-four colleges. Five had developed graduate programs. Over two decades (1925–45) PhD students graduated with degrees in mathematics, music, pharmacology, bacteriology, embryology, pathology, civil engineering, public health, agronomy, nutrition, geology, and chemical engineering. The United Negro College Fund was founded in 1944. For the first time, Black presidents were installed at Black institutions, beginning with Howard University in 1926.[45]

Blacks correctly perceived President Hoover to be indifferent to their cause and a proponent of white supremacy. They were correct in their analysis of a president who believed that Blacks were mentally inferior and lacked the

supposed higher cognitive ability of whites. They could make limited societal advances, but only gradually and through the acquisition of an education
and the socialization that wealth afforded one. His 1909 *Principles of Mining*
claimed that "White workers (are) of a higher mental order and possess higher
intelligence than Asiatics and Negroes. They are better coordinated and more
likely to take initiative, and for this reason, it (is) cheaper and more efficient to
hire white rather than nonwhite workers. Much observation leads the writer
to the conclusion that, averaging actual results, one white man equals from
two to three of the colored races, even in the simplest forms of mine work
such as shoveling or tramming." It was the responsibility of the superior white
race, the "white man's burden," to civilize and control the colored races of
the world.[46] Hoover unsuccessfully nominated for the Supreme Court North
Carolina judge John Parker, who had previously stated that Black participation in politics presented an "evil and danger to both races."[47] He removed
Blacks from previously held leadership positions in the Republican Party.

President Hoover did nothing to earn their votes and increased the alienation
of Blacks from their past political loyalties, and at this time many Black people
made a clean break from the Republican Party to the Democratic Party. He
possessed neither the intuition nor the interest to notice their dissatisfaction with
Republicans. As the party moved further away from issues relevant to the race,
Blacks moved further away from the party. He was completely oblivious to the
fact that Blacks were conscious voters, not driven by blind loyalty but voting
for what was in their best interest. He lost his 1932 reelection bid to Democrat
Franklin Roosevelt, due in large part to Blacks voting for Democrats.[48]

It would take the administration of President Franklin D. Roosevelt (1933–
45) to implement meaningful policies and produce a national forum for social
change. For Blacks, this was a time of increasing political influence. While
disenfranchised in the South, their efforts to lobby presidents were becoming
more effective. This generation's parents switched political parties wholesale,
moving from being Lincoln Republicans to Roosevelt Democrats. Shirley Taylor Haizlip, in *The Sweeter the Juice*, remembered her family's transition:

> When Franklin Roosevelt was elected president in 1932, politics
> began to capture Julian's attention. From his father he had learned
> that having political power could help him change the laws of the
> country and the lives of his people and, equally important, would
> give him access and clout that he could translate into financial gain.
> Most of the members of the Stratford Church were Republicans,
> but admiring Roosevelt and his New Deal, Stratford's new minister
> decided to throw his lot in with the Democrats. It was a break not
> only with the church's congregation, but with his father's Abe Lincoln
> Republicanism.[49]

Roosevelt came into office with the country facing the greatest economic calamity in its history, the Great Depression. By the time he took office, the Depression had inflicted three years of damage on the nation's economy. Unlike his predecessor, his powers of observation were extremely astute, and he responded with energy and vitality in the face of widespread pandemonium on almost every front. He deployed the full resources of the federal government to prop up the economy and propelled the United States onto the world stage as a global leader. He provided capable leadership as he hid the crippling effects of his disability from polio from the public eye. As the country grappled with the devastation of the Depression, he instilled hope and confidence in the hearts of millions of fearful and impoverished Americans of all races. He acted boldly to install New Deal programs to kick-start the economy by generating resources for the one-quarter of Americans who were unemployed. Effective New Deal programs included the Works Progress Administration, the National Labor Relations (Warner) Act, and the Social Security Act.[50]

New Deal programs were beneficial to Blacks. There was an increase in farm and home ownership as well as education and vocational training opportunities. The New Deal provided relief through the National Youth Administration, Civilian Conservation Corps, and the Works Progress Administration. In the thirteen years between 1933 and 1946, FDR increased the number of Black federal employees from fifty thousand to two hundred thousand. And the Works Project Administration (WPA) made a valuable contribution to history when it collected the oral histories of two thousand formerly enslaved men and women. But these advances were hampered by racism when southern Democrats insisted on limiting Black participation in the economy. Locally, Black farmers received less subsidies, if any. Blacks received lower wages via a lower pay scale, and families received less assistance.[51] For the first time, Blacks received federal assistance during a time of calamity, even though they were not the intended recipients and received less than whites. New Deal programs were of tremendous benefit to those fortunate enough to receive them. In response, Blacks credited Roosevelt and the Democratic Party for extending assistance and rewarded both with the bulk of the Black vote. Political estimates are that Blacks constituted between 5 and 13 percent of the presidential votes cast in Delaware, Illinois, Indiana, Kansas, Kentucky, Maryland, Michigan, Missouri, New Jersey, New York, Ohio, Pennsylvania, and West Virginia, votes that would help win the election for the party that received them.

Roosevelt never openly advocated for racial justice but acted in the direct interest of African Americans as a means to leverage his political power and dominance over the Democratic Party. He was always a politician first and measured his actions by how they would impact his political fortunes. He was rather timid when it came to southern Democrats and did not desire to give the impression that racial justice was foremost in his agenda. After two terms, he remained reticent, avoiding controversy and failing to take action in the pursuit of racial progress. He instructed his staff to reject invitations from Black leaders. He demurred when Walter White of the NAACP pushed him to lobby for an anti-lynching bill and never instructed the Justice Department to investigate hate crimes. White referred to the agency as the "U.S. Department of White Justice," charging that it did little about the crimes inflicted on Blacks. But his silence was noticed by the Black and global communities. When the president, touring Gambia, was shocked by the poverty he witnessed and suggested to British Prime Minister Winston Churchill that the United Nations ought to investigate the way the colony was being ruled, Churchill responded, "All right, the United Nations will send an inspection committee to your own South in America."[52]

The president was fortunate on the racial frontier, as Blacks were able to provide him with leaders capable of assisting him with the promotion of reasonably progressive and politically strategic policies. They were also more than willing to push him beyond his comfort level to go further than any presidents before him. Several individuals were pivotal to the actions taken during this administration. They included his wife, Eleanor Roosevelt; Mary McLeod Bethune; Secretary of the Interior Harold Ickes; and A. Philip Randolph. Eleanor Roosevelt went out of her way to align herself with the Black community on issues of social justice. Her influence on her husband was immense, unrelenting, and effective. She befriended Black women and considered Mary McLeod Bethune a close friend and confidant; they shared meals together in the White House.

Bethune (1875–1955) was the most influential Black woman of her age, with few white peers who could equal her influence. She founded the Daytona Literary and Industrial School for Training Negro Girls in 1904 in Daytona Beach, Florida. She was president of the State Federation of Colored Women's Clubs and later served the National Association of Colored Women in 1924. She was a member of Roosevelt's "Black Cabinet" and led the administration's Negro Division of the National Youth Administration. She was appointed an organizing delegate for the United Nations. She was honored with a statue in Washington, DC, in 1974, the first for a person of color in the nation's history. Due to Bethune's influence, Eleanor Roosevelt resigned from the Daughters of the American Revolution when they refused Marian Anderson use of Constitution Hall for a concert. She and Ickes arranged for it to be held at the Lincoln Memorial, with 75,000 people in attendance. She was outspoken when it came to the rights of Blacks and women and acted when her husband was reticent to act.[53] A. Philip Randolph (1889–1979) was one of the most resourceful and effective leaders of his day who led one of the most effective unions, the Brotherhood of Sleeping Car Porters.[54] Together they influenced presidents, utilizing the dual strategies of threat and compromise. He was a major collaborator with other civil rights organizations and leaders and a major architect of the 1963 March on Washington.[55]

FDR's recognition of the importance of his Black allies grew over his four terms. Black Democrats frequented the White House in the persons of Robert L. Vann, Julian Rainey, William T. Thompkins, and F. B. Ransom. The president visited Black institutions and corresponded with several organizations. It was in his appointments to the federal courts where he had long-lasting impact. He appointed eight progressives to the Supreme Court and William Hastie as the first Black federal judge. He appointed a "Black Cabinet" which advised him on matters affecting the lives of Black Americans. Members included Mary McLeod Bethune, William H. Hastie, and Eugene K. Jones. Presidents had in the past sought the counsel of Black leaders. Lincoln met with a group of Black clergy asking about colonization, and Booker T. Washington advised three presidents. But this was different; it was not a one-time or one-person conversation. They had the ear of the most powerful man on the planet and were bound by oath in an official capacity. They were true advisors and the fulfillment of Du Bois's dream of a talented tenth. They were referred to as his "Black Brain Trust."[56]

Paired with the economic upheaval, FDR's presidency also faced the greatest international threat to world peace since World War I: the destruction of World War II (1939–45). Domestic issues became secondary when on December 7, 1941, the Japanese bombed the American armada docked in Pearl Harbor and the United States was drawn into World War II. Roosevelt, Winston Churchill, and Joseph Stalin merged to create the Big Three aligned against the Axis powers led by Nazi Germany. He rose to the occasion, encouraging the American people that this enemy would be defeated with words that still speak loudly today: "Yesterday, December 7, 1941, a date which will live in infamy."[57]

The global war provided employment opportunities through military service as well as in domestic defense industries. Segregation was rampant in the industries that produced weapons for the war. North American Aviation openly proclaimed that it would not hire anyone Black for positions other than maintenance positions. "While we are in complete sympathy with the Negro, it is against the company policy to employ them as mechanics or aircraft workers." Labor unions were gaining sway, and two hundred thousand Blacks joined integrated unions. Randolph threatened a March on Washington in 1941 to demand fair treatment in the defense industry and throughout the federal government.[58] Even Eleanor Roosevelt urged him not to do it. Randolph stood firm and told the president directly, "Something must be done now!" The president issued Executive Order 8802 that outlawed racial discrimination in defense industry employment. It was the first executive order pertaining to race since the Emancipation Proclamation. The order established the Committee on Fair Employment Practice, which led to the training of 323,000 Blacks. Between 1938 and 1942 the number of Blacks employed by the federal government increased from 8.5 to 18 percent, many hired to white-collar jobs and many of them Black women.[59]

With the start of the war, the president needed the support of Blacks as voters, laborers, and troops. Black leaders agreed to assist in recruiting, but with the stipulation that the country would implement historic reform. Led by Black newspapers and the *Pittsburgh Courier*, the "Double-V" campaign marketed military recruitment as a means to end discrimination in America. Two Vs stood for two types of victory: over enemies at home and abroad. Despite some reticence to serve in a segregated army and for a Jim Crow country, Blacks demonstrated loyalty to the Roosevelts and a sense of intense patriotism; but they also fought because it would offer the race new opportunities. Blacks responded by enlisting in high numbers, working in the defense industry, and voting Democratic.[60] Historian Benjamin Quarles wrote, "As a result of the unrelenting pressure of Negroes of every creed and class, America began a slow retreat from the bastion of white supremacy. Negroes were accepted into the Air Force, Marines, and WAACS. Segregated officer candidate schools were abolished; and . . . Negroes fought with white men in combat units to roll back the bulge (of racism)."[61] They served in every capacity in the military. Black paratroopers trained in Fort Benning, Georgia; naval cadets trained at Manhattan Beach Training Station, Brooklyn, New York; and army recruits, including the Forty-First Corps of Engineers, trained at Fort Bragg, North Carolina. The Tuskegee Airmen trained successfully as pilots in Tuskegee, Alabama, and provided superior protection for bombers. The Marine Corps desegregated, and the Army accepted Black women for the first time into the Women Auxiliary Army Corps (WAAC). Benjamin O. Davis was promoted to become the first Black general; his son, Benjamin O. Davis Jr., followed in his father's footsteps as general and commanded the Tuskegee Airmen.

The young men who fought against Nazi Germany returned as war veterans determined to continue the fight for freedom at home. Many were aware that the fight on foreign soil must be repeated in their homeland. They were confident and determined to resist racist discrimination. In 1940 the NAACP recorded a membership of fifty thousand; by 1946 veterans swelled it to four hundred thousand. They helped found the Congress of Racial Equality (CORE) in 1942 and were of vital importance to civil rights organizations.[62]

Many Black athletes and artists, while publicly silent, hoped their achievements would inspire both their people and the nation. Jesse Owens won Olympic gold medals at the 1936 Olympics, and boxer Joe Louis defeated the German Max Schmeling in 1938. A more militant element criticized both men and anyone else they considered to be Uncle Toms. Oscar winner Hattie McDaniel rebuked criticism over her roles playing maids by saying, "I'd rather make $700 a week playing a maid than earn $7 a day being a maid."[63]

Despite untiring efforts of Black leaders, white supremacy was difficult to eradicate, and Jim Crow would not die easily. Jesse Owens commented on the reception he received upon returning to the United States after the 1936 Olympics. He lamented, "I came back to my native country and couldn't ride in the front of the bus. . . . I had to go to the back door. I couldn't live where I wanted. . . . I wasn't invited to the White House to shake hands with the president either. . . . Hitler didn't snub me—it was our president who snubbed me. . . . The president didn't even send me a telegram."[64] Black frustrations boiled over in 1943 when rebellions exploded in forty-seven American cities. Detroit erupted in one of the worst instances of violence in the nation's history. Tempers flared and tension were high as Blacks and whites competed in job and housing markets with few openings. After thirty hours of unrest, thirty-four deaths, and $2 million in damage, federal troops finally intervened.[65]

Black men and women appear as a footnote in military history despite their enormous war presence of over a million troops. Megan Rosenfeld of the *Washington Post* observed, "The African Americans who fought valiantly despite having to live with a segregated military are represented by one Johnny Holmes, a nice man who spent his postwar life making good on a combat promise to God that if he was spared, he would help others. But their stories are not really included, either."[66] They are a neglected part of "The Greatest Generation" and charged their white peers with racial hypocrisy, as those who fought for European freedom supported racial discrimination on the home front. Many white soldiers, on returning home, quickly forgot that they were a band of brothers overseas. Historian Howard Zinn wrote,

> If there is to be a label "the greatest generation," let us consider attaching it also to the men and women of the sixties: the black people who changed the South and educated the nation, the civilians and soldiers who opposed the war in Vietnam, the women who put sexual equality on the national agenda, the homosexuals who declared their humanity in defiance of deep prejudices, the disabled people who insisted that the government recognize the discrimination against them.[67]

When Roosevelt succumbed to his illness in 1945, the entire country grieved, but especially Black Americans. Many considered him a friend and an ally.

According to John Hope Franklin, "Many regarded him as the best president since Lincoln."[68] The New Deal provided more economic security than the race had ever experienced. Under his administration, the earning ability of the average Black worker tripled. After his death, a letter was discovered that he wrote to North Carolina Democratic Senator Josiah W. Bailey. "If some of my good Baptist brethren in Georgia had done a little more preaching against the KKK, I would have a little more genuine American respect for their Christianity."[69]

SUMMARY OF THE MOTOWN GENERATION

In 2024, this generation was between seventy-nine and ninety-nine years of age. The Administration for Community Living's report, "2019 Profile of Older Americans," provided valuable statistical information on adults sixty-five years or older living in the United States. In 2018, more than one in every seven Americans was an older adult (sixty-five years and older). In the second decade of the twenty-first century, those sixty-five years and older increased from 38.8 million in 2008 to 52.4 million in 2018, a 35 percent increase in population. Twelve percent of all African Americans were in this age range. By 2060 it is estimated that there will be 94.7 million older adults. Racial ethnic minorities comprised 23 percent of the total in 2018, with 9 percent being African American. Their numbers grew to 7.5 million in 2008. They constituted 23 percent of all older adults, up from 19 percent in 2008. By 2040, they are projected to make up 34 percent, with a population of 27.7 million residents. The 2018 median income for families headed by Black persons sixty-five or older was $47,149, lower than the $67,904 for white families. Almost 19 percent lived below the poverty level. By 2019, some 79 percent had achieved a bachelor's degree or higher. This was an increase of 70 percentage points since 1970, when the percentage rate was 9 percent.

Overall, every race reported at least one chronic health condition, with many having several conditions. Forty-five percent reported that their health was excellent or very good as compared to 65 percent of those ages 18–64 years of age.[70] In 2016, about 50 percent lived in eight states: New York, Florida, Georgia, Texas, California, North Carolina, Illinois, and Maryland. That same year families led by Blacks 65 or older reported a median income of $43,554. In 2017, some 75 percent had completed high school, with 18 percent having a bachelor's degree or higher. Thirty-seven percent were married, 27 percent widowed, 19 percent divorced, 5 percent separated, and 13 percent had never married. Between 2012 and 2014, over 65 percent reported having good to excellent health with at least one chronic health condition. In both 2016 and 2017, reports indicated that between 39 and 40 percent had one or more disabilities.[71]

The top causes of death were heart disease, cancer, stroke, diabetes, and chronic lower respiratory diseases.[72]

This complex generation can be subdivided into subgenerations. This is a war generation, as members witnessed international violence that few other generations have experienced so intensely or personally. They were born into a global community sandwiched between two world wars within two decades of each other. There was always a battle going on. Life was one fight after another, and they fought for a better life. Those who came back from World War II continued to fight on the battlefields of America. They took seriously the fight to save democracy. Veterans joined and helped provide invaluable leadership for the Civil Rights Movement. World War II veteran Joe Lewis (not the boxer) remembered,

> I'm an old infantryman, a platoon sergeant. And yeah, the war changed me, changed us all. . . . I figured if those old guys could do it (register to vote), we could do it. The rest of them, they'd say, "Man, no, I ain't going down there and have those white folk getting hold of me." I begged people. At my church I begged the people. But there were only five of us went—John, Sidney, Vann, Thurston, myself. All of us had been in the service and come back home. . . . In the Army when the going got rough, you just get where it doesn't bother you. Same thing happened about this case. We didn't care what happened. We just made up our mind that we were going to register, and we went on and did it. We weren't afraid.[73]

Members of this generation created the Civil Rights Movement and have been referred to as the civil rights generation. This generation changed America. This generation believes in the right to protest and in its efficacy. Their commonality with whites of their generation ends when it comes to social and political rights. Aware of the nightmare of American racism, they did not accept it stoically. While many of their white peers were silent, and even resistant, to the injustices of their day, they refused to disengage. Ellis Cose countered *Time*'s description by attributing to Blacks during this period the possession of "militant beliefs." He contended that the two racial groups were opposites in life experience and worldviews. Blacks were fully aware that their white peers were complicit participants in American apartheid and were not silent in their support of white supremacy. Despite the ability of Blacks, if permitted, to participate functionally in society, their white peers denied them the chance. The Silent Generation was uncomfortable with a Black presence in southern universities and in corporate offices in the North. They refused to acknowledge that Blacks had the ability to compete if allowed an opportunity and did little to open doors for competent and qualified Blacks.[74] Philadelphia's first Black television news reporter, Trudy Haynes, described her work career as plagued by discrimination in 1965 when she was hired by KYW-3. Most of the resistance to her was not from viewers but from her work colleagues. "The crew didn't care to work with me, they'd do little things to make it uncomfortable."[75] This generation's parents' struggle to make ends meet filled them with a determination that change was going to come to America. Their childhood memories of racial violence and discrimination resulted in a people ready to engage to bring forth progress. It produced both the movement and its leadership as they marched in the streets, endured water cannons sprayed into their backs at high velocity, and went to jail. Contrary to their parents' instructions, they hit the streets. This is the generation of Berry Gordy Jr., Coretta Scott King, Martin Luther King Jr., Malcolm X, Medgar Evers, Ralph David Abernathy, John Lewis, Miles Davis, Hosea Williams, Barbara Jordan, Jesse Jackson, Maya Angelou, Tina Turner, and countless others. It was a generation of martyrs and risk-takers. Celebrities jeopardized precarious careers in industries just learning to accept Black performers. Ruby Dee, Ossie Davis, James Baldwin, Harry Belafonte, Sammy Davis Jr., Aretha Franklin, Dick Gregory, Berry Gordy Jr., and Sidney Poitier performed tirelessly in the movement. Sammy Davis Jr. raised $750,000 for the NAACP and Southern Christian Leadership Conference. Harry Belafonte fought in the South Pacific during World War II, and once home, he joined the movement. He adopted King's message about the power of nonviolence. "Have you ever tried to get your arms around a white man in a white sheet? You say that's not possible. I say, 'yes, it is.'"[76] This generation as a whole believes in the right to self-defense—never to initiate violence but to respond in kind when it is threatened. This generation taught their children to defend themselves and warned them that if they were assaulted and did not fight back, they would receive another beating when they came home. Robert F. Williams and other radicals refused to adopt nonviolent tactics and defended marchers and activists threatened by racist terrorists. In a 2012 interview in "Daughter of a Sharecropper," activist Frankye Adams-Johnson remembered, "I always felt that we were fighting for something. We were fighting for our freedom, we were fighting for justice, we were fighting for human rights, we were fighting for civil rights, and that became so important that the thought of giving up never really occurred. . . . I've always believed that things change if we help make them change."[77]

Members of this generation have appropriated and applied the lessons their grandparents taught to their parents. They affirm that life is hard and demands hard work and that if they are going to succeed, they have to stay committed and focused on their goals, despite resistance from white America. They expected similar commitment from others and from their children. They learned that loyalty begins with family and is extended beyond the doors of the home. It finds expression in workplaces as members remained on one job, within one profession, often for a lifetime. They often did one thing, did it for a long period of time, and did it well. They relied on hierarchy to provide order and structure. They respected authority in an authoritarian world and expected punctuality and structure. Respect for oneself and society was highly regarded and insisted on. They were risk-takers and wanted to expand the legacy of family. Thirty-one-year-old Weyling White returned to his hometown of Ahoskie, North Carolina, and became the first African American mayor in 2018. He spoke of the inspiration of his deceased grandfather. "My grandfather was by far the hardest working person I have ever known and also the funniest. Well into his late 60s, he would still crawl under houses and dig ditches, as he took his plumbing business very serious. My grandfather had a third-grade education and boasted about it like it was a PhD. He was a well-respected businessman in the community and often employed many men that couldn't find a job elsewhere. He taught me how to work hard, be fair, and most importantly take care of family."[78]

The Motown Generation aligns with various values of their white peers dubbed "The Silent Generation" by *Time* magazine in 1951. Both generations share a commitment to silence when it comes to affairs of the family and do not publicly discuss their personal matters. *Time* wrote in 1951,

> The most startling fact about the younger generation is its silence. With some rare exceptions, youth is nowhere near the rostrum. By comparison with the Flaming Youth of their fathers and mothers, today's younger generation is a still, small flame. It does not issue manifestoes, make speeches, or carry posters. It has been called the "Silent Generation." But what does the silence mean? What, if anything, does it hide? Or are youth's elders merely hard of hearing?[79]

The Motown Generation matured in a time when hard work demanded reserves of inner strength and silent resilience. Complaints were unspoken, especially if you were a man. They learned lessons of sacrifice witnessed firsthand by their parents' selfless lives. These life lessons were intensified by the difficulties contained within Black life and, due to Jim Crow repression, family took on greater significance. Motown Generation member Elizabeth Ohree commented on her family:

> Our parents were very hard-working people. They spent most of their lives working on the farm in Nash County. Our father owned a mule and a horse, and he gave one-fourth to the person who owned the land. They wanted us really to be somebody, and they worked very hard to make sure that we went to school as much as we could. We had to stay out of school for tobacco harvest, and then we stayed out to pick cotton and shake peanuts, and the boys stayed out to plow.[80]

Lives revolved around work and family, and it was considered anathema to speak ill of kin to outsiders. There was a commitment to offer support and compliance in the maintenance of its survival. When things weren't going well, one had to suck it up and do what was needed to ensure its survival. Alvin Ailey remembers a story his mother told him: "I told my father, I was going to separate from him (Alvin's father). And my daddy told me, you married him, you were going to stay with him. There will be no divorces in this Cliff family."[81] All children, even those born out of wedlock, were part of the nuclear family.

Because of being denied educational resources, this generation affirms the benefits of an education and readily makes sacrifices to support others in their desire to obtain academic training. Mayor Bunny Sanders followed in her father's footsteps when she became the mayor of her hometown in 1997. Elmer Vanray "E. V." Wilkins served Roper, North Carolina, for twenty years. His motto, "Don't get mad, get smart," was put on his tombstone. He was an educator and passed out the checks for the teachers but had to wait for the white chair of the school board, who couldn't read or write, to put his X on the checks, for hours at a time.

> My daddy used to say they had to "stoop to conquer." In my later years, I thought to myself how scriptural that is. And I'm telling you, he not only said that, I saw him stoop in many ways. He was often torn between what he knew he had to do in order to move Black people forward, especially to get money for the school, and what was kind of a humiliation for him. That is not something he wanted to do. He hated it. In fact, as a little girl, my sister and I used to lie in our bedroom and late at night I would hear my dad cursing in his sleep. He would be cursing white men. I guess in his dreams is where he got to do it. But he recognized it as a strategy, and it did not fail him. It was for a season that he had to do that, and then he got bolder and bolder as the years went on.[82]

This generation has a commitment to service and making a positive difference in the world. They feel blessed by their accomplishments and want to help others to be successful in their own right. They believe in a commitment to something other than yourself and your needs. If you have been blessed, you are called to bless others. Andrew Young wrote in his memoirs: "My parents lived through the depression. And their first thought was for security. It usually takes at least two secure generations for people to have a sense of responsibility toward others. I was that third generation. My grandfather had been a successful businessman and a well-respected leader in Louisiana's Prince Hall Masons. My father was a dentist. I was the generation destined to make a contribution to the world at large. My contribution was to go beyond my family and include a contribution to my race and humankind."[83] This generation inherited their parent's indefatigable spirits and continued the resistance they started. Don Stith was a firefighter in Warrenton, North Carolina, in the first fire department crewed by African Americans in the state. It was established by former slaves in 1868 and named the Plummer Hook and Ladder Company. Blacks would serve the Black section of town and whites the other. Following integration, whites wouldn't want a Black fireman in their home, even to put out a fire. Some would insist on going in to check if something was stolen. Don Stith remarked, "Chief Cheek and them heard it all, but they didn't care. They were here to protect the citizens of the town of Warrenton. They held their heads high, and they were the best of the best."[84]

As this generation grays, there is a resentful feeling that racism prevented them from achieving all that they were capable of accomplishing, a sense that America cheated them out of the advances available in a race-neutral society. They saw white colleagues being offered opportunities who lacked their drive and ability, simply because of the color of their skin. It was a sadness that their life could have been more meaningful if they were not limited by systemic racism, which refused to play by the rules it claimed to follow, that ability earned one the right to advance.[85] Sevone Rhynes grew up in Charlotte, North Carolina, and remembers the "colored" library, a segregated school with secondhand books and a three-hour school day. He reflected, "People who are white want as little to do with Black people as they can get away with."[86] Sheila Kingsberry-Burt lamented,

> We weren't afraid of white people. We knew what our place was. . . . If we suffered, we suffered from feelings of inferiority, not from fear of our safety. I was always clear that I was the inferior. That's what was so pervasive: It locked people into an inability to believe that they could hope for much more. Nobody told us different, not even in school. And even if somebody told you different, reality would prove it wrong. Like, the books that we had always had somebody's name in them—white people's names in them—before we got them. Like, that white people had a nice brick school down the street, and we had this little one here. Like, the white people live in this nice big house with running water and everything, and we don't even have a toilet in the house. Remember, none of the people who sharecropped had indoor plumbing or indoor toilets. None of them.[87]

They have seen the country change but remain skeptical and suspicious. Jim Crow left them with an unwillingness to fully trust in the genuineness of whites. The *Washington Post*'s George Floyd series resurrected a sense passed down through the family that no matter how hard you tried, the system was always dragging you down. There was a "more ominous sentiment" that each generation inherited. The Black community felt an "unshakable fear of White exploitation" and "a skepticism toward a system that had treated the family's dark skin as a permission slip for oppression." Floyd's brother wisely reflected the words sung by Louis Armstrong and Lou Rawls, "Your skin is your sin."[88] Ellis Cose titled this "Gen 1 Fighters" who "took on a society that was wedded to the notion that Blacks, no matter how brilliant and highly accomplished, are lesser beings. And in breaking through the walls that Jim Crow had built, they did indeed get scars. Those scars, deep and painful, left many of them unwilling to fully trust in the kindness and goodwill of white folks."[89] They are not surprised that racism still exists in so many areas of society. A 2019 *Washington Post* story recorded the comments of the daughter of a father who was lynched in Wytheville, Virginia: "Them old white people, I hate 'em all. I just don't want 'em around me. I don't trust 'em. The only thing I think about when I see 'em is bringing blood."[90]

The members of this generation are very religious. According to Pew Research Center, this generation registers high when it comes to religious commitment, as 88 percent identify religion as of vital importance in their lives. Only 4 percent deem it to be "somewhat" or "not too important." The predominant religion is Christianity, with 92 percent claiming it as their faith base; only 5 percent identify as being Catholic. Sixty-three percent are in a traditional Black Protestant denomination or association. Sixty-five percent attend worship services "at least once a week" and 25 percent once or twice monthly. Seventy-one percent read Scripture weekly, and 67 percent believe that the "Word of God should be taken literally." Eighty-four percent report that they pray "at least daily." Sixty percent participate in a formal faith-oriented activity each week, such as Bible study or Christian education. A significant number participate in meditation: 74 percent. Weekly an equal number report a level of "spiritual peace" or "wellbeing" rounding out at 75 percent. Half express a sense of wonder about the universe, spending time in speculation and awe, and 81 percent believe in heaven. This corresponds with 73 percent stating a belief that hell is a real place. A slightly higher number find guidance in their faith institution (48 percent) than merely utilizing "common sense" (41 percent). A high percentage (68 percent) believe in situational ethics and determine the proper course of action depending on the situation.[91]

The contributions of the Motown Generation are found in their determination to overcome the injustices that Black people faced for centuries of existence in the United States of America. They were only a generation from slavery, with family members who were enslaved. Their plight was only slightly better. They were determined to advance the race by any means necessary. They utilized a variety of strategies and tools, from the music of Motown to protest, advocacy, and entrepreneurship. They are advanced in age but have a resolve to make this world a better place by sharing their story and encouraging young people to aspire for greatness. They are inspirational, with a positive attitude and a love of life. They have lived a long time and have learned to value life as a gift from God that should not be wasted.

3

Black Power Generation (Baby Boomers)

1946–64

[G]enerations matter—hugely—and not just as a reflection of age. Ever since the civil rights generation shook things up, whites and American society have been undergoing a metamorphosis, and those changes have had different effects on blacks' expectations and aspirations depending on when they were born.[1]

—Ellis Cose, *The End of Anger*

The Black Power Generation is the most ideologically diverse generation and was impacted by America's transition to a more democratic nation. The signature song of the Civil Rights Movement was "We Shall Overcome"; this is the generation that overcame. Their nine million members emerged out of the struggles of the fifties and sixties with the doors of opportunity pried slightly open. Unique to this generation's experience was the historic conversion from segregation to integration. They lived in a transitional moment when God answered the prayers of the slaves that one day freedom would come, and with it, opportunity. As they evolved into adulthood, so did the nation. They were keenly aware that before them was a *kairos* moment where the change their ancestors prayed for was at hand. They were born into an openly racist, deeply segregated society slowly progressing into one that was to be the first to publicly reject racism. White supremacy had revealed its true nature as an evil blight on the soul of America, and for the first time it was disavowed by a majority of white Americans.

This generation grew up during the civil rights revolution, one of the most remarkable periods in the history of American life. As children who lived during the movement, theirs was a tumultuous environment filled with protest and revolutionary resistance often resulting in violent reprisal. This generation grew up in one of the most impactful periods for Blacks as they witnessed the change prior generations had struggled to bring to realization. It was the culmination of all previous struggles for freedom as American Jim Crow customs and norms experienced legal defeat. Black activism achieved a level of professionalism as community organizing against racial injustice became more widespread. The political prowess of this generation of African Americans reflected the lessons they learned from the previous generation. Access to presidents was accelerated, with Black leadership pushing even more aggressively for the dismantling of systemic racism. Not only were Black rights defended, but by extension human rights were advanced, including acceptance of gender and sexual identities.[2] *Ebony* magazine summarized,

> With WWII ending the previous decade, the '50s found the United States and its NATO allies firmly entrenched in the Cold War. Both "Colored" people who had fought abroad for U.S. interests and those who stayed behind would no longer tolerate a denial of citizenship through voter suppression, nor would they comply with the legal structures erected by entrenched racist powers to prevent them from building economic wealth. Confident of their rights as full citizens, they continued to chip away at racist practices and policies by challenging the laws that held them firmly in place.[3]

Ellis Cose described this generation as "children of the dream" but also as "children of the riots." They were willing to march but their patience was not eternal, and they were tired of waiting for change. If nonviolent marching didn't do it, then fighting back suited them just as well. Cose referred to columnist Clarence Page, who was asked during a conference if he received any advantage from the tumultuous sixties. Page responded, "Yes, a program called urban riots . . . thirty years ago, in 1965 to '68, we had over 400 urban riots in this country." He stressed that it was urban insurrection that forced newspapers and other businesses to recognize the need for Black faces on their staff in order to encounter urban communities.[4] David Forbes, a founding member of the Student Nonviolent Coordinating Committee (SNCC) chapter on his campus at Shaw University in Raleigh, North Carolina, commented, "But no matter how different people were, there was total agreement that the United States was not going to continue like it was on the race issues. Either they were going to be prepared to kill us all or something had to give. That time had come."[5]

This generation believes in the promise of America, even today. They were the first to catch a glimpse of what America could look like without Jim Crow. It was their parents' dream that they enroll in college, graduate, and secure a good job to escape the hardships they endured. As college graduates, they climbed the corporate ladder and assumed unprecedented positions in upper management and administration. They crafted the first permanent Black professional class and enlarged the size of the Black middle class. They had more interaction with whites than any of their forebears in open workplaces and desegregated neighborhoods. They had tremendous impact on racial views as they defied the stereotypical images that many whites believed represented the Black community. They learned to suppress their frustration and withheld lashing out when faced with blatant racism that was delivered under the cover of "just messing with you" or "don't be so sensitive." They were called "Affirmative Action babies" as white coworkers sought reasons to disqualify them from having earned their positions.

Just as this generation experienced an increase in Black activism, they also lived through a violent and virulent backlash from a racist society. For Blacks, terror continued to be a part of everyday living. African Americans had to contend with the constant threat of being assaulted, even murdered, for the crime of being Black, daring to vote, or simply registering. The murder of Blacks for simple offenses was a daily occurrence. Willis Williams remembered the times in which he grew up and the danger it posed for African Americans. He was a witness to the abduction of North Carolina Agricultural and Technical State University student Joe Cross, who was kidnapped and murdered by sheriff deputies who thought he was dating a white girl. They chased his car into the Williams front yard, dragged him into their car, and drove away with him. He was found dead.

> People still talk about Joe Cross. The other black men that were killed here did not have the affluence or family connections Joe did. Carl Grimes worked in the logwoods. King Hyman was military, shellshocked. Button Jackson was a Weyerhaeuser worker. But Joe was going to do something with his life. He was going to get his college degree, then work in his father's carpentry business. Outside of the ones that killed him, there was nobody black or white that didn't like him.[6]

The threat of nuclear war loomed, causing people to dig bomb shelters in homes, schools, and businesses. A cartoon PSA with Bert the Turtle taught young children to "duck and cover." Senator Joe McCarthy frightened the public with wild accusations of communist infiltration of the government and movie industry. He ran amuck for four years screaming of communists in the government, to the alarm of many Americans. Between 1953 and '54, he accusingly asked members of "The Hollywood Ten," "Have you ever been a member of the Communist Party?" Blacks were impacted, as Paul Robeson and Jackie Robinson were called before his committee, with repercussions for

Robeson in having his passport confiscated and career curtailed.[7] Most Blacks were careful not to associate with communists, out of loyalty and concern for their careers. William A. Nolan wrote a column, "Communism Versus the Negro," in which he revealed that after thirty years of solicitation, only five thousand Blacks joined the Communist Party.[8] Lena Horne commented, "Communism offers nothing to the Negro and the United States offers everything."[9]

The economy of the 1950s was strong, employment was high, and inflation was low. It was a time of economic prosperity accompanied by technological advances. Called the "Golden Age of American Capitalism," humongous government spending propelled a doubling of the gross national product in the fifteen years between 1945 ($200 billion) and 1960 ($500 billion).[10] A rise in wages allowed Americans to purchase home appliances for a life of comfort. The advent of television, transistor radios, drive-in movies, liberated fashions, low unemployment, and 2 percent inflation marked a new era of high living standards for millions of whites. The American dream was available to a wider range of people than ever before, and the hope of a house in the suburbs was becoming a reality for white America. Despite hard fought gains, Blacks were hampered by poverty, unemployment, low-wage jobs, and shorter life spans. They remained burdened under racist discrimination in the North and Jim Crow oppression in the South. The 1950s saw a decrease in Black wealth, a widening of the wage gap, and a disproportionate increase in unemployment. Every area of Black life was hampered by inadequate financial resources as well as discrimination in education, healthcare, housing, and employment. Dilapidated housing for Blacks increased and, in a decade, Black residents in thirteen cities had twice as many ruined homes with a lower financial worth. Those able to afford better homes were limited in their options.[11] Leola Spann remembered, "As a young woman I had a lot of prejudice. I did not understand why this white young woman was able to go here and do this and look pretty. In the South, I had this example. Here was this beautiful house and here was this shack. I had a good focus on how divided we were. It was a resentment, I'll put it that way. Not of the persons themselves but at the difference of the quality of life. I'm sure there's a lot of Black people that felt the same way."[12]

This generation experienced the Great Migration as a slow steady movement that grew each decade. Many families experienced the loss of fathers, siblings, and extended family. The Black population blossomed to 14,900,000 as a greater number of Blacks moved to the nation's northern and western regions. This relocation had enormous political and economic implications. For the first time, the Black vote could determine local, state, and national elections. Black home ownership doubled, and wages increased by three and a half times their former rates. Black college attendance percentages outpaced those of whites.[13] A higher percentage of Blacks younger than twenty-five years of age married, but they suffered higher divorce rates than whites. In some areas, their divorces outnumbered those of whites. One in every two thousand marriages was between whites and Blacks. The Black death rate decreased at a faster rate than whites. There was improvement in the wage ratio between northern Black and white laborers as southern low-paying positions were abandoned for higher wages in the North. The number of farm laborers greatly shrank until farm laborers were one of every six wage earners. Those in semiskilled trades increased from 380,000 (1940) to one million.[14] Legislation limited hiring discrimination, resulting in job acquisition, and in 1945 the minimum wage was increased. Blacks benefited from jobs in the defense industry making tanks, planes, jeeps, and other military vehicles and weapons. Despite discriminatory distribution of the GI Bill, Black veterans took advantage of the opportunity to attend college, and thousands received degrees.[15] They were hired into the ranks of police officers. In the South, 82 municipalities hired 450 Black officers. In 12 states there were 381 uniformed officers, another 44 were in plainclothes, with an additional 18 serving as policemen. Miami was a forerunner with its "Negro-Officers-for-Negros" program that produced 41 officers, followed by Louisville, Kentucky, with 36. Miami's chief credited the new recruits with lowering crime by 50 percent.[16]

THE PRESIDENTS

This generation lived during the most pro-civil rights presidential administrations *ever!* Presidents who governed during this period were Harry S. Truman (1945–53, thirty-third president), Dwight D. Eisenhower (1953–61, thirty-fourth president), and John F. Kennedy (1961–63, thirty-fifth president). The Lyndon Johnson administration, although belonging to the next generation, can be viewed with the same progressive lens. Truman, Eisenhower, and Kennedy faced international pressure as the victory of World War II quickly chilled into a Cold War.

President Harry S. Truman (1945–53, thirty-third president) came into office under a cloud of suspicion in the eyes of the Black community. They were well aware that he ascended to the presidency due to the death of President Roosevelt just five months into his fourth term. He was born in 1884, just nineteen years after the end of the Civil War. His family history included slaveholders as well as Confederate sympathizers.[17] His mother embedded in him the Confederate perspective on the Civil War and taught him to believe in white supremacy. She hated anything northern and racially progressive.

She so reviled Abraham Lincoln that, on her first visit to the White House, she stated that she would sleep on the floor before sleeping in the Lincoln bedroom.

Throughout his presidency, Truman used racial slurs and told racist jokes. Between 1911 and 1939, his letters to family were filled with racial epithets and demeaning statements about Black inferiority. "I think one man is just as good as another so long as he's honest and decent and not a nigger or a Chinaman. Uncle Will says that the Lord made a white man from dust, a nigger from mud, and then threw what was left and it came down a Chinaman. He does hate Chinese and Japs. So do I. It is race prejudice, I guess. But I am strongly of the opinion that Negros ought to be in Africa, yellow men in Asia and white men in Europe and America." In other letters he commented, "All these things were in courses, deftly placed and removed by an army of coons. . . . Well, this is a n***** picnic day."[18]

It was rightly assumed that Black rights were not his immediate priority nor was he their candidate of choice. A May 1946 Negro Digest Poll revealed that 91 percent of Black voters preferred Henry Agard Wallace, FDR's previous vice president, in the upcoming Democratic presidential campaign. Many doubted his ability to be the successor to the most popular president in their lifetime. Democrats held together a fragile coalition of voters often at odds with one another: Blacks, southern whites, small farmers, and laborers. Many in his own party initially rejected his leadership and called for his resignation.[19] In 1946, fifty Black women demonstrated in protest in front of the White House holding signs reading, "Speak! Speak! Mr. President!" and "Where Is Democracy?"[20]

The fight for civil rights led to the founding of organizations that were amazingly effective at galvanizing the population. Springing up almost overnight was the Montgomery Improvement Association (MIA), National Association for the Advancement of Colored People (NAACP), the Southern Christian Leadership Conference (SCLC), Student Nonviolent Coordinating Committee (SNCC), Congress of Racial Equality (CORE), the Council of Federated Organizations (COFO), and the Alabama Christian Movement for Human Rights (ACMHR). These organizations created a variety of strategies in the fight to overcome racial discrimination. As the movement gained momentum around the country, marches and rallies were primary tactics in Southern cities. Nonviolent protest occurred at sit-ins, Freedom Rides, and voter registration drives. Sit-ins occurred in restaurants, libraries, swimming pools, and businesses.[21]

The NAACP played a major role in bringing lawsuits through its Legal Defense Fund. Attorney Charles Hamilton Houston argued that *Plessy v. Ferguson* mandated that segregated facilities had to be equal. He successfully

sued the Universities of Texas and Oklahoma State for inequitable education. Another tactic promoted the idea that the cost of discrimination was a
mental and emotional one. The importance of racial identity and the damage inflicted on it by Jim Crow could be used as means of measuring the
impact of discrimination. Twenty Black organizations, led by the NAACP and
the National Urban League, published a "Declaration of Negro Voters" that
included a call for military desegregation.[22] In 1951, Josephine Baker raised
quite a ruckus at the New York Stork Club when she waited for an hour to
be served while whites seated all around her table received their meals. She
wrote to President Truman, who responded by inviting *New York Post* reporter
Ted Poston to the White House to brief him on the incident. The incident
was resolved to the dissatisfaction of the Black public, with no apology from
a recalcitrant owner.[23] In 1951, Dr. Frederick Wertham testified in an anti-
segregation lawsuit that segregation harmed both Black and white children.
They theorized that such an "anxiety-producing factor" could be interpreted
as a "punishment" and produced "social disorientation." It taught white children that they were superior to others.[24]

While Black rights were not originally at the forefront of Truman's agenda,
his conscience was pricked by lynchings occurring across the country and by
the treatment of Black soldiers. On September 19, 1948, Truman met with
clergy and leaders of the National Emergency Committee Against Mob Violence to discuss ways to curb racial violence. After listening to Walter White,
head of the NAACP, the president was shocked and exclaimed, "My God.
I had no idea it was as terrible as that. We've got to do something!"[25] The
abuse and beating which left World War II veteran Sergeant Isaac Wood-
ard blinded had a particularly strong impact on the president. "My stomach
turned over when I learned that Negro soldiers, just back from overseas, were
being dumped out of army trucks in Mississippi and beaten. Whatever my
inclinations as a native of Missouri might have been, as President I know
this is bad. I shall fight to end evils like this."[26] "The will to fight these crimes
should be in the heart of every one of us."[27] These were emotionally strong
statements that the Black community had not heard before from a president
of the United States. But still, many wondered if actions would follow the
words. Eventually, they did.

An effective tool in the freedom struggle was the growing influence of the
Black press. Notable newspaper reporters and editors were Wendell Smith of
the *Pittsburgh Courier*, Fay Young of the *Chicago Defender*, Joe Bostic of the *People's
Voice* in New York, Sam Lacy of the *Baltimore Afro-American*, and Lester Rodney,
sports editor of the Communist paper the *Daily Worker*. Between 1945 and
1948, the Black press advocated for the desegregation of Major League Baseball. They utilized every journalistic tool at their disposal. They wrote and

published open letters to owners challenging the racist policies keeping Blacks out simply due to the color of their skin. Some published conversations with white managers and players who confided that they would not object to playing with Black players even though it might be at the sacrifice of their positions. They ushered Black players into spring tryouts even though the teams had not scheduled a workout. They did everything they could to keep the issue in the public eye. Because of their leadership, several white journalists picked up the refrain and rallied around Black entry into the major leagues. Once Jackie Robinson was picked up by the Brooklyn Dodgers, the advocacy of the press was so consistent that it provided free publicity for the team in the promotion of desegregation.

As president, Truman demonstrated one characteristic of great value to the Black community: he was a man of his word. He took seriously his pledge to govern by "a simple formula: to do in all cases without regard to political considerations what seems to me to be for the welfare of all our people."[28] Truman established the President's Committee on Civil Rights on December 5, 1946. At a meeting at the White House, he gave them his reasoning: "Because of the repeated anti-minority incidents immediately after the war in which homes were invaded, property was destroyed, and a number of innocent lives were taken."[29] He charged it with safeguarding the rights of every American, regardless of race, creed or religion. "I want our Bill of Rights implemented in fact. We have been trying to do this for 150 years. We're making progress, but we're not making progress fast enough." The committee produced the report "To Secure These Rights," which recommended an end to racial discrimination, segregation, and police brutality. He was the first president to speak at the annual meeting of the NAACP on June 29, 1947, before ten thousand attendees from the steps of the Lincoln Memorial. The NAACP was considered a radical organization, and to many southerners, it was also a communist pawn. "There is no justifiable reason for discrimination because of ancestry, religion, race, or color. We cannot wait another decade or another generation to remedy these evils. We must work, as never before, to cure them now." He repeated the phrase several time to heartfelt applause, "When I say all Americans, I mean, all Americans."[30] NAACP president Walter White was moved by the president's word and told him on the platform that it was a stunning speech. Truman replied, "I said what I did because I mean every word of it— and I am going to prove that I do mean it."[31] Southern Senator Strom Thurmond led his fellow southerners out of the Democratic Party. The Dixiecrats formed the States Rights Democratic Party with segregationist Thurmond as its presidential candidate.[32] When asked by a reporter why he left when Roosevelt had used similar rhetoric, Thurmond replied that the difference was that "Truman really means it."[33]

Truman responded in a more decisive manner than did most presidents. He was the first president since Abraham Lincoln to confront and publicly denounce the country's history of racial discrimination toward Black Americans. He was the first president to make the fight against racial injustice a priority in his administration. He believed that the federal government should protect the rights of all citizens, regardless of race. He challenged the South's long-utilized justification for discrimination based on states' rights theory and stated plainly that the federal government has an interest in and the authority to protect the rights of citizens when they are abused. "The full force and power of the federal government must stand behind the protection of rights guaranteed by our federal constitution."[34] He refused to back down when southern Democrats threatened to not support the rest of his programs and even leave the party. He expanded on Roosevelt's theory of expanded government: "The extension of civil rights today means not protection of the people against the government, but protection of the people by the government."[35]

On February 2, 1948, Truman became the first president to send a special message to Congress endorsing civil rights legislation and called for a ten-point program. He was unmovable. "We cannot be satisfied until all our people have equal opportunity for jobs, for homes, for education, for health and for political expression, and until all our people have equal protection under the law."[36] He proposed voting protections, a permanent Fair Employment Practices Commission (FEPC), an anti-lynching law, and the creation of a permanent Commission on Civil Rights. To end intimidation at the polls, he asked for legislation banning interference by either public officials or private citizens with the free exercise of suffrage.[37] He went even further, calling for "home rule for the District of Columbia; statehood for Hawaii and Alaska and more self-government for other U.S. territories; equalizing opportunities for residents of the United States to become naturalized citizens, and settlement of the evacuation claims of Japanese-Americans."[38] As Congress debated his civil rights bills, he vetoed a 1951 school construction bill that mandated that all schools constructed on military bases were to be "in conformance with the laws of the states where the defense installations are located."[39] This bill would have segregated all southern bases. He affirmed that "discrimination is a disease, we must attack it wherever it appears."[40] He asserted that if the United States wanted to be a leader on the world stage, it had to begin at home. "Step by step we are discarding old discriminations. We must not adopt new ones."[41]

He was the first Cold War president and undertook his responsibility as the leader of the free world with a grave determination. During his time in office, he confronted, in his own deliberate manner, a series of consequential international events: the decision to drop atomic weapons on Japan, confrontation

with Stalin at Potsdam, sending troops to Korea, the firing of General MacAr-
thur, the Marshall Plan, and the Truman Doctrine. The Soviet Union increasingly criticized the United States over the way it treated people of color,
primarily African Americans. Truman considered the criticisms with great
thoughtfulness: "The top dog in a world which is half Colored ought to clean
his own house."[42] When Congress failed to pass any of his civil rights legislation, Truman acted through executive orders. In a single day (July 26, 1948),
he signed Executive Orders 9980 and 9981 that enforced equality in federal
employment and integrated the military. He boldly stated, "There shall be
equality of treatment and opportunity for all persons in the armed services
without regard to race, color, religion or national origin." Executive Order
10210 prohibited racial discrimination under the War Powers Act of 1941.
EO 10308 prohibited federal contractors from practicing hiring discrimination. He stated, "There shall be equality of treatment and opportunity for
all persons in the armed services without regard to race, color, religion or
national origin."[43]

His 1948 reelection campaign contained a platform endorsing human
rights that shocked southern Democrats. While campaigning, he became
the first president to canvass Black voters with a visit to Harlem, New York.
On the campus of Howard University, he reaffirmed his position, "You can't
cure a moral problem, or social problem, by ignoring it."[44] He received a
letter from a friend beseeching him to desist in his efforts for racial equality.
He responded, "The main difficulty with the South is that they are living
eighty years behind the times and the sooner they come out of it the better it
will be for the country and for themselves. I am not asking for social equality, because no such thing exists, but I am asking for equality of opportunity
for all human beings and, as long as I stay here, I am going to continue that
fight."[45] It was an extremely bold move leading up to an election. He won
with heavy support from Black voters in key electoral states (California, Illinois, and Ohio) over Republican Thomas Dewey.[46] He called his win one
of his greatest achievements because he achieved it without the support of
the Dixiecrats. His 1949 inauguration was one of the most integrated in
presidential history.

When asked about what appeared to many to be an abrupt turnaround, he
replied that he was never racist in his personal feelings toward African Americans and talked about growing up around Black people. He confided to Carl
Rowan that despite his conservative voting record in the Senate, his positions
on race were consistent. "My views in the White House were exactly the same
as when I was back in Jackson County, Missouri. I grew up with Negroes. I
was always friendly with them. And they were just like part of my family. I
learned a long time ago that the composition of the human animal was about

the same no matter what color your skin is."[47] To Truman's credit, he demonstrated early indications of leaning toward racial equality during his 1940 Senate reelection campaign. Before a largely white crowd he said, "I believe in brotherhood . . . of all men before the law . . . if any (one) class or race can be permanently set apart from, or pushed down below the rest in politics and civil rights, so may any other class or race . . . and we say farewell to the principles on which we count our safety. . . . The majority of our Negro people find but cold comfort in our shanties and tenements. Surely, as free men, they are entitled to something better than this."[48]

When he left the White House, he had low poll ratings, and many whites considered him a failure as a president. But for the Black community, he had secured a place of respect for his quiet dignity and determined will to do the right thing regardless of the political consequences. Many Blacks considered him an ally in the cause of Black rights. His actions were heralded as "the greatest contribution to the cause of human rights." As president, he intimately understood that he was president of the entire nation. The Interdenominational Ministerial Alliance of Greater New York honored him with the annual Franklin D. Roosevelt Award. He received the American Democracy Legacy medal from the Anti-Defamation League of B'nai B'rith.[49] The Negro Newspaper Publishers Association awarded him the John B. Russwurm Award. Black newspapers wrote a fitting eulogy to his presidency that the outgoing president had "awakened the conscience of America and given new strength to our democracy by his courageous efforts on behalf of freedom and equality for all citizens."[50] He was fondly called, "Mr. Civil Rights." At the 1956 Democratic national convention, Black Democrats considered the platform to be too conservative. Truman declared, "I say that this is a good civil rights plank and I'm the greatest civil rights president the country ever had."[51] Carl Rowan agreed, writing, "No president in the nation's history stuck his neck out further or risked more in terms of his own political future or the nation's well-being in order to espouse the first-class citizenship for the Negro than did Harry Truman."[52]

His reputation with Blacks and whites from Missouri was unsurpassed. According to Representative J. Frederick Neal, he single-handedly changed his home state for the better. "Missouri has made more progress in civil rights than any other southern or border state. School integration is completed in all but three counties in the state." He remarked on the change in Independence which "immediately integrated both students and teachers." The Howard Johnson Hotel and the Kansas City Convention center both allowed Blacks to be served as a result of the former president's influence.[53] He demonstrated a will to uphold the rights of all citizens despite the fact that he was born and bred in white supremacist Missouri. He overcame racist sentiments and defended the rights of Blacks to be free from violence and discrimination under the protection of the constitution. In a speech in Sedalia, Missouri, he said, "I believe in the brotherhood of man, not merely the brotherhood of white men, but the brotherhood of all men before law. I believe in the Constitution and the Declaration of Independence. In giving the Negroes the rights which are theirs, we are only acting in accord with our own ideals of a true democracy."[54]

In many ways Truman completed the party shift that saw Blacks leaving the Republican Party to become Democrats. The transition began with Franklin D. Roosevelt, but it was Truman's focused determination to address racism that paved the way. *Jet* magazine reflected this reconsideration in an article it published in its second issue in 1951. "At a pro-Truman, non-segregated Democratic breakfast held in Dallas, Texas, a white son of a slave owner stood beside a Negro son of a slave. As they shook hands, the white man said: 'It took 90 years and Roosevelt and Truman to bring this about.' He then suggested that all sons and daughters of slaves should join the Democratic Party."[55]

After he left office, Truman openly disapproved of interracial marriages, criticized the sit-ins by young adults, and threatened to throw out anyone who disrupted his business. He accused the protesters of spreading "ill will."[56] He publicly branded Martin Luther King Jr. a troublemaker. In a letter, King wrote to Truman that he held him in high esteem and reminded the former president that he had sent him an autographed copy of his first book, *Stride Toward Freedom*. He expressed his disappointment in his condemnation of the sit-ins as communist inspired. "It is a sad day for our country when men come to feel that oppressed people cannot desire freedom and human dignity unless they are motivated by Communism. . . . When the accusations come from a man who was once chosen by the American people to serve as the chief custodian of the nation's destiny then they rise to shocking and dangerous proportions."[57]

Two misguided wars to halt the spread of communism, the Korean Conflict (1950–53) and the Vietnam War (1955–75), disillusioned white youth while Black youth became enamored with the protest of the Civil Rights Movement. Blacks leveraged their growing voting strength to sway executives to endorse their issues. The importance of the Black vote, in the South as well as the North, reached its apex in influence and value to administrations. Presidents who responded with executive orders or lobbied Congress were rewarded with overwhelming Black support. The presidents of this generation responded despite personal misgivings and even racist beliefs held in reserve. Brody Shields's thesis, "The Civil Rights Presidents: FDR to Nixon," revealed, "Presidents throughout the civil rights era had different ideas and strategies on how to handle the issue and bring about equality for African Americans. When evaluating the different presidents in the era, from Franklin D. Roosevelt to Richard Nixon, it is often found that the main driving forces among them to act on civil rights were necessity and political gain. Factors such as domestic unrest, political aspirations, and political influence forced these presidents to act on, or delay, civil rights legislation whether they had the desire to or not."[58]

Blacks were well aware of the influence of the international community and appealed to the global family of nations to put pressure on America's leaders. They widened their target audience, no longer solely focused on an American theater, but also pursuing world leaders and the foreign press. They were aware of American political sensitivity to foreign propaganda and criticism, especially by the Soviet Union. They used the global stage to address apartheid in European colonies, South Africa, and America. United Nations ambassador Ralph Bunche stated, "There cannot be any sound foundation for peace in the world unless 200 million colonial people may look forward to freedom." Former U.N. delegate Edith Sampson remarked candidly, "The sole reason America is finding difficulty in winning the confidence of eastern powers is due to racial discrimination at home."[59] Darius L. Swann, the first Black missionary sent to China, relayed stories of the high acceptance he received where race was a non-factor. He shared with his fellow Presbyterian missionaries that the Chinese displayed no racial enmity and considered tolerance to be a worthy attribute.[60]

President Dwight David Eisenhower (1953–61) assumed the office of the presidency in 1953 with a promise to end the war in Korea. He came into office one year before the Supreme Court's *Brown v. Board of Education* decision and the emergence of the coming Civil Rights Movement. He was not a proponent of civil rights. The country was in the midst of racial transformation, and he struggled to manage the transition from what it was to what it was going to be. He publicly opposed legislation that would compel states to end discrimination, naively stating that states should handle race relations. He affirmed his belief that most southerners were "of good will, united in their efforts to preserve and respect the law." He was very sympathetic to white southerners who complained that their way of life was being destroyed. He justified his own racist beliefs that white southerners were simply ensuring that "their sweet little girls were not required to sit in school alongside some big Black buck."[61] After meeting with South Carolina Governor James Byrnes, the president wrote in his diary,

> He is well aware of my belief that improvement in race relations is one of those things that will be healthy and sound only if it starts locally. I do not believe that prejudices, even palpably unjustified prejudices,

will succumb to compulsion. Consequently, I believe the Federal law imposed upon our states in such a way as to bring about a conflict of the police powers of the states and of the nation, would set back the cause of progress in race relations a long, long time.[62]

Martin Luther King Jr. tried to induce him to use his bully pulpit in support of racial integration. He remained silent.

Similar to his military forebear, General Ulysses Grant, Eisenhower was meticulous, methodical, and painstakingly cautious before taking action. His leadership can be summed up by his call for "patience and forbearance." On May 17, the 1954 *Brown v. Board of Education* Supreme Court decision legally ended segregation in public schools. After a magazine reported that he had voiced personal reservations about the Brown decision, the president clarified to say that he had "said something about slower." Attorney Thurgood Marshall responded that progress was so slow that the country was almost going backward. Civil rights leaders urged him to be more vocal on the rising tide against white supremacy and Jim Crow policy. He would not. NAACP president Roy Wilkins said, "President Eisenhower was a fine general and a good, decent man, but if he had fought World War II the way he fought for civil rights, we would all be speaking German now."[63]

He personally edited his Attorney General's speech to indicate that segregation would be a permanent reality and that desegregation could take upwards of twenty years.[64] He attempted to keep civil rights leaders at a distance and privately believed that most were closet communists, or at the very least aligned with those who were. He had only one meeting with civil rights leaders during his two terms in office. In 1958 King wrote the president for a second time requesting that the president meet with Black leaders to use his bully pulpit to prevent the domestic terrorism occurring in all quarters of the South. The president's response was to question whether his making a speech would make a difference. Mamie Till, the mother of slain Emmett, wrote the president asking for his intervention in seeking justice for the murder of her son. He never replied.[65] The president continued to remain silent and took no actions. The president's failure to respond was an indication to segregationists that they could resist desegregation efforts. He later insisted that his intention was to enforce the ruling of the courts; it was never to enforce integration.

That wouldn't last for long. During his time in office, pivotal civil rights events erupted to let him know that the fight for justice would be held under his watch. The resistance to the Black protest movement was overwhelming; southern white society reacted with a fierce determination to defeat the movement for Black rights by means both violent and extralegal. Mississippi, with a 45 percent Black population, was one of the deadliest places to live as a person of color. On August 28, fourteen-year-old Emmett Till was murdered in the township of Money, which brought the state unwanted national attention. Reverend George Lee and Lama Smith were murdered for political activism. On December 1, Rosa Parks's refusal to give up her seat was met with arrest, initiating the Montgomery Bus Boycott.

A key line of resistance was drawn at school doors. One hundred southern congressmen responded to the 1954 Supreme Court ruling with a "southern manifesto" and a pledge to resist the *Brown* decision. When the Little Rock Nine attempted to attend Central High in the fall of 1957, the White Citizen's Council and the Central High Mothers' League organized a protest. Governor Orval Faubus sent the National Guard and state troopers to prevent their enrolling. President Eisenhower nationalized the National Guard, which granted the students entry. For the first time in eighty-one years a president of the United States ordered the presence of troops in the South to protect the rights of Black people. Ernest Green graduated on May 27, 1958. The governor closed the schools from August 1958 until September 1959. In Virginia, Prince Edward County closed every public school under its authority the school year of 1959–60. Whites responded to *Brown* with violence and a mass withdrawal of children from public schools called "massive resistance." When the schools opened, not one white student enrolled. Their parents enlisted them in segregation academies with a lasting legacy of mostly racially divided schools still in operation.[66] In 1962 the southern states of Mississippi, South Carolina, and Alabama created white and Black schools. Two years later only 2 percent of Black students in eleven states attended integrated schools. Mississippi declared that rather than integrate its school systems, it would finance segregated facilities at a cost of $141,000,000 over twenty years.[67] Governor George Wallace stood in the door of the University of Alabama adamant that Black students would not be enrolled at the university. When James Meredith attempted to attend the University of Mississippi, Governor Ross Barnett blocked the door.[68]

By 1957 Eisenhower could no longer ignore the movement, as some of the most progressive Supreme Court rulings joined with congressional legislation in favor of King and the movement.[69] A 1951 Supreme Court decision declared segregation unconstitutional in DC restaurants. Thurgood Marshall won the 1954 *Brown v. Board of Education* case by convincing the court that segregation did measurable damage to the psyches of Black children. Drs. Mamie and Kenneth Clark tested the self-esteem of Black children using Black and white dolls. Consistently the children associated beauty and niceness with the lighter-skinned dolls. The Clarks convinced the Supreme Court that segregation caused lifelong mental deterioration for Black children.[70] A year after the 1954 *Brown* decision, the Supreme Court determined guidelines in *Brown II*. Similar anti-discrimination rulings occurred in public education (1951), housing (1954), and transportation (1956). Congress followed suit with the Civil Rights Act of 1957, creating the Civil Rights Division of the Department of Justice and the Federal Civil Rights Commission.[71]

When nine Black students were prevented from integrating Little Rock Central High School, Eisenhower redefined the role he was to play. No longer was it just a fight for Black equality but a question about the authority of the federal government and American democracy itself. While he was not a passionate proponent of civil rights or school desegregation, Eisenhower was adamant that the authority of the federal government had to be maintained. When the Supreme Court ruled against the state he was determined that states had to adhere to its decision. The president, reluctantly, sent in the National Guard to protect the students for the remainder of the school year. The administration arranged it so that only white troops were sent to the school. *Jet* magazine reported that "the pride of the integrated U.S. Army was being re-segregated for this mission."[72] It was the first time that a president had sent federal troops into the South since the Reconstruction Era. The president justified his decision on national television on the grounds that the Soviet Union used the incident for propaganda purposes. Despite his wavering, Martin Luther King Jr. affirmed the president's stance on maintaining "law and order. . . . You should know that the overwhelming majority of Southerners, Negro and white stand firmly behind your resolute action." Governor Orval Faubus retaliated by closing every public high school in Little Rock.[73]

Eisenhower quietly initiated several vital actions in the advance of racial justice. He desegregated the District of Columbia. His appointment of Earl Warren as the Chief Justice of the Supreme Court on September 30, 1953, gave civil rights a major impetus, even though the president later regretted the choice, referring to it as the greatest mistake of his life. He appointed moderate to progressive federal judges to federal courts and a total of five Supreme Court Justices, none of them segregationists. He signed several significant pieces of civil rights legislation into law. He lobbied for the passage of the Civil Rights Bill of 1957, and with his signature it became the first civil rights legislation since Reconstruction. It established the Civil Rights Commission and the Civil Rights Division in the Justice Department. It was weakened by an amendment inserted by southern Democrats intended to deny African American suffrage.[74] He signed a second bill in 1960 and used his constitutional authority to challenge segregation. He made into a reality Truman's desegregation of the military, which had taken five years to fully implement.

In the last year of his term in February, the sit-in movement started when four Black students in Greensboro, North Carolina, were refused service at a lunch counter. Both President Eisenhower and Vice President Nixon gave informal endorsements of the protests. In November six-year-old Ruby Bridges was escorted into school in New Orleans by four armed federal marshals.

The argument over whether Eisenhower was a reluctant hero or a clandestine racist continues to this day. Two of his biographers strongly disagree on his purpose and stance on civil rights. Stephen E. Ambrose stated firmly that the president was not a civil rights leader and that his "refusal to lead was almost criminal." David A. Nichols insisted that the man must be measured not by his words, but as a soldier, by his deeds. He quoted Ike as reflecting on his civil rights record, "We have been pursuing this quietly, not tub-thumping, and we have not tried to claim political credit. This is a matter of justice, not of anything else."[75] E. Frederic Morrow was the first African American to serve as a White House executive staff member. He relentlessly demanded that the administration do more to pursue racial justice. He was often frustrated and warned that the country was bordering on the edge of a racial confrontation. In his book *Black Man in the White House* he wrote, "The failure of any prominent member of the administration to speak out and deplore the present condition of terrorism and economic sanction against Negroes is causing deep concern among Negro leaders in the country today. . . . [The administration] has completely abandoned the Negro in the South and left him to the mercy of state governments."[76]

Black frustration was suitably summed up by a letter to the president from Val J. Washington that he received on July 16, 1957. Washington was the Republican National Committee Director of Minorities. He wrote,

> I am not a radical or extremist, but as a Negro I have always sought and demanded my rights within the orderly processes of the law. I shall continue to do so. There are many of us who have worked and patiently waited years for a Republican regime willing to change unlawful traditions which rob us of our rights as first-class citizens. We knew that in you we have a leader who would, when given an opportunity, rectify the flagrant injustices and inequities by which we have been penalized. This situation has existed for years through no fault of our own. I refuse to believe that you would ever compromise any basic right because of pressures from those so prejudiced that they wish to continue humiliating loyal citizens. We have a right to share and share alike in all that is a part of the Americans way of life—the sweet as well as the bitter. I know you will not let us down.[77]

The debate is still being waged.

Black colleges and universities contributed to the increase of a growing percentage of the populace being educated. A 1950 U.S. Office of Education survey determined that one out of every 221 Blacks in the South were in college; twenty years earlier it was one out of every 364.[78] Between 1950–51, an additional nine colleges were founded, adding to a record number of students attending. "The U.S. Office of Education reported 2,624 students in 1900, and 74,526 in 1950. Baccalaureate degrees awarded: 156 in 1900; 13,108 in 1950. Faculty membership, however, has increased more slowly. Number of instructors: 1,555 in 1900; 5,851 in 1950."[79] Illinois college educators voted unanimously to recommend to their universities the eradication of all racial barriers in the admittance of students as well as segregation in "classrooms, housing, recreation, food and health services, scholarships, grants, campus employment, graduate placement, and charter for new college social organizations."[80] When the University of Louisville eliminated its racial prohibitions in all academic programs, President Philip Davidson reported that 270 Black students transferred to the school.[81] *Jet* magazine reported that in 1951, "For the first time in modern history of the South, colored and white grade school students are attending a publicly supported elementary school on a completely unsegregated basis." It occurred on the Fort Bragg, North Carolina, army base as 33 Black students were quietly integrated with 1,175 white students.[82] The North maintained a sizable percentage of Black students, 30 percent, who attended schools that were at least 90 percent Black.[83] A number of private graduate schools began accepting Black students, especially those affiliated with a religious denomination: Columbia (Presbyterian) Theological Seminary and two Episcopalian schools in Sewanee, Tennessee, and Lexington, Kentucky.[84] A decade before, Atlanta University President Rufus Clement predicted that it would only take a decade or two before academic segregation would be ended in the country. He urged his colleagues to raise their standards to be ready to accept students of all races.[85]

The 1960s was the decade of victories toward the desegregation of public schools and protection of Black voting rights. A series of Supreme Court victories boosted voting rights, fair housing, school integration, and college enrollment. The decade came to life out of the 1950s boom amid great promise and excitement. It was during this period in time that the freedom movement evolved into a radicalized protest movement. Each generation produced its own freedom fighters, from slave revolutionaries to combatants against racist violence and discrimination. Marked as beginning in 1954 with the inspirational Montgomery bus boycott, the Civil Rights Movement introduced to the world Rosa Parks and Martin Luther King Jr. The protests became more public and abandoned the veil of secrecy. Even the nonviolent and patient Martin Luther King Jr. expressed frustration with the Vietnam War and the slowness of change. In 1960, NAACP president Roy Wilkins announced the adoption of a more confrontational policy. "We have always used persuasion through various means of political and economic pressure, but now we're going to use it much more intensively than in the past because the membership has become restless over the slow pace of the civil rights proceedings."[86] Young Blacks adopted "Black Power" as a platform and confronted racism by sitting down in restaurants and places with "whites only" signs. Nonviolence was rejected for the right to self-defense and militancy. A new, more radicalized vocalization of self-defense was adopted by the Nation of Islam and its chief spokesman, Malcolm X. The Black Panther Party grew into a national movement advocating for Blacks to arm themselves and seek self-reliance. White youth around the country protested the war and refused the draft. SNCC's chairman, Stokely Carmichael, popularized the term *Black Power* to demonstrate a determination to demand, not ask for, equal rights.[87]

Much of the focus for civil rights protest was positioned in the southern theater, but the North had its own brand of discrimination. "Protecting the neighborhood school was the northern equivalent of preserving the southern way of life. Thus, many Northern school boards were as guilty of perpetuating segregation as those in the South."[88] Racial segregation in schools existed until the 1950s. State-by-state integration was adopted in New York (1938), Indiana (1949), and New Mexico and Wyoming (1954). Housing for northern Blacks was dilapidated and barely livable. High unemployment and low salaries were a constant irritant as overcrowding pushed tempers to the limit. Police brutality was rampant, as policemen were free to abuse the population however hostile officers saw fit. When the entire family of Marquette Frye was arrested, including his mother, after a traffic stop, chaos erupted in Watts, California. Over six days, thirty-four mostly Black Americans lost their lives. Four thousand men and women were arrested, one thousand were injured, and upwards of $100 million in businesses and homes were destroyed.[89]

In three and a half years, President John F. Kennedy (1961–63, thirty-fifth president) became an immortal to Black Americans. During his administration, the Civil Rights Movement was in full swing, but he was much more invested in foreign policy than domestic affairs. The Cold War, the threat of nuclear war, the Soviet Union, the Cuban Missile Crisis, Vietnam, and the race to space dominated much of his intellectual capacity. Initially the Black community was very skeptical about the young candidate running for president in 1960. He was a Catholic seeking to woo Black Protestant voters. He was from American royalty with no real knowledge or experience of what Black life entailed. Jackie Robinson endorsed Richard Nixon believing that he was "better qualified" and would do more for the Black community. During his election campaign against Nixon, Kennedy posted a list of promises. *Jet* magazine listed them as "What Kennedy Promises Negroes": "Full employment, protection of voting rights and elimination of poll taxes and literacy tests, boost in teacher salaries and school construction, an end to housing discrimination, federal protection for civil rights, cabinet positions, healthcare coverage and increased Social Security payments."[90] He was the first television president, and his polished appearance contrasted with Nixon's stoic demeanor and enhanced his appeal to Black voters.[91] Television's influence went beyond the simple broadcast of shows or events; it shaped attitudes and culture. The televised debate between presidential candidates John Kennedy and Richard Nixon gave Kennedy the edge due to his charisma. In 1960 the youthful John F. Kennedy was elected president and the country was on the verge of global dominance as America's economy and culture were the envies of the world. His New Frontier legislation was racially progressive but was blocked at every avenue by southern legislators. The Civil Rights Movement received televised coverage of the brutality inflicted on marchers, and this changed white America's perceptions of the movement. The Soviet Union was a constant irritant, showing its influence in the Cuban Missile Crisis and the failure of the Bay of Pigs coup.[92]

Kennedy made a calculated move that won the hearts of Black Americans. When Martin Luther King Jr. was sentenced to six months hard labor in prison in Reidsville, Georgia, the candidate called Mrs. King, who was pregnant at the time. He told her, "This must be pretty hard on you. I want to let you both know that I'm thinking about you and will do all that I can to help."[93] That same day he called the Georgia governor, Ernest Vandiver, lobbying for King's release. The Black community exploded with gratitude, especially considering that Richard Nixon, who knew King, decided not to make the same call. From that point on the call tilted Black voters in his favor. King Sr., a Republican, pledged to deliver as many votes to Kennedy as he could. King, when released, praised Kennedy and chastised Nixon. Black newspapers followed suit. He overwhelmingly won 70 percent of the Black vote in eleven key states. King and the community expected his support in return. But other than accepting a congratulatory phone call from King, the newly elected president considered him too controversial and limited any contact with him for months.[94]

The first two years of Kennedy's presidency were filled with one incident of injustice after another. At the time of his election in 1960, Black life was hemmed in by social and political barriers. Northern Blacks endured housing, education, and employment discrimination. In the South, segregation, voter disenfranchisement, and racial violence were rampant. Alabama was a deadly state for Black people. Birmingham, Alabama, was commonly referred to as "Bombingham." On September 15, 1963, a bomb exploded outside Sixteenth Street Baptist Church and killed Denise McNair, Cynthia Wesley, Carole Robertson, and Addie Mae Collins, all between eleven and fourteen years of age. Days later, sixteen-year-old Johnnie Robinson was shot and killed by police during the violent insurrection of Black people who were filled with grief and rage.[95] Carolyn McKinstry was a survivor of the bombing. She remembered,

> We had had over 60 unsolved bombings in Birmingham, and no one had ever been brought to justice for those bombings. And it appeared that black people were just powerless to do anything about it. No one had been brought to justice. So here is the first bombing where some-one has been killed. And we waited. No one was arrested after the first year. When they were renovating the building, someone said, well, they just have never taken anybody white to justice or a trial for the death of someone black.[96]

Minnijean Brown-Trickey, one of the Little Rock Nine, reflected, "Seg-regation was everywhere, and meanness was everywhere, and violence was everywhere. So, wherever you moved, you could touch anywhere, you would be touching it. Because it was so pervasive, no matter what you did you were in opposition to it." She commented on integrating Central High School and the vehemence the nine students faced.

> People were shouting, "Kill them! Lynch them!" I mean, horrible things. It was more frightening than anybody can ever imagine. It's like some kind of monsters coming at you. You don't really want to see it. . . . Oh, kick you downstairs, throw garbage, spit, drop acid—not that kind—off the third floor and make holes in your clothes. Melba Pattillo got acid in her eyes. . . . Name calling, it was just constant. So, I mean it was designed to break your spirits.[97]

Fifty thousand activists, mostly college students, were active in sixty-five cit-ies in twenty-two states as sit-ins interrupted segregated dining. Throughout 1961, Black and white Freedom Riders were assaulted by white mobs as they attempted to end segregation at southern bus terminals. Riders were arrested in North Carolina and brutally assaulted in South Carolina and Alabama. In 1962, James Meredith's effort to integrate the University of Mississippi was met by a recalcitrant governor and white mobs and resulted in the death of two white protesters. Medgar Evers was murdered on the same night Kennedy spoke to the nation on civil rights. In early 1963 King was arrested in Birming-ham and imprisoned for over a week. On June 11, 1963, Governor George Wal-lace blocked two students from enrolling at the University of Alabama and was forced by the administration to allow their enrollment. [98] These events deeply affected a president who struggled throughout his term over the decision to take a public stance for the movement and against racial discrimination.

Despite increasing violence against protesters, Kennedy was a reluctant warrior for civil rights. Even after Blacks helped to deliver him the presidency, he did little to reward them for their votes. For two and a half years, the president made no public pronouncements confronting the issues of racial injustice. He refused to speak out publicly against the brutal violence inflicted on peaceful marchers. The president had a wavering attention span concerning civil rights. King and the other leaders beseeched the president to make a statement that the protest movement was a moral one and to make a strong statement to the nation supporting the movement. He did not. Fear of southern reprisals, local and congressional, caused him to pause before acting decisively. Steven Levingston wrote in *Kennedy and King*,

> Kennedy perhaps need not have cowered before Congress. If he had shown some backbone right after the election and challenged segregationist senators, he might have been able to subdue them. . . . In a further sign of a potential opening on civil rights, the Republican Party was becoming more liberal and progressive. Nixon's loss suggested that Republicans in Congress needed to soften their conservatism and focus more on social justice to attract northern Blacks. . . . Some Senate Republicans went so far as to say that their party would support Kennedy on civil rights. . . . *Newsweek* declared that if Kennedy "jumps right in with a broad new legislative program, he will find Congress so receptive that his record might well approach Franklin D Roosevelt's famous 'One Hundred Days,' when FDR pushed through 15 major bills in 1933 to combat the dire circumstances of the Great Depression. Yet Kennedy shrank from asserting his leadership."[99]

He delegated the task of addressing civil rights issues to his brother Robert ("Bobby"), who was his Attorney General and served as a quasi-assistant to the president. It was also Bobby's job to engage with civil rights leaders. When a problem arose, it was Bobby who made the phone calls, sent in federal marshals, called governors, and informed the president. Bobby arranged federal marshals to escort the Freedom Riders after attacks and brutal beatings in Alabama.[100] It was Bobby who negotiated on King's behalf in Montgomery when he was barricaded in First Baptist Church along with one thousand supporters and surrounded by hostile, violent whites. He gave a speech at the University of Georgia on civil rights at the same time that Charlayne Hunter and Hamilton Holmes bravely walked with federal marshals to class.[101] He took on the governors of Mississippi (Ross Barnett) and Alabama (George Wallace) to compel them to allow James Meredith, Vivian Malone, and James Hood to register as students. He also evolved in his commitment to the movement and joined the voices urging his brother to issue a strong definitive statement of support.[102] The president ordered federal troops to protect Meredith. Roy Wilkins accused the president of not doing much to help the movement while wanting to receive credit for actions he did not take. The president resented such sentiments and felt that he had done more in support of Black rights than any previous president.[103]

The complex relationship he shared with Martin Luther King Jr. is a tale of two men radically different in personality yet amazingly similar in life details. Neither experienced dire poverty as children, as both grew up in well-respected families with strong, domineering fathers. Both were eloquent speakers and handsome men. Both were extremely intelligent, with high levels of education. But King had an unwavering commitment to justice, while Kennedy's courage failed him at pivotal moments concerning domestic affairs. Internationally, he was able to back down Soviet premier Nikita Khrushchev during the Cuban Missile Crisis but faltered in his fear of southern senators who might derail his efforts. Kennedy approached King during his candidacy asking for an endorsement. They met twice privately, but King refused, as it was his policy not to endorse candidates. After he was elected, Kennedy refused meeting requests from King on at least four occasions. The president and his brother Bobby approved the tactics of FBI director J. Edgar Hoover, who wiretapped and attempted to blackmail King into submission. In late 1963, Kennedy transitioned from avoiding King to echoing his talking points, especially those in "Letter from Birmingham Jail," and sought King's approval. After the president's murder, King acknowledged that he had reconsidered his refusal to make endorsements and probably would have endorsed Kennedy for reelection.[104]

There were less publicized measures that he did take. His Executive Order 11063 attacked housing discrimination in federally financed housing projects. He issued Executive Order 10925 and coined the term *Affirmative Action* to increase Black hires across the nation. He gave time and effort to erasing resistance to cross-racial hiring, especially in his cabinet. Six months into his presidency, there were fifty Blacks holding high-ranking positions in his administration. He met with 1,700 persons in twenty-one meetings on that one subject. He created a Committee on Equal Employment Opportunity to monitor fair hiring practices. His appointments of high-ranking Blacks were the highest ever to positions attained by a person of color: Robert Weaver (Housing and Home Finance Agency), Carl Rowen (Deputy Assistant Secretary of State), Clifton Wharton (Ambassador to Norway), Andrew Hatcher (Deputy Press Secretary), George Weaver (Assistant Secretary of Labor), Andrew Brimmer (Federal Trade Commission) and Leon Higginbotham (Postmaster). He appointed the highest number of Black lawyers, five, to the federal bench, surpassing the previous total of three. One of them was Thurgood Marshall. Attorney General Robert Kennedy wrote forty-five law schools inquiring about potential Black graduates. His Justice Department filed four times as many civil rights suits claiming racial bias than the previous administration. In addition, it filed thirty-seven voter registration suits in Mississippi, Alabama, Georgia, Louisiana, and Tennessee. J. Edgar Hoover increased the number of Black agents from two to twenty-eight by 1964. Kennedy arranged the selection of the first Black Secret Service agent in a presidential detail.[105]

The same people who helped to propel him to the White House compelled him to confront the racist brutality against Black people. It was after the stand-off with Alabama governor George Wallace that the president decided to issue a televised statement to the nation. According to Levingston,

> He wanted to deliver a major civil rights speech; he was determined to speak on Black rights in a manner he had never done before—in language no president had uttered. . . . Afterward, he explained what came over him. "I may lose the legislation, I may even lose the election in 1964. But there comes a time when a man has to take a stand and history will record that he has to meet these tough situations and ultimately make a decision."[106]

On June 11, 1963, President John Kennedy appeared on live television to emphasis the importance of dismantling white supremacy.

> I hope that every American, regardless of where he lives, will stop and examine his conscience about this and every other related incident. . . . This nation . . . was founded on the principle that all men are created equal. . . . Next week I shall ask the Congress of the United States to act, to make a commitment it has not fully made in this century to the proposition that race has no place in American life or law. . . . This is not a sectional issue. . . . This is not even a legal or legislative issue alone. . . . We are confronted primarily with a moral issue. It is as old as the scriptures and as clear as the American Constitution.[107]

Martin Luther King Jr. leaped out of his chair. Both he and Jackie Robinson sent congratulatory telegrams to the president. John Lewis was speechless and later shared that he would never forget the president's words. A. Philip Randolph's dream of a march on Washington came to fruition on August 28. Civil rights leaders were congratulated by a previously reluctant president in the White House, where they posed for pictures. He followed up his speech with a fierce effort to lobby Congress for the passage of a civil rights bill that would be the most far-reaching anti-discrimination legislation ever created.[108]

He needed to win reelection to ensure passage, and he embarked on a two-day, five-city tour of Texas to mend broken relationships with southern Democrats. But on November 22, 1963, President John F. Kennedy was shot in Dallas. For the first time ever, network television was interrupted as news of a national tragedy was reported live. Three days later, the president was laid to rest.[109] This was a deadly period, as President John F. Kennedy was murdered in 1963, Malcolm X in 1965, Martin Luther King in 1968, and Bobby Kennedy in 1968. In 1965, Bloody Sunday was the term used to describe the brutal beating of civil rights marchers, including future congressman John Lewis.

This period saw the introduction of television as the major media outlet. Scholars consider the 1950s to represent the "Golden Age of Television." By the end of the 1960s, 96 percent of households owned a set. Black celebrities made headway into the new entertainment fields of television and radio. In 1951, the first Black doll was produced and sold in the United States, Saralee Negro Doll.[110] Black cultural societies were in full swing as middle-to-upper-class Blacks held their own social events, with racial and class exclusions. In Pittsburgh, the Cavalcade of Fashions extravaganza was sponsored by the Urban League. The Royalties cocktail party (Chicago) and the Rinkey Dinks Club (New York) held annual fundraising events and social galas.[111] Black celebrities were few and far between, but several managed to showcase their talents in a variety of fields. Eartha Kitt, Lena Horne, Harry Belafonte, Nat King Cole, Ruby Dee and Ossie Davis, Jackie Robinson, Sammy Davis Jr., Bill Cosby, Muhammad Ali, Diahann Carroll, Leslie Uggams, Cicely Tyson, Flip Wilson, Redd Foxx, Pearl Bailey, George Kirby, Ben Vereen, Marilyn McCoo, Billy Davis Jr., and Ivan Dixon presented a new image for Blacks on the small screen. Serious shows with Black stars and costars appeared for the first time, including *Sing-Along with The Nat King Cole Show, I Spy, The Sammy Davis Jr. Show, Julia, The Bill Cosby Show, Hogan's Heroes, The New People, Star Trek, The Mod Squad, Mannix, Mission Impossible, Land of the Giants, The Flip Wilson Show, Peyton Place, Gentle Ben, Matt Lincoln, The Outcasts, Room 222, Daniel Boone, Rawhide,* and *High Chaparral.* Despite most being short-lived, they garnered special attention and pride in the Black community, which eagerly anticipated each show's weekly episode. Most shied away from discussion of issues of race or white supremacy. This period introduced a new representation of Black people in the media as detectives and nurses in both comedy and dramatic series. The world of Black entertainment their parents grew up in was one of minstrelsy and buffoonery. This generation grew up seeing themselves presented as respectable human beings on the television set. While the stars they saw on television were from the previous generation, this generation took the inspiration they received and propelled it onto the small and large screens to star, direct, and produce.[112] Sociologist Rodney Coates summarized Sidney Poitier's life,

> The roles he played during a time of discrimination and vast inequalities infused Black people, who had mostly seen demeaning roles in movies and television, with pride and hope that would ultimately lead to a change and diversity in the film industry. I am one of those growing up who was able to see a strong, positive Black man on the screen whose roles were powerful and sent the message that Black people matter, that we are to be respected. It seemed every one of his movies was 30 years ahead of its time. You just did not see Black actors in lead roles, standing up for themselves, which was also standing up for Black people. And he did this at a time when they were lynching Black people, having dogs attack them, sprayed with water hoses on the streets.[113]

SUMMARY OF THE BLACK POWER GENERATION

This is sentimentally the Reverse Migration Generation. Many were children born in the North to parents who had migrated from southern enclaves. Some were nostalgic and wanted desperately to retire in the land of their birth. They were moving back to the places that helped nurture them via summer visits to the hometowns of their parents. For many, they were never emotionally removed from the South and still considered it home. Extended family members beckoned them to return to the land of their parents and forebears, and they responded. They were aware that as they aged, there would be family support there, as well as a lower cost of living. After selling their homes they purchased retirement homes, gaining more land for less money. George Graham grew up in East Arcadia along the Cape Fear River in North Carolina. He had good motivations to return to the South.

> I'd rather be right here on Cape Fear River than anywhere else I know of. I'm serious. I went up New Jersey and stayed a long time—four and a half months! I said, hey, this is not my place. I'd see squirrels out there, man, I'd get so sick, I'd want to eat me a squirrel. I said I'm going back home. I ain't leaving no more. I ain't gonna go too far where I can't get back the same day. And that's the way I am with home. And I guarantee you, as long as a shad come up this river in the spring of the year, I'm going to eat one.[114]

For those who were not born in the South, the call of hometowns where their parents originated was enough to bring them back. Timuel Black, a retired high school teacher in Chicago, reflected on his family's journey from South to North.

My family came to Chicago in the first Black migration from the South right after World War I. My father had few skills, but he had a strong back and a willing mind. Many of them came for the same reason people left Europe, a better life. . . . We came in 1919, right after the race riot. . . . Most of the children and grandchildren of my generation, of those who came from the rural South after World War I, are doing fairly well. The others, who came after the Second War, are in bad shape.[115]

Judith Shaw was told, with pride, about the accomplishments of her grandfather, Eugene Jim Shaw, who was a Pullman porter. He was the first in his community to have indoor plumbing, a grand home, and an automobile. She grew up in New York City to a family that ventured to her father's hometown, La Grange, North Carolina. She decided to make the journey one final time and relocate back home. "I have just always had a feeling about this town. When I first came back, I stayed three or four months in the same house where my great-grandfather and great-grandmother lived. It felt like home. Ever since I was small, I had a feeling that I would move here. There was just something about this town that was in my blood since I was born."[116]

This generation knows how to maneuver in two worlds, a Black one and a white one, with two faces. They mastered the art of hiding their true feelings, whether at work or home. When in the white world, they could not give the perception of being too assertive or they would be labeled an angry Black person. When in the Black world, they could never appear to fit in too comfortably and risk being labeled an Uncle Tom. They reached many of the same conclusions as those who came before them. America was a land wherein a person was not judged by qualification or competence but by the color of one's skin. They recognized that society had changed but were ever cautious, even angry.

They were able to maintain conflicting loyalties. They loved their country yet were highly critical of it. Vietnam veteran Kenny Davis remembered, "When I got back to America, coming from Vietnam, I could relate to how the Black veterans of Korea, World War II, World War I, maybe even the Spanish-American War felt. They believed that defending this country would make them equal in society—and it didn't. You become bitter. You become hostile. . . . I was a sergeant in the U.S. Army then, a Vietnam veteran. And I said to myself, 'I can't believe this is happening in America.'"[117] They marched in the civil rights revolution but walked to the beat of Black Power ideology. They loved Martin Luther King Jr. but wanted to be like Malcolm X. They admired the dream but realized that the nightmare of racism would not end without a fight. The documentary *By Any Means Necessary* shared important commentary from a former activist: "I had already been active in my local

NAACP youth group doing sit-ins. There are times that pacifism is an excellent tactic, but there was no way in hell you were gonna get me to lay down on the floor, put my hands over the back of my neck to protect myself from people trying to kill me with billy clubs and bats, because I'd rather shoot somebody." Another replied, "Martin Luther King at that time, with all due respect, was not one of Harlem's favorites. Harlem, we were Malcolm's children." A young man pondered, "Martin Luther King, is he our leader? Martin Luther King I can't completely go along with. You know, he will be so nonviolent, that it would, that the white man can sic the dogs and the ammunition and blow us all up, and we'll all die for—you know, for this peace and brotherly love and all of this."[118]

Eddie McCoy was active in Oxford, North Carolina, in protest of the killing of Henry Marrow in 1970 and participated in burning downtown businesses. He remembered the attitude of many young Blacks who were involved in the revolt.

> We said, the only way this is going to work is, you either have to burn somebody's buildings down or break some windows or do something violent. It wasn't the right way, but I didn't think nonviolence would work. Martin Luther King was never my favorite. I admired him. I liked what he stood for. But I was in the sit-ins. I was in the marches. And after awhile, people just weren't listening to us. So, I was like Bobby Seale and all those guys—burn, baby, burn.[119]

Deacons for Defense activist Robert Hicks's daughter spoke of her father's philosophy: "Martin Luther King was a good man. He had a dream. But my Daddy fought for the dream. And it was his right to fight for the dream. You have a Constitutional right, and that's what Daddy said, 'I have a right to bear arms. And if I need to protect my family,' especially when the police did not protect us, then he had a right to do that."[120] Peniel Joseph stated,

> Malcolm's bold critique of white supremacy, Western colonialism, and anti-Black racial violence embodied the Black Power movement. All this seemed to contrast with the passionate call for Black citizenship through nonviolent suffering extolled by Dr. Martin Luther King, Jr. . . . Contemporary social justice movements, ranging from Black Lives Matter (BLM) to efforts to end mass incarceration, stand on the shoulders of Black Power activists who led a sprawling, intersectional, multigenerational human rights movement whose universal call for justice has been obscured by its basis in the particular struggle of Black people.[121]

This generation is undeterred and does not believe in quitting anything once they have started. It lived through the dismantling of Jim Crow policies

but understood that racial discrimination did not go quietly away but continued to persist. They didn't eradicate racism from the American landscape;
they succeeded despite its overarching presence. They lived with an unspoken
tension as they attempted to tread new ground in this transitioning America.
They were aware that they were constantly watched and being judged. Dr.
Derrick Darby of Michigan State University explained, "At the time, it was
really difficult, knowing that they changed the rules. You climb this ladder—
but then, when we start climbing that ladder and we get into those spaces,
the rules change."[122] Scoutmaster Gary Grant and his troop of Boy Scouts
attended the first integrated jamboree in the United States in 1976. They were
the only Black troop of the five thousand scouts in attendance. They were
given a campsite far into the woods, and each tent had an American and Confederate flag flying over it. When Grant asked that they come down, leaders
refused. They made their own black, green, and red flag with a black fist and
the words, "Black Power." After a compromise, no secondary flags were flown.
His boys felt a tremendous sense of pride and were recognized for having the
"best campsite, best layout and best maintenance." Ten of his patrols were
awarded blue ribbons.[123]

This generation told their children that if they worked hard, they could do
anything they set their minds to. They pushed their children to achieve greatness and repeated that one day, their children could be president, even when
they themselves did not believe it. They went on to elect one of their own as
the first Black president, alongside a Black First Lady. Another, Kamala Harris, rose to the rank of vice president as the first person of both Black and
South Asian descent to do so. She represents the diversity of experience of this
generation and their endless belief in the opportunities available to Black people. As vice-president-elect, she said on the night they were pronounced the
victors in the presidential election, "Tonight I reflect on their struggle (Black
women), their determination and the strength of their vision to see what can
be unburdened by what has been. While I may be the first woman in this
office, I will not be the last."[124]

Dr. James Slade entered the University of North Carolina Medical
School in 1951 as the second Black medical student. His friendly and warm
demeanor concealed a serious determination to finish what he started. His
experience at UNC, while novel, was one where professors treated him
fairly on the whole, and he did not encounter vicious racist opposition. He
reflected that he did face circumstances the white students did not have to
deal with. He couldn't do pelvic exams on white patients, was limited to
Black patients on the third floor, and stayed in a different dorm than the
other freshmen, white students.

> I went along with it. It wasn't anything I would have put a stamp of
> approval on, but, by the same token, I was willing to go ahead, at that
> point in time, and see what would work out. My white patients didn't
> resent my taking care of them, but the administration just wasn't
> ready for it. They were in the growing stages of integration. One of
> the advantages of being young was that things like that didn't bother
> me that much. I was there for studying. I saw a need, and I wanted to
> learn medicine.[125]

They have noticeable generational differences with younger generations,
politically and attitudinally. Members of this generation do not feel as if young
Blacks appreciate the struggles they have been through. They are concerned
about their individual legacy and the story of the struggle being retained and
appreciated. In turn, young adults have argued that the previous generation
is reticent about openly talking about their experiences.[126] During the 2020
presidential election, polls indicated that members aged sixty-five or older
shared favorable feelings toward candidate Joe Biden, a sentiment they shared
more with young whites (eighteen to twenty-nine years old) as opposed to
younger Black voters. Polling by HIT, AARC, and Democracy Fund found a
generational gap as Biden received endorsement from older voters in contrast
to some younger voters who went for Trump. Older voters had made their
mind up about whom they were going to vote for.

> Older Black people are more clearly partisan Democrats than younger
> Black people, both viewing the Democratic Party and its leaders much
> more favorably than younger Black people and viewing the GOP with
> more disdain than younger Black people. Among Black registered
> voters age 50 and older, 75 percent said they thought congressional
> Democrats were doing a good job, compared to just 22 percent who
> thought congressional Democrats were doing a poor job, according
> to a HIT survey conducted in June . . . among Black people over 65,
> 77 percent had a favorable view of Harris and just 10 percent viewed
> her unfavorably, according to HIT polling conducted in late August
> and early September (after her selection as Biden's running mate).
> Among Black people ages 25 to 34, 28 percent viewed her favorably
> and 44 percent unfavorably. (The rest were neutral or didn't know.)
> Similarly, in AARC polling, older Black Americans expressed more
> anti-Trump views and more pro-Democratic Party views on a num-
> ber of measures than their younger counterparts. They also seemed
> more enthusiastic to vote, in part because they seem to view voting as
> part of lifting up the broader Black community."[127]

This generation is filled with many first-time achievers who were the first
of their race to attend predominantly white universities and work in white

professions. Judge Karen Bethea-Shields was one of the first African American women to receive a Duke University law degree and was the first female judge in North Carolina's Fourteenth District. Straight out of law school, she defended Joan Little, who was charged with the murder of a white male jailer she accused of trying to rape her. It was considered a hopeless case to try to free a Black woman accused of murdering a white officer of the court. Attorney Bethea-Shields reflected,

> When it came time for jury argument, I didn't write anything down. I just felt it and gave the jury argument. What I did was put the jury in Joan's cell the night of the rape and made them feel what she felt. Yes, she was a convicted felon. Yes, she had had problems in the past. But she still was a young woman, and she was vulnerable with all that power and control he had. . . . And then I led the jurors through the rape scene. As I gave the argument, some of the jurors started crying. Now, I'm young. This is my first jury argument. I thought I had done something wrong. And when I finished, the courtroom was silent. Nobody was saying anything, and the judge is looking stunned. I didn't realize that I had succeeded, at least to some degree, in making them feel what Joan felt in that prison cell. The verdict was not guilty. And when I finished, I went straight to the bathroom and just cried and cried and cried.[128]

This generation is successful in that they built homes and lived stable, professional lives but struggled to create generational wealth, as their children had difficulty maintaining a middle-class existence. The doors pried open for them were meant for only a few to enter, leaving multitudes impoverished. Maura Cheeks, in "American Wealth Is Broken," maintained that Black wealth is fragile.

> As a whole, Black wealth is delicate, because for generations lawmakers and power wielders attempted to prevent African Americans from building it. . . . A raft of policies responsible for building the American middle class destroyed opportunities for Black people to build intergenerational wealth . . . the injustices that have kept Black families without a safety net for generations still reverberate throughout our history.[129]

They view their success less through an individual lens, instead tracking it as progress for the entire race. They understand that much had been sacrificed to guarantee their presence in venues forbidden to previous generations. Educator Charlie Nelms wrote in *HuffPost*, "As Americans who came of age in the 1960s and '70s and who played a crucial role in the Civil Rights movement of that era, many of us became the first of our race to be employed in our respective careers and to be promoted to positions of leadership. I recall eagerly awaiting the arrival of *Jet*, *Ebony*, and *Essence*—all national magazines devoted to showcasing the accomplishments of African Americans."[130]

They are eternally hopeful because they inherited their parents' optimism. They are the living examples of what determination and perseverance can do. They entered an unfriendly business world and managed to gain employment and were rewarded for their faithfulness to the firm. They took advantage of the opportunities before them and earned their way. They believed in the mottos of men and women such as Golden Frinks, called "The Great Agitator" and "Mr. Civil Rights."

> I came by the fields of battles where our forefathers fought wars to make fast these truths that all men are created equal—I came holding high the hopes and dreams of America—ever ready to defend what some men have died for. We must be determined to live for, in the instance upon respect for these rights, not just for the weak, or the strong, but for the unpopular as well as the popular—the minority as well as the majority. . . . Asking that no special treatment I ask, we want as equal part to enjoy the fruits of America.[131]

Growing up during the militancy of the sixties, many never lost their spirit of activism and engaged in it throughout their lives. When surveyed by AARP, they identified that social justice issues were vitally important. Topping their lists was access to quality healthcare (91 percent), economic security (91 percent), and information on healthcare (89 percent). Retirement was a priority, as many were nearing that moment of decision. Even then, quality education ranked near the top. They stated the greatest level of pessimism over issues pertaining to employment. They prescribed their age and race as barriers leading to a lack of employment opportunities.[132] During the recession of the 1980s, when as many as 35 percent of her community was unemployed, Bessie Mizell worked in her elementary school cafeteria. She recognized that hungry children dominated the ranks of those she encountered and decided to open a food pantry during a time when they were not nearly as commonplace. She started in her husband's abandoned Masonic hall and later relocated to a family resource center. She described the people she helped:

> Some say, my job has closed down or we're off until summer. We have a lot of single parents, a lot of the elderly, a lot of the sick. I know somebody who is on dialysis three times a week and they can't get any other kind of help. They come to the food closet. All of the homeless need us. . . . Some come from families that are pretty well-to-do . . . I say, we are just trying to make a difference here. We don't want

anybody to feel ashamed. We want everybody to feel comfortable. We are all in this together.[133]

On May 19, 2019, billionaire investor Robert F. Smith delivered the commencement address for Morehouse College in Atlanta, Georgia, an all-male HBCU. The founder of Vista Equity and one of the world's richest men committed to liquidate each graduate's college debt. African American students leave college indebted $7,400 more than white students. He said, "Let's make sure every class has the same opportunity going forward, because we are enough to take care of our own community. We are enough to ensure we have all of the opportunities of the American dream, and we will show it to each other through our actions and through our words and through our deeds."[134]

This generation maintains a commitment to community service and consistently volunteers in a multitude of organizations, especially churches, sororities, and fraternities. They are philanthropic and give back by creating opportunities for others. They define their success as being able to leave a legacy that continues to help those who follow. Joyce Johnson was a part of the second class of Black undergraduates to attend Duke University. Her parents were hard-working members of the Richmond, Virginia, community. Her mother was a domestic worker and her father labored in the steel mill. She was ever mindful of the responsibility placed on her shoulders by being one of the few Blacks to attend Duke, or any majority white academic institution. She reflected, "When I went to Duke, I went with the blessing and the responsibility of the whole community. Personal advancement was what I sought to do, but it was very closely linked with advancement for my entire race. It makes you very serious about your work, but it is an awesome thing."[135]

They have reached retirement age with differing opinions about it. While some support early retirement, others hope to continue to work past retirement age. Across all racial demographics, members of this age range plan to work years past sixty-five, understanding that there are financial penalties imposed the earlier they retire. Cuts in medical and pension benefits are partly to blame, as reduced payments increase the chance of retirement being delayed. Members of the Black Power Generation have postponed retirement due to economic hardships. Traditional blue-collar workers can't afford to retire, have minimal insurance, and deal with sprawling family burdens. Despite all of their hard work, there is a tremendous wealth gap with whites their own age. Making less money in combination with family responsibilities, many will have decided to delay retirement.

This could be referred to as a caretaker's generation. Even though their parents are mostly deceased (43 percent), they carry the responsibility of caring for aunts, uncles, brothers, sisters, and especially, grandchildren. According to Melinda Chateauvert of the University of Maryland, there are differences between Blacks and whites concerning family duties for this generation that impact the dispersal of family income.

> African American families taking care of children goes on much longer, and to a much greater extent, than it does among white families. And it's not just the children, it's also the elders, and the grandmothers, and the grandfathers. There is more dispersal of a single African American family income to greater number of relatives, and sometimes even neighborhood folks and churches, etcetera, than there is in the white community. So that accounts for some of the difference in the wealth gap, but it also accounts for a quite large network of possible resources that might be drawn upon after retirement.[136]

They have personal concerns over healthcare and high prescription costs. Dr. JeffriAnne Wilder on NPR commented that those "who lived through the Jim Crow era and the turmoil of the Civil Rights movement often find they don't have the skills to successfully navigate the vagaries of retirement."[137] Despite this reality for so many, others intend to work fewer years before entering full retirement, regardless of reduced benefits. This sentiment is expressed regardless of education, health, wealth, and other influencing factors. The reasons expressed are defined as lower educational attainment, which limits promotional ability, health status, and earnings. Family responsibility plays a role too, as they wish to spend more time with grandchildren and extended family.[138]

The Black Power Generation has remained one of the most forward looking of all the generations in the Black community. They remain skeptical that life will ever be perfect, but they have not given up. Their excitement over the gains they made is something they have tried to pass on to today's generation of young people. They are extremely realistic and driven by a desire for a better life than the one they experienced. Theirs is the experience of living in a multiverse, a different reality, from what they saw and lived as children and as young adults. Their ability to adapt to changing realities has been a gift they readily share with family and friends, always stressing the need to keep on moving and to keep their heads up.

4

Hip-Hop Generation (Generation X)

1965–80

Young Black Americans born between 1965 and 1984 are the first
generation of Black Americans to come of age in the era of globalization. . . . Both rappers [Notorious B.I.G. and Tupac], like their
peers who saw hope and promise in their short lives, were hip hop
generationers—those young African-Americans born between 1965
and 1984 who came of age in the '80s and '90s who share a specific
set of values and attitudes. At the core are our thoughts about family,
relationships, child rearing, career, racial identity, race relations, and
politics. Collectively, these views make up a complex worldview that
has not been concretely defined.[1]

—Bakari Kitwana, *The Hip-Hop Generation*

The Hip-Hop Generation inherited the radicalism of the Black Power
Generation combined with the idealism of the Motown Generation. Its name
is derived from what started as a form of entertainment in urban centers. Hip
hop is a music genre that originated in the African American community in
the 1970s in the Bronx in New York City. It's characterized by a strong, rhyth-
mic beat, rapping vocals, and other artistic elements including break dancing.
It has grown to be a cultural movement with tremendous impact nationally
and globally, influencing fashion, music, language, and poetry.

As members of this generation matured, they focused on a positive image
of Blackness yet never adopted the sacrificial nature of previous generations.
They are unapologetically Black in their affirmation of loving the skin they
are in. They are style setters in fashion, with great focus on presentation. They
identify positivity with being Black. Celebrities were early adopters in promoting Afrocentric attributes. Yet not all their ingenuities are throwbacks, as they
created their own creative style.

The Hip-Hop Generation is the generational counterpart of Generation X and possesses opposite traits. Gen X was labeled by *Newsweek* as "the [lost] generation that dropped out without ever turning on the news or tuning in to the social issues around them."[2] Hip-hoppers are generationally included in the cohort referred to as the Unknown Generation, or Gen X. Many complain that this is the worst possible identifier, as it lacks any real descriptors. Vena Moore wrote under the moniker "The Invisible Black Gen-Xer." She determined, "If you're a Black Gen-Xer as I am, none of this fazes you. Black people, in general, are used to being ignored and hyper visible, sometimes at once. Many of the alleged traits of my generation (or any other generation for that matter) don't really apply to Black folks because for the most part, the supposed characteristics of any cohort are steeped in privilege, which we don't have."[3]

Bakari Kitwana, author of *The Hip-Hop Generation*, celebrated this generation as having an extensive influence on mainstream society through hip-hop culture. He said in a 2002 NPR interview, "The most important thing that captured the essence of this generation and nothing has impacted this generation more significantly and across class than hip-hop."[4] He proposed the idea that hip-hop politically mobilized young African Americans to voice unspoken frustration. Hip-hop culture, the defining element in their identity formation, reflected their perspectives, attitudes, and frustrations.[5] He issued a sober assessment, describing the world as illusionary because it dangles promises at the same time it places roadblocks. He characterizes integration as a deception that allowed a handful to advance while the masses were paralyzed by racial discrimination.

> The worldview of hip-hop generationers has been influenced by persisting segregation in an America that preaches democracy and inclusion. This contradiction has been particularly hard for us to swallow. Our generation is the first generation of African Americans to come of age outside the confines of legal segregation. We certainly live in a more inclusive society than existed in pre-civil rights America. However, continuing segregation and inequality have made it especially illusory for many young Blacks.[6]

Yet, for many of this generation, paradise has proven to be a mirage. The dream was not yet fulfilled, as America continued to write a bad check to Black people. Despite the promise of opportunity, they have been denied for the same reasons that their parents and grandparents were: racism. Resentment has risen to a high level as this generation has experienced frustration over normalized injustice in every sector of society.[7] They grew up believing that America's promise of equality was meant for them but experienced the reality of racism in every area of life. De facto desegregation has given way to de jure inequality in housing, schools, employment, and police shootings. They are trapped in a vicious cycle that has been the curse of white supremacy for generations of Black Americans. Vena Moore wrote, "Black Gen-Xers, more than anyone else, start out knowing that life isn't fair. We don't expect a handout or a hand up. We learn well before adulthood that we have to work twice as hard to get half of what the dominant society has. Our resilience and adaptability have helped us withstand adversity not just for belonging to a generation that is forgotten but for the oppression that we are still subjected to."[8] Brian Jones, associate director of education at the Schomburg Center for Research in Black Culture, wrote in *The Guardian* of having obtained "second sight" due to growing up with a light complexion in a white world.

> I write this as a Black person who also knows the white American world. There is ignorance and prejudice there, but there is also pain, suffering and struggle. I am grateful to my parents and teachers who helped me to notice and name racism and discrimination. They have helped me to understand my personal experience and, just as importantly, to see beyond it. I have become convinced that black liberation is bound up with true human liberation.[9]

They are the children and grandchildren of the Great Migration. Like their parents and grandparents, they are willing to relocate for greater opportunity. Unlike them, they don't leave to escape persecution but to pursue improvement of their circumstances. They will relocate two to three times within their lifetime. They are frustrated that there are not more opportunities available and are prone to wander for years as they figure out what they want to do with their lives. Large numbers of this generation struggle with debt and anxiety over being unable to make ends meet. Those from first-generation middle-class families have a fragile economic base, teetering between middle and lower economic class status. Even Blacks who grew up in wealthy families have a difficult time retaining wealth, especially compared to white wealth inheritors. Many are burdened by the obligations of family plus expanded responsibilities due to aging parents, grandparents, and children. AARP conducted a survey of members of this generation who lived in New York City. Many felt that they would be able to retire fully at the age of sixty-five and not have to work late into life. Despite this optimism, many questioned their ability to afford life in the Big Apple. The mounting expenses of healthcare and housing led to increasing debt. Stressful big city living created anxiety and worry, and 70 percent expressed doubt that they could afford to retire in the city.[10]

They are the first Blacks in America to feel that the words of the Declaration of Independence held meaning for all Americans, not just whites.

They grew up in a society that modestly lived up to its promise of equality. They matured believing that anything was possible. They saw firsthand the ways in which whites and Blacks could positively interact. They continued the legacy of being the first Black person in their profession, school, or neighborhood. Many lived in integrated communities and negotiated between two worlds, one white and the other Black. Baratunde Thurston, born in 1977, wrote,

> [Mom] moved us out to Takoma Park, Maryland, to a single-family home with a massive deck and even more massive front yard. With long, extracurricular heavy school days, a one-hour public transit commute on both ends, and limited time in my new friendless neighborhood, my social life was increasingly defined by Sidwell [School], which meant I had white friends! I had Black friends, too, but the numbers made not having white friends nearly impossible, and these friendships offered new opportunities to share my blackness with others, not always voluntarily.[11]

Many in this generation are the children of single-family households or divorced parents. They retained their parents' suspicion of everything being just fine and dandy. They refused to allow their children to be naïve or lulled into complacency. They continuously warned them of the dangers of white supremacy. They taught that the privileges available to whites don't necessarily apply to them. As a result, Hip-hoppers are self-aware and highly independent. Baratunde Thurston wrote, in *How to Be Black*, of his mother's insistence that he and his sister demonstrate independence:

> Under my mother's tutelage, I was becoming a miniature Black activist myself. When I was eight, she gave me a book about apartheid, because, how else am I supposed to learn how the world really works? . . . My mother's parenting strategy was consciously designed to pass on the lessons she'd learned in life. . . . The *Question Authority* bumper sticker that would face my locker and notebooks from seventh through twelfth grade is one she gave me, always reminding me that just because someone had authority over me does not mean they deserve my respect. This was clearly counter to the programming she'd received in her own upbringing, and she was determined to break the cycle.[12]

Hip-hoppers never had the luxury of daycare and were often on their own after school. They had to manage for themselves from an early age and were highly self-reliant. Gen Xers were latchkey kids, daycare offspring, and children of divorce. Mother Norma Stevenson commented,

> I think Black children see more of what's going on than white kids the same age. They see their parents struggle a little more. White people hide a lot from their kids. Black people do not hide their feelings. When they're hurting it's no crime to show it. They let you know exactly where they're coming from. White people don't. Blacks also know when to put on the act, if necessary. So Black children at an early age become more hip to what life's about.[13]

They are informal, casual, and direct, extremely loyal to family, friends, and community. They refer to other Blacks as family despite a lack of biological connections.

They are the first Americans whose future will not be economically better than that of their parents. They are the first to live in a nation that required a secondary degree for job entry. A higher percentage acquired advanced academic degrees, even as college costs have more than doubled since the 1980s. The Great Recession and high cost of college decreased their earnings and, for many, neutralized their savings. Erin Currie of Pew Charitable Trusts has a harrowing prediction for all members born within this generation regarding upward mobility. Race plays a significant role in limiting members to the bottom of the economic ladder, she writes. Blacks were hardest hit since they lacked factors that increased mobility, such as two-parent households with college degrees.

> A whole host of things influence whether a person will end up in the bottom, middle, or top of the economic ladder as an adult. Family background clearly plays a sizable role, but so does educational attainment, family structure, and race. . . . College-educated, partnered, or white Gen Xers typically have higher income and wealth totals than do their counterparts who have less education, are single, or are Black. . . . These data represent an existential threat to the notion of the American Dream, to the belief that America is indeed a land of opportunity for even the least financially secure. Broad, national data on economic mobility already challenged the often-accepted notion of equality of opportunity in the United States, but the specifics of the Gen X experience are an exclamation point to those broader trends. This generation is not better off, and efforts to improve upward mobility from the bottom must grapple not just with income and education, but also with race.[14]

Like every other Black generation, this one places great value on the right to vote. Gen Xers have the lowest voter participation rates of any generation, but the Hip-Hop Generation participated in the political process and voted for Barack Obama in overwhelming numbers.

THE PRESIDENTS

Presidents during this period were Lyndon Baines Johnson (1963–69, thirty-sixth president), Richard Milhous Nixon (1969–74, thirty-seventh president), Gerald Rudolph Ford (1974–77, thirty-eighth president), and James "Jimmy" Earl Carter Jr. (1977–81, thirty-ninth president). Presidential leadership in the field of race relations reached its apex during the presidency of President Lyndon Johnson and afterward began a slow but steady decline in support. A renaissance occurred concerning Black electability and presidential appointments, but there began a slow decline in legislative victories. President Kennedy's 1961 Executive Order 10925 instructed federal contractors to utilize "affirmative action to ensure that applicants are treated equally without regard to race, color, religion, sex, or national origin." Presidents Johnson (11246) and Carter (12138) strengthened the policy with their own executive orders and included women as recipients of protection. Reagan opposed it vehemently. President Clinton stated his administration's position as, "Mend it, don't end it." Within a decade of Kennedy's executive order, white students sued, claiming "reverse discrimination."

President Lyndon B. Johnson (1963–69) was one of the most unlikely candidates to be a presidential hero and advocate for Black Americans. He was one of the most complicated personalities ever to sit in the president's chair in terms of his relationship with Black people. He is difficult to dissect, as he demonstrated conflicting traits throughout his life.

Early in his political career he demonstrated strong opposition to bills supporting Black civil rights. He was never able to accept systemic racism as a cause of police brutality and blamed Black poverty on Black inadequacy. During his Senate career he voted against any progressive bill, including those that pertained to anti-lynching, anti-poll tax, and a federal school lunch program put forth by Adam Clayton Powell. As a Texas senator he was known for his colorful language and demeaning attitude toward Black people. When a senator, his biographer Robert Caro wrote that the president used the N-word as a regular part of his vocabulary. "Johnson would calibrate his pronunciations by region, using 'nigra' with some southern legislators and 'negra' with others. Discussing civil rights legislation with men like Mississippi Democrat James Eastland, who committed most of his life to defending white supremacy, he'd simply call it 'the n***** bill.'"[15] He voiced opposition to Harry Truman's civil rights program:

> The Civil Rights Program is a farce and a sham—an effort to set up a police state in the guise of liberty. I am opposed to that program. I have voted AGAINST the so-called poll tax repeal bill; the poll tax should be repealed by the states which have enacted them. I have VOTED against the so-called anti-lynching bill; the state can, and

DOES, enforce the law against murder. I voted against the FEPC; if a man can tell you whom you must hire, he can tell you whom you can't hire.[16]

Politicians and the Black media were willing to publicly expose those they considered to be the enemy. He faced immediate replies from Black leadership in Texas in opposition to his states' rights and free speech justifications. The Houston NAACP director responded to his March 9, 1949, "We of the South" speech with a sharp rebuke through a telegraph: "The Negroes who sent you to Congress are ashamed to know that you have stood on the floor against them today. Do not forget that you went to Washington by a small majority vote and that was because of the Negro vote. There will be another election and we will be remembering what you had to say today."[17] Black Texas leaders traveled to Washington and confronted the senator in an angry argument fueled by both sides. NAACP chapters passed censures on Johnson.[18]

Unfortunately, the president had a mounting Cold War against communism that split his attention. Fed by rabid politicians, Americans grew anxious about Russia and its threat to capitalism and the American way of life. Many viewed the Civil Rights Movement as a double threat, believing it to serve as an agent of communism and a menace to society's equilibrium. By late 1967 over half a million American troops were in Vietnam, with one hundred thousand injured and fifteen thousand dead. Johnson was consumed by Kennedy's commitment to prevent the spread of communism to South Vietnam and was determined to win. The opinion of the American public was split, with half for and the other half against the war.[19] Muhammad Ali was stripped of his boxing title when he refused to serve in the army during the Vietnam War. He linked the war to racism in America. "My conscience won't let me go shoot my brother, or some darker people, or some poor hungry people in the mud for big powerful America. And shoot them for what? They never called me n*****, they never lynched me, they didn't put no dogs on me, they didn't rob me of my nationality, rape and kill my mother and father. . . . Shoot them for what?"[20] During the 1968 Mexico City Summer Olympics, Tommie Smith and John Carlos won gold and bronze medals. They raised their fists in a Black Power salute during the medal ceremony and became a symbol of a growing awareness of Black defiance to oppression. They were suspended and expelled from future participation in the Olympics. They received years of death threats from the white public and were blackballed from gaining meaningful employment.

Despite outward appearances, Johnson was personally troubled and moved by the never-ending reign of violence directed at Blacks. As vice president and then as president, he witnessed firsthand, through the power of television, the most epidemic episodes of violence in the Civil Rights Movement. Southern violence moved him to usher in the most progressive civil rights agenda of any president before or since. On September 15, 1963, a bomb murdered four young girls getting ready for Sunday school at the 16th Street Baptist Church in Birmingham, Alabama. President John F. Kennedy was murdered in Dallas, Texas, on November 22, 1963. James Chaney, Michael "Mickey" Schwerner, and Andrew Goodman were murdered by racist terrorists assisted by a sheriff's deputy in June 1964. On February 21, 1965, Malcolm X was assassinated. On March 7, 1965, Bloody Sunday occurred when police brutally beat marchers in Selma, Alabama. When Martin Luther King Jr. was murdered on April 4, 1968, the nation's cities erupted in flames and violence. Prior to King's death, Washington, DC, was known as "The Colored Man's Paradise." For four days, in Washington, DC, nine hundred businesses were damaged, burned, and looted, and many were destroyed, never to reopen. Flood's Shoe Repair, Columbia Carry Out, F. W. Woolworth, People's Drug, Maxis Men's Wear, and Your Home-Town Newspapers did not survive the nights of burning. Most were drugstores, pawnshops, markets, shoe stores, laundromats, and clothing, furniture, and appliance stores. Liquor stores were a common target, with half of the 383 entered and emptied. Seven hundred homes were set aflame, mostly in the Shaw neighborhood along 7th Street. Homes were not intentionally targeted; many were next door to a burning business that shared the flames. There were 7,600 arrests, mostly men and juveniles who were charged with rioting. Thirteen lives were lost. The financial cost was estimated in 2020 dollars as $175 million.[21] The largest number of federal troops (army, marines, and national guard) to occupy the nation's capital since the Civil War arrived as a contingent of 13,000 troops were called to quell the uprising. Former DC councilwoman Charlene Drew Jarvis remembered the days and the mood of Black people. "There was a confluence of anger and hurt about the death of Martin Luther King. But there was also a way of breaking out of a cage in which African Americans felt they had been contained. A lot of it had to do with, 'We've been contained here. We're angry about this. We owe nothing to people who have confined us.'"[22]

As president, Johnson ushered through some of the most progressive human rights legislation ever passed. He was a major force in the passage of the Civil Rights Act of 1964, which outlawed discrimination due to race, color, sex, religion, or national origin. The Voting Rights Act (1965) directly attacked oppressive policies that prevented political participation by Blacks.[23] He utilized his persuasive personality to bully Congress into passing the 1965 Voting Rights Act, which ended literacy tests and provided federal poll monitors in southern states. The 1964 Civil Rights Act passed because President Lyndon B. Johnson lobbied diligently for it in memory of his slain predecessor,

John F. Kennedy. He told a joint session of Congress, "No memorial oration or eulogy could more eloquently honor President Kennedy's memory than the earliest possible passage of the civil rights bill for which he fought for so long."[24] On July 2 the president signed into law the Civil Rights Act of 1964, which provided enforcement for school integration, open interstate accommodations, uninhibited voter registration, and fair employment practices. The Voting Rights Act of 1965 outlawed the poll tax and literacy tests and empowered the federal government to intervene when southern states suppressed Black voting rights.[25] The passage of the Civil Rights Act (1964) and the Voting Rights Act (1965) dismantled the legal framework for segregation and increased Black enfranchisement. Blacks were appointed to prominent positions in the federal government and were elected to office. Presidential administrations were forced to take into consideration the ability of the Black vote to sway an election and responded by hosting meetings with leadership and offering high-level appointments.[26] Johnson's social programs were of great benefit to Black families. His War on Poverty and Great Society programs produced Medicare, Medicaid, Head Start, Job Corps, the Office of Economic Opportunity, federal aid for education, environmental protection laws, the Kerner Commission, consumer protections, public radio and television, and his Model Cities program.[27] The Kerner Commission investigated the cause of Black unrest and reported that racism and inequality was the primary cause. *Smithsonian Magazine* reported in 2018, "'White society is deeply implicated in the ghetto. White institutions created it, white institutions maintain it, and white society condones it.' The nation, the Kerner Commission warned, was so divided that the United States was poised to fracture into two radically unequal societies—one black, one white."[28]

The president was naturally verbose and loved being listened to. He would call civil rights leaders and talk about the movement and pending legislation. He insisted that his earlier resistance to civil rights bills was due to an insistence on the rights of states to deal with states' problems and argued that he was consistent in his support of civil rights.[29] He was to play a direct role in the most impactful civil rights legislation ever passed in the nation's history. He made direct references to civil rights on at least 232 occasions. No president during his term in office more personally identified himself or the office with the rights of Black Americans. He was far more aggressive earlier in his presidency in the movement for racial justice than his slain predecessor. Tape recordings reveal White House conversations with a variety of Black leaders. Blacks had not had such direct interaction with a president since the Roosevelt administration. National Urban League Director Whitney Young spoke with him on November 5, 1964, after the FBI discovered the bodies of three slain civil rights workers in Mississippi.[30] Civil rights leaders were photographed in the Oval Office of the White House on several occasions. In January 1964, Johnson was photographed with Martin Luther King Jr. Roy Wilkins, James Farmer, and Whitney Young.[31]

He had a compelling relationship with Martin Luther King Jr. whom he admired yet was ultimately frustrated by because of his opposition to the Vietnam War. Like Kennedy before him, he uttered unattributed but evidentiary quotes of King in his remarks made at the one hundredth anniversary of Gettysburg on May 30, 1963. "One hundred years ago, the slave was freed. One hundred years later, the Negro remains in bondage to the color of his skin. . . . The Negro today asks for justice. We do not answer him—we do not answer those who lie beneath this soil—when we reply to the Negro by asking, 'Patience.' It is empty to plead that the solution to the dilemmas of the present rests on the hands of the clock."[32] King had said in his earlier 1963 *Letter From a Birmingham Jail*, "One hundred years ago, the slave was freed. One hundred years later, the Negro remains in bondage to the color of his skin. . . . For years now I have heard the word 'Wait!' It rings in the ear of every Negro with piercing familiarity. This 'Wait' has almost always meant 'Never.' We must come to see, with one of our distinguished jurists, that 'justice too long delayed is justice denied.'"[33] Johnson's most memorable utterance in relation to civil rights was his usage of the phrase "we shall overcome" in a joint address to Congress on March 15, 1965. It was titled, "The American Promise" but was remembered under the moniker "We Shall Overcome." He stated,

> There is no Negro problem. There is no Southern problem. There is no Northern problem. There is only an American problem. . . . What happened in Selma is part of a far larger movement which reaches into every section and State of America. It is the effort of American Negroes to secure for themselves the full blessings of American life. Their cause must be our cause too. Because it is not just Negroes, but really it is all of us, who must overcome the crippling legacy of bigotry and injustice. And we shall overcome.[34]

John Lewis shared that he witnessed Martin Luther King Jr. wipe away a tear after hearing the president utter the phrase.[35]

Historian Monroe Billington surmised that the president was neither a racist nor an opportunist but a morally changed man. By the time he became president, he, like Truman, did what he thought was in the best interest of the nation.

> Critics say that Johnson moved from anti-civil rights stands in the 1930s and 1940s and the late 1950s because he was ambitious, expedient, opportunistic, and politically motivated. . . . The record shows that over three decades in public life Johnson was not consistent. But

the record shows less expediency than the growth of an individual in public life. . . . His role as national leader compelled him to ask for the interest not only of the oppressed minority but also for all the people of the country. The story of Johnson's public stance on civil rights is one of evolution, of maturation, of growth.[36]

His Black chauffeur, Robert Parker, recorded in his memoir that when considering the former president in light of his civil rights accomplishments, "I loved that Lyndon Johnson." Of Johnson the racist he commented, "I hated that Lyndon Johnson."[37]

Ebony magazine captured the changing mood of middle-class Black America in its 1969 special edition on the state of Black America. For centuries the country had racial quotas, to benefit whites in employment, academia, and business. Stores and entire industries would not hire Blacks or Hispanics. Blacks were prohibited from attending white universities and later only a handful at a time. Every opportunity was denied to people of color until the 1960s sought to turn that tide. The 1960s ushered in a period of progressive legislation that outlawed discrimination in the hiring, firing, wages, promotions, and working conditions of Black workers. The gains were noteworthy in the South, where for the first time, wages and employment opportunities increased markedly. The most beneficial political decision was the one that created Affirmative Action as a policy to rectify discrimination in education and employment. Between 1961 and 1995, Affirmative Action programs influenced college admissions and employment practices. Title VII of the Civil Rights Act of 1964 prohibited employment discrimination by any employer with over fifteen employees. There is an ebb and flow to rulings that uphold it while others deem it unconstitutional. *Ebony*'s 1962 cover featured a picture of the Reverend Dr. Martin Luther King Jr. under the caption, "The Black Revolution." Between 1962 and 1968, King only appeared on its cover twice, being considered too militant in contrast with its preferred image of Booker T. Washington. By 1969, opinion changed. *Ebony* founder John H. Johnson declared,

> Black people have been forced now into the position where they must either fight for their rights or be reduced to a permanent second-class citizenship. Black people have chosen to fight, and this special issue examines the many facets of that fight. Here Black leaders, Black philosophers, Black activists, and Black historians discuss the Black Revolution in terms that Black people can understand. We feel that this issue is a must read for anyone seeking insight into Black America in its most crucial period in history.[38]

The issue contained articles by John Conyers, Bayard Rustin, and Huey P. Newton.[39]

Richard Nixon (1969–74), was perhaps the greatest presidential hero-villain in the nation's history. His 1971 trip to China is still marveled at today, and it was said that only Nixon could go to China. However, the Watergate break-in disgraced him personally and forever marred his presidential legacy. He is forever reviled for being the first president of the United States to resign from office.

In his first term, Nixon tried to walk a fine line concerning civil rights. Early on he stated he wanted to bring the country together. "We want to bridge the generation gap. We want to bridge the gap between the races. We want to bring America together. And I am confident that this task is one we can undertake, and one in which we will be successful."[40] Traditional Black Republicans such as Jackie Robinson expressed that he believed that Nixon was the "better man" and would name a Negro to his cabinet.[41] Martin Luther King, Jr. had several encounters with Nixon when he was Eisenhower's vice president. King shared that Nixon's conservative voting record gave him an "initial bias" that the vice president was aligned against civil rights. On an occasion when they both were in Ghana in March 1957, they connected. King said to Nixon that with "persons like you occupying such important positions in our nation I am sure that we will soon emerge from the bleak and desolate midnight of man's inhumanity to man."[42] Nixon later extended an invitation to a summit conference where King asked the vice president to lobby for a civil rights bill to be voted on in Congress. King said to the vice president, "How deeply grateful all people of goodwill are to you for your assiduous labor and dauntless courage in seeking to make the civil rights bill a reality."[43] King, however, later said, "If Richard Nixon is not sincere, he is the most dangerous man in America."[44] This was as close as they ever came to forming a relationship. When King was arrested and Nixon made no statement or efforts to secure his release, he was extremely disappointed. "When this moment came, it was like he had never heard of me. (He) was a moral coward and one who was really unwilling to take a courageous step and take a risk."[45]

Nixon was never able to overcome his racist beliefs in a racial hierarchy that placed Blacks and Latinos on the bottom and whites and Asians on the top.[46] He strongly believed in theories that linked intelligence to race, especially those propagated by Richard Herr Stein and Arthur Jensen. He confided in an interview with Daniel Patrick Moynihan, "I have reluctantly concluded, based at least on the evidence presently before me . . . that what Herr Stein says, and what was said earlier by Jensen, is probably . . . very close to the truth."[47] After the United Nations voted to seat a delegation from China instead of Taiwan in 1972, Nixon blamed African nations. In a recorded conversation, California Governor Ronald Reagan referred to United Nations African delegates as cannibals. Nixon repeated Reagan's racist remark to Secretary of State William Rogers and said that the governor "spoke for racist (white) Americans who needed their ear."[48] As a repercussion, he canceled all appointments with African heads of state who voted for China, despite the fact they were not responsible for the vote's outcome.[49]

He had several programs and hires that benefited the Black community. He hired Robert J. Brown as a White House special assistant to the Black community, to serve as advisor in the areas of civil rights legislation, job funding, HBCUs, and housing. He doubled the funding for HBCUs and eliminated the tax credit for donations to segregated schools.[50] He attempted to increase Black business ventures though his Black capitalism initiative and desegregated more schools during 1970 than since the effort had begun. He signed the Voting Rights Act of 1970 as well as the Equal Employment Opportunity bill in 1972.[51] His creation of the Family Assistance Plan, the Environmental Protection Agency, attempts at universal healthcare, and ending the military draft to create a volunteer army were more than many presidents accomplished.

He had willful failures in judgment concerning the issues important to the Black community. When the Congressional Black Caucus (CBC) formed in 1971 to create legislation and policy, the president rejected their invitation to meet. They, in return, publicly announced a boycotting of his State of the Union address. They presented the president with a list of sixty-one recommendations aimed at eliminating poverty and systemic racism.[52] His Black capitalism campaign had racist roots, as his motivation was to decrease Black radicalism rather than increase Black wealth.[53] He reversed social policies he inherited from Johnson, voiced opposition to busing, and was a "law and order" president. It was his highly advertised War on Drugs that completely destroyed his relationship with the Black community, as many blamed him for the resulting high and disproportionate rates of young Black male incarceration with long prison sentences. Nixon's former domestic policy advisor, John Ehrlichman, who experienced public disgrace after serving time in federal prison, stated in 1994 that the goal was to disrupt both the Black and hippie communities by "associating them with drug criminalization and crime."[54] In a 2016 interview Ehrlichman revealed,

> You want to know what this was really all about? The Nixon campaign in 1968, and the Nixon White House after that, had two enemies: the antiwar left and Black people. You understand what I'm saying? We knew we couldn't make it illegal to be either against the war or Black, but by getting the public to associate the hippies with marijuana and Blacks with heroin, and then criminalizing both heavily, we could disrupt those communities. We could arrest their leaders, raid their homes, break up their meetings, and vilify them night after night on the evening news. Did we know we were lying about the drugs? Of course, we did.[55]

His War on Drugs was initiated to target young whites and Blacks and led to the mass incarceration of African Americans and Hispanics. His coded "silent majority" appeal was a shout-out to white America later adopted by the Trump campaign in 2020. "So tonight, to you, the great silent majority of my fellow Americans, I ask for your support."[56] The war he inherited from Johnson became Nixon's war as he escalated troop buildup in Vietnam by two hundred thousand.

Blacks suffering under the hardship of impoverishment had little hope for advancement in life beyond poverty due to high incarceration rates, racialized policing, un- and underemployment, and high crime rates in their neighborhoods. They grew during the nation's tough-on-crime response to the drug trade. Drugs were a normal part of life, with experimentation leading to addiction and incarceration. The War on Drugs had a devastating impact on Black communities and incarcerated family members and friends. Many sought employment by selling drugs as the only means to escape poverty. It was a double-edged sword, as those with a felony conviction were branded as outcasts with no potential for a meaningful career. Michelle Alexander wrote,

> As a result of his conviction he may be ineligible for many federally funded health and welfare benefits, food stamps, public housing, and federal educational assistance. His driver's license may be automatically suspended, and he may no longer qualify for certain employment and professional licenses. If he is convicted of another crime, he may be subject to imprisonment as a repeat offender. He will not be permitted to enlist in the military, or possess a firearm, or obtain a federal security clearance. If a citizen, he may lose the right to vote; if not, he becomes immediately deportable.[57]

This generation's cynicism about American justice was justified by a criminal justice system that persecuted them more than other Americans. Men with felony convictions gave up hoping that life would be better. They were left with few options and a simmering internal anger. They longed for a better life but didn't know how to get there. One of the unforeseen consequences of northern migration was the loss of nearby family support. Females who entered parenthood early found themselves the primary nurturer and provider for their children. Many struggled to meet childcare, rent, and transportation expenses.

By his second term, Nixon was obsessed with enemies, real and imagined. His relationship with civil rights leaders had evaporated, and he was irritated that he had to contend with the issue at all. He was confronted by Ralph Abernathy and expressed his true feelings of being "pretty fed up with Blacks and their hopeless attitude."[58] His frustration with all who opposed him led to his downfall when the Watergate tapes came to the surface. It can be said that a Black man ended his presidency, for it was Frank Wills, a Black security guard, who discovered the break-in and disclosed it to the world. Investigations revealed that the president was guilty of many illegal actions: break-ins, cover-ups, slush funds, wiretaps, and an enemies list that resulted in arrests, imprisonment, and his resignation. On August 9, 1974, Nixon boarded a helicopter, his favorite mode of transportation, and rode away into infamy.[59]

There was a wider scope to Black life by this time as greater participation in every area of life opened up. Tremendous strides were made in the fields of politics, business, and entertainment. Black politics gained a maturity and respectability not witnessed since the days of Reconstruction. Black mayors governed cities and towns in Los Angeles, Chicago, Detroit, Philadelphia, and New York. Maynard Jackson, mayor of Atlanta, affirmed that "politics is the civil rights movement of the seventies."[60] Black students enrolled in white state universities during the late 1960s in large numbers. Most Predominantly White Institutions (PWI) were resistant and required federal intervention to enroll their first students. Private institutions practiced de jure segregation and never formally excluded Black students but did not enroll any. They proclaimed that they judged the man and not his color. They felt mounting pressure from the Civil Rights Movement, the Great Migration, World War II racial advances, military desegregation, and the *Brown v. Board of Education* ruling. By the end of the 1960s, the tide had turned, and more Black students were headed into white universities than traditional Black schools. Studies discovered greater educational resources in these predominantly white institutions, but racism often neutralized many of those benefits. Studies have shown that Black students exhibit a greater level of success at Black schools due to a nurturing environment for first-generation students. The assassination of Martin Luther King Jr. prompted an increase in Black studies programs, Black faculty, and student enrollment.

While the latter part of the 1960s was reputed to be a time of chaos and pain, the 1970s were filled with their own turmoil. By the 1970s white flight was the law of the land as whites fled inner cities for the suburbs. The city of Detroit lost 350,000 white residents, while the suburbs grew in population by the same number. For the first time in American history, a U.S. president resigned. College students were shot on three campuses (Jackson State, Kent State, and South Carolina State College) by national guard and police. The carnage of the Vietnam War ended with a bloody defeat in 1973. The widening of wealth disparity ballooned because of Reaganomics and the faulty concept of trickle down economics. The conservative movement, the "Silent Majority," emerged, partially in reaction to the 1960s; it challenged the increasing advocacy for equal rights for Blacks, women, gays and marginalized groups. The "New Right" sought to wipe away all the gains of the sixties and attacked the federal government's right to raise taxes and produce regulations.

Gerald R. Ford (1974–77) was elevated to the presidency in 1974 due to two resignations. Spiro Agnew, Richard Nixon's vice president, resigned in 1973, and Ford was picked as a replacement. When Nixon resigned a year later, he became the thirty-eighth president of the United States. He is the only person to serve as both vice president and president without being elected to either office.

Extremely well-liked and respected, he tried to bring positivity and honor back to the country. Ford was personable and comfortable around all races, which was of vital importance to Blacks in the 1970s. He quietly committed two acts of racial advocacy, one early in life (1934) and the other near the end (1999). Willis Ward, an African American, was Ford's friend and travel roommate on the University of Michigan football team. The team was told the visiting team from Georgia Tech insisted Ward not play in their game. Ford protested and threatened to boycott the game. Ward convinced him to play, and Michigan won its only game that year. In 1999, he wrote a *New York Times* op-ed in support of the university's affirmative action program, which was embroiled in two lawsuits.[61] He was the first president to celebrate Black History Month, in 1976, and he asked Congress to extend the Voting Rights Act for another five years.

During his term he survived two assassination attempts in one month, September of 1975. His veto of sixty-six bills earned him the moniker Mr. Veto. The economy crashed under the weight of high unemployment, high interest rates, and severe inflation, the worst in the peacetime history of the nation. On September 8, 1974, he pardoned Richard Nixon, and it was the beginning of the end of his presidency. He tried to play it safe by saying little about civil rights. He refused to either support or condemn busing even as forced busing resulted in whites rioting in Boston and refusing to accept the enrollment of Black students in local schools. He compounded his missteps by stating that the *Brown* decision had been decided incorrectly. He commented, "Most Blacks wouldn't vote for me no matter what I did."[62] He would lose his bid for reelection in 1976 to Jimmy Carter, becoming a one-term president known more for his unceremonial falls than for his accomplishments.

By the late 1970s, affirmative action trends would be reversed as anti-discriminatory policies were not enforced. Industries that did not require high levels of education relocated from urban centers to the suburbs. The remaining jobs required applicants to hold college degrees in order to be competitive in the job market. Inner-city residents lacked available transportation to go where the jobs were and were unable to obtain the jobs that were nearby. Those who could afford to leave did, leaving communities struggling with high unemployment and poverty. Within the Black community, gender gaps increased as Black women were more likely to be employed than both Black men and white women. Black families possessed only a quarter of the wealth of white households.[63] The environmental movement gained national prominence with the successful passage of the Clean Air Act and Clean Water Act of 1972. Women rallied unsuccessfully for the passage of the Equal Rights Amendment.[64]

This generation witnessed the transformation of the public school system. According to Brookings, "On every major national test, including the National Assessment of Educational Progress, the gap in minority and white students' test scores narrowed substantially between 1970 and 1990, especially for elementary school students. On the Scholastic Aptitude Test (SAT), the scores of African American students climbed 54 points between 1976 and 1994, while those of white students remained stable."[65] The number of Black students who attended majority white schools rose from 23 percent in 1968 to 37 percent in 1981. Sixty-four percent attended Black schools (those with a 90 percent minority majority) in 1968; by 1974 the number had decreased to 39 percent. By the end of the 1980s the experiment had stalled, as most schools remained segregated, and those that had made strides were reversing course.[66]

James "Jimmy" Earl Carter Jr. (1977–81) was the first president elected from the South since 1844 and owed his presidency to the Black vote. His parents, Earl and Lillian, raised him in the small, mostly Black community of Archery, which is close to Plains, Georgia. The family owned hundreds of acres of farmland where Black sharecroppers farmed peanuts and cotton. His father was a staunch conservative, but this was contrasted by his mother's progressive attitudes, especially concerning race. She raised her four children to never use the N-word and insisted that they treat people kindly. She modeled her beliefs as she serviced both Black and white patients as a registered nurse, often as a midwife. Carter grew up playing with Black children but was separated from them by Jim Crow laws and school segregation.[67]

He served two terms as a Georgia state senator, 1963–67, and fought against voter suppression. He ran for governor and lost as segregationists flocked to the polls to vote for his opponent, Lester Maddox, a white supremacist. He won the race for governor of Georgia in 1970 by appealing to the racial attitudes of the constituents of former Governor George Wallace in support of white supremacy and upholding its status quo. He opposed busing, sought the endorsement of segregationists, did few appearances before Black audiences, and supported the Vietnam War. The *Atlanta Constitution* caricaturized him as "an ignorant, racist, backward, ultra-conservative, red-necked South Georgia peanut farmer."[68] To the horror of many who voted for him, once in office he unveiled a racially aggressive policy. In his inaugural address he pronounced that racial segregation should no longer be tolerated in the country. He hung a picture of Martin Luther King Jr. in the rotunda of the state capitol in Atlanta. He increased the number of Black hires in state government by 40 percent and facilitated appointments to boards and commissions previously barred to Black applicants. Funding for schools was equalized.[69] He was the shining example of the New South and was portrayed on the cover of *Time* magazine in 1971.

Although a virtual unknown when he ran for president in 1976, he appealed to Blacks due to his Christian faith, which he talked about openly on the campaign trail. When his home church held a vote on receiving Black members, the vote resoundingly failed. It did tally three votes in favor, and two of those came from the Carter family, he and his wife, Rosalynn.[70] In the election, he rceived four out of every five Black votes cast. After winning, he affirmed that the Black vote had been "instrumental in helping me to become elected to the highest office in our land."[71] In June 1976, the *New York Times* reported,

> The major reason that Jimmy Carter appears to be leading President Ford as the choice of the electorate at this point is the former Georgia Governor's overwhelming support among Blacks . . . the latest national political survey conducted by *The New York Times* and CBS News suggests that the Black vote would be pivotal if the election for President were held today between President Ford and Mr. Carter. The Georgian was chosen by Blacks in the survey by more than 5 to 1. . . . Mr. Carter's lead this year is all the more significant, because he seems to be retaining that strong Black support, even though he is a white Southern politician, and because the white vote is so evenly divided. The survey results strongly suggest that the President and Mr. Carter would run about even among white voters, with Mr. Ford possibly edging out the former Governor by a slim margin. However, when Blacks are added, Mr. Carter would win by about 6 percentage points.[72]

Once in office, he tripled the number of Blacks on the federal bench and penalized mortgage institutions that utilized racially discriminatory policies. He established a Black College Initiative that increased funding significantly. He increased business opportunities to close the Black-white wealth gap. He was a dependable supporter of Affirmative Action. He placed several Blacks in his cabinet: Wade H. McCree (solicitor general), Clifford L. Alexander (Secretary of the Army), Mary Berry (Department of Education), Eleanor Holmes Norton (Equal Employment Opportunity Commission), Franklin Delano Raines (White House staff), Andrew Young (Ambassador to the United Nations), and Donald F. McHenry (Young's replacement).[73] As president, he appointed more Black women than any previous administration, including

Ersa Poston and Patricia Harris. A major rift between him and the Black community came when he fired United Nations Ambassador Andrew Young for meeting with the Palestinian Liberation Organization in 1979. Rep. Shirley Chisholm charged that the president sacrificed Young for his failure to bring about peace in the Middle East. He replaced Young with another African American, Donald F. McHenry.

A pair of catastrophes destroyed his presidency, neither of his creation. The energy crisis and the Iran hostage crisis were insurmountable challenges he couldn't overcome. When he lost his reelection bid in 1980, Black voters were the only constituency to remain faithful and vote for him. His image was repaired post-presidency, and in 2002 he was awarded a Nobel Peace Prize.

SUMMARY OF THE HIP-HOP GENERATION

Many hoped that hip-hop's cultural influence would translate into political power.

> Ironically, the very cultural movement that has often been on the receiving end of much criticism and disdain from the civil rights/ Black power generation, due to its sometimes anti-Black, sexist, and homophobic lyrics and seemingly endless celebration of bling bling, consumer culture, just may be the vehicle for Black America's next major political movement. . . . In Little Rock, Selma, San Francisco, LA, etc., young activists are calling on hip-hop's influence and hip-hop kids to work for change at the grassroots level and beyond. . . . What's less known, outside of youth culture circles, is the extent of a growing political activism among America's hip-hop kids.[74]

Rap music entrepreneur Russell Simmons hosted a series of hip-hop summit town hall meetings in Philadelphia, Detroit, Los Angeles, and New York. P. Diddy, Nelly, Snoop Dogg, and Eminem served as hosts and encouraged young people to vote and participate in the political process. Previously, Diddy had sponsored a Vote or Die campaign registering voters. Foundations sponsored by rappers include Chingy for Change, Ludacris Foundation, G Unity, Shady Foundation, Daddy's House, and the Shawn Carter Foundation.[75]

This was the first generation in which individuals achieved financial viability in a variety of industries. This generation grew up with more uninhibited Black celebrities than any previous generation. When prominent athletes of this generation protested, they became symbols of a new celebrity resistance. Many celebrities spoke for the experience of everyday Blacks who understood the truth of their words and applauded their resistance, especially when it came at a price. Black individuals of this generation were celebrated for their achievements, amassed tremendous wealth, and achieved true celebrity status. White children wanted to "be like Mike" (Michael Jordan). Oprah Winfrey was the most popular talk show host in the world. *The Cosby Show* gave America a Black dad. Michael Jackson was an entertainment phenomenon with worldwide appeal. Eddie Murphy made movies everyone wanted to see that earned billions in revenue. Rap took over the music industry and invaded the suburbs. This generation grew up in a time when, even though racism was still evident, opportunity seemed more available than ever before.

In business, this was the first generation to not only occupy a seat at the table but to own the table. Their business acumen, including million-dollar salaries, produced remarkable growth for the Black middle class. Many mastered their industries, founded businesses, and invested in empire-building by successfully marketing their brand. Globalization contributed to corporations becoming worth billions of dollars and birthed a mindset that wealth makes right. Materialism is a characteristic of this generation. They are much more materialistic than any previous generation, perhaps influenced by the fact that they are the first generation with a realistic chance to quickly accumulate enormous wealth. They are much more individually oriented than other generations and have formed their values from a society that teaches individualized survival, as each one looks out for number one. Tiger Woods received a slew of criticisms for labeling himself "Cablinasian," a mixture of Caucasian, Black, Indian, and Asian heritage. He was viewed as attempting to disassociate himself from being Black. (Authorities who arrested him in 2017 did not agree and labeled his race as Black.) Rappers of this generation rap about bling, flicking dollars, and drinking champagne.[76] Rappers of this generation identified with Donald Trump long before his presidency, with more than three hundred references in lyrics. Lil Pump, Ice Cube, Lil Wayne, and 50 Cent all stood with Trump during his reelection campaign. Ice Cube ridiculed his critics by saying that he was working with Trump on financial investments in the Black community without providing any details. Fifty Cent initially endorsed Trump for reelection, as he feared Joe Biden would raise his taxes. He backtracked after criticism from others, including his former girlfriend, Chelsea Handler. On *The Tonight Show Starring Jimmy Fallon*, she stated plainly, "I had to remind him that he was a Black person, so he can't vote for Donald Trump, and that he shouldn't be influencing an entire swath of people who may listen to him because he's worried about his own personal pocketbook."[77] Fiddy responded to the controversy by tweeting, "F*** Donald Trump, I never liked him."[78]

This is a paradoxical generation: it wants to do the right thing, but it is seduced by the glare of riches. Some describe this one as a generation at war with itself. The desire to change the world has been seeded by parents, but it has not taken deep root. They live with a sense of service, but the bulk of their time is spent securing wealth and power. Significant numbers have climbed to the top of their professions and are now insiders with much to lose. They have a brand to protect and are fully aware of how fickle the white public can be, especially when it comes to persons of color engaged in public activism. Their desire to succeed goes beyond being simply successful; they want to win all the marbles. They want to sit at the head of a table with their names emblazoned in gold. They describe themselves as being civic minded and aware of the importance of giving back to the communities from whence they originated, as long as it does not endanger their financial pursuits. Charity is the manner through which they give back, as it contains high returns and little risk to their reputation. They donate generously but are rarely socially provocative, not willing to challenge the system publicly. They don't utilize their voice or image outside of personal marketing opportunities. They tweet but are rarely seen advocating at rallies, vigils, or protests. Sean Combs (P. Diddy, Puff Daddy) walks a fine line between entrepreneurship and philanthropy. The last paragraph on his webpage, Combs Enterprises, lists his "philanthropic work and political activism" as providing water for Flint and $2 million to New York public schools and states that he has registered millions of young adults through his "Vote or Die" project in 2008. The other ten paragraphs are about his life and professional accomplishments. Jay-Z said in 2013 in response to criticism by Harry Belafonte, "I'm offended by that because first of all, and this is going to sound arrogant, but my presence is charity. Just who I am. Just like Obama's is. Obama provides hope. Whether he does anything, the hope that he provides for a nation, and outside of America is enough. Just being who he is."[79]

The Hip-Hop Generation experienced misogyny within the Black community, amplified by rap music. Constant references to Black women in lyrics depicted them as "bitches, gold diggers, hos, hoodrats, chickenheads, pigeons" and other offensive labels. Kitwana highlighted several prominent reasons for the hip-hop generation's sexism: male-to-male loyalty to the exclusion of others; a lack of interest and/or understanding of feminism; a growing objectification of women; cultural focus on materialism; sexism passed down from previous generations; and fan dismissal of bad behavior. Black male resentment targeted Black women, who responded with mutual resentment. Men resent women for having to carry less of a burden and supplanting them as heads of households. Women resent men for giving up too easily and accepting defeat at the hands of racism. In response, Kitwana asks, "Where did our love go for each other and, some might argue, ourselves?"[80]

Amazingly, hip-hop generationers display the same type of sexist rhetoric evident in the behavior of previous generations to keep Black women in their place by any means necessary. Kitwana charged Black women of his generation with failing to challenge the attitudes of men, even justifying it to a degree. Many contemporary artists, surprisingly many of them female, gave voice to misogynist lyrics. Beyonce's 2019 Netflix special, *Homecoming*, had background voices singing, "Bitch, I'm back by popular demand. I did not come to play with you hoes. I came to slay bitch!" as she mouthed the words.

This generation reintroduced a tradition in which Black parents provided unique naming patterns for their children, often to promote racial pride and identity. During slavery, it was not uncommon for an enslaved child to have two names. The enslaver would provide a public name, and the parents would provide a name used by intimates. Biblical names were extremely popular. The tradition resurfaced in the 1970s with the Black Power Movement and the TV miniseries *Roots*. Kizzie became a popular name for several years. Studies have indicated that a unique name identifying one as African American can have impact on employment opportunities by as high as a 50 percent decrease in job interviews. Harvard professor Latanya Sweeney revealed that Google searches with "Black-sounding names" produced ads focused on criminality.[81] Another study determined that it is not the name that caused a denial of opportunity or produced an impoverished outcome for children, but that unique naming patterns arose out of impoverishment. According to Fryer and Levitt in their study of California naming practices, there was a connection between pride in Black identity and the naming process of Black children. In the early 1970s, Blacks who lived in segregated communities originated names for their children. "Blacks, much more than other minorities, choose distinctive names for their children. The distinctiveness of Black names has risen greatly over time, most notably in the late 1960s and early 1970s."[82] The more racially isolated Blacks were from whites, the greater the uniqueness in their children's names. During the 1960s, parents living in integrated and segregated communities followed the same naming patterns, that is, adopting Anglo names. But by the early 1970s, those living apart from whites created original names or adapted those already in existence. In California, some of the most frequently used were DeShawn, Tyrone, Reginald, Shanice, Precious, Kiara, and Deja.[83]

The Hip-Hop Generation combined the creativity of the Harlem Renaissance and the radicalism of the Black Power movement to create a new brand for Black America. They have not given up on the idea of America as a free nation, but they are frustrated that more progress has not been made. Nevertheless, they are relentless in their pursuit of the American Dream, regardless of how illusive and illusionary it might be for Black people. They have seen progress within individual success, but not for the whole of their people. Yet they refuse to quit and will continue to push forward for economic, political, and spiritual progress for Black Americans.

5

#BlackLivesMatter Generation (Millennials)

1981–96

The hip-hop and post-hip-hop generations, the first groups to grow
up in legally desegregated America, possess a worldview that has not
been shaped by the sociopolitical institutions that our parents and
grandparents were a part of, many of which, because of desegregation, have since withered away. Where the Black church, community
centers, and family were once the primary transmitters of values and
culture, today it's a potent mass media concoction of pop music, film,
television, and digital content—all of which are produced and dis-
seminated through a small handful of multinational corporations.[1]
—M. K. Asante Jr., *It's Bigger Than Hip Hop*

The #BlackLivesMatter Generation is comprised of socially aware men and
women who rally against discrimination and social injustice. This generation founded the 2013 Black Lives Matter Movement when Patrisse Cullors,
Alicia Garza, and Opal Tometi organized a campaign against systemic racism and violence against the LGBTQ+ community. According to the Pew
Research Center, since May 2018, the Black Lives Matter hashtag has been
retweeted thirty million times, an average of 17,002 times each day.[2] M. K.
Asante Jr.'s book, *It's Bigger Than Hip Hop*, labeled this generation the "post-
hip-hop generation."[3] Asante defines this generation as highly critical of hip-
hop culture, defining it as a deflated movement, a money-making monstrosity
detached from social justice. This generation desires more than dance beats,
wealth, celebrity, and a television moment. Their celebrities are far more prone
to speak out against racial injustice and feel obligated to advocate on behalf
of millions struggling in systemic poverty. Social media and the Black Lives
Matter Movement are central to their lives. They utilize technology and social
media as their primary tools to organize civic and political protest. A 2016 *Los*

Angeles Times article described the young Black activists: "The newer generation is rawer and more spontaneous, focusing on personal emotions and therapeutic ideas of healing more than political debate and policy proposals."[4] While their parents voted for Hillary Clinton in 2016, they voted for Bernie Sanders.

Demographer Tom Exter wrote that in 2016 members of the #BlackLivesMatter Generation numbered 10 million adults (13.7 percent) out of the 73 million in their age range. They are located in large metropolitan cities including New York; Atlanta; Chicago; Washington, DC; and South Florida. They are similar to whites in that most are either single or in a relationship without children. Eighty percent have never married. Many are transitioning into home ownership and establishing families. Thirteen percent hold a bachelor's or graduate degree. Fifty-three percent have spent time in college, with 25 percent enrolled in an undergraduate or graduate institution. Annually, they have the tremendous collective buying power of $162 billion.[5]

In 2020, there were 3.1 million households headed by this generation. According to Jill N. Filipovic,

> White millennials are almost three times as likely as Black millennials to own their homes. And it's getting harder for African Americans: according to New America, the homeownership rate for Black Millennials is lower today (2020) than it was for African Americans of the same age in 1960. An African American member of the Silent Generation, born between the late 1920s and early 1940s, and living, as an adult, in an era in which Jim Crow laws were still enforced, was more likely to own a home than a Black Millennial is now.[6]

Black home ownership has remained unchanged since the 1960s, with just over 40 percent owning homes, while whites experienced a slight increase to 70 percent home ownership. Whites are five times more likely to be bequeathed an inheritance than Blacks, primarily the inheritance of family homes.[7]

The Great Recession cost this generation almost 60 percent of its acquired wealth while white millennials lost only 16 percent.[8] Millennials endured an economic downfall, but the #BlackLivesMatter Generation endured much worse economic devastation. After the onset of the coronavirus pandemic, 43 percent reported difficulty in paying their household bills and 33 percent visited a food bank.[9]

This generation absorbed what it meant to be Black in America at an early age. Unlike their white peers, the #BlackLivesMatter Generation was neither accommodated nor doted over. The world never revolved around them, and they didn't get participation trophies. They did not have play dates or sleepovers. They were not told how special they were as children but were taught that life is rough and only the strong survive. They learned they would have to work twice as hard in order to be half as successful. They were taught to handle difficult situations, to be resilient, and not to fear failure. Their parents had "the talk" with them concerning how to deal with police encounters: don't resist, talk back, or make any sudden moves. While most other races in America had stopped using corporal punishment, their parents practiced "spare the rod and spoil the child." #BlackLivesMatter Generation members did not grow up in a democracy but a dictatorship. They differ from white post-Millennials, who often were raised in dual-income families with high levels of involvement in family decisions. While feeling valued, they did not get a vote in family decisions.[10]

The 2015 Black Youth Project revealed stark statistics and disturbing racial discrepancies in employment, workplace, racial, and gender discrimination within this age group. They face wage discrepancies, difficulty obtaining mortgage financing, and low rates of home ownership. They are paid less than their white peers and are more often denied credit approval. In 2020, whites earned an average of $60,800 annually while Blacks earned $37,300. A mere 5.5 percent earn more than $100,000.[11] Blacks are more likely to earn lower incomes, as Black workers make only 82.5 cents on every dollar a white worker makes. Thirty-six percent of young Black women reported much higher workplace discrimination compared to white women (13.9 percent) and Latinas (21.2 percent). Black youth (ages 20 to 24) experienced a 16.6 percent unemployment rate compared with Latino (10.3 percent) and white (8.5 percent) youth. They carry more student debt too, with 86.6 percent indebted via a federal student loan. Only 59.9 percent of whites are similarly burdened.[12]

A 2020 Cigna "Loneliness at Work Survey" reported that 30 percent of #BlackLivesMatter employees felt abandoned by coworkers at work, and 30 percent felt alienated. Employees reported experiences of microaggressions and were blocked from receiving assignments on a fair basis.[13] The 2019 report by the Center for Talent Innovation think tank called "Being Black in Corporate America: An Intersectional Exploration" determined certain important facts about the experience of African Americans in corporate America. "Black professionals see barriers to advancement that are largely invisible to white professionals. Few have access to senior leaders. They are more likely than any other group to encounter racial prejudice at work and experience certain microaggressions at higher rates than all other professionals. Over one in three Black employees intend to leave."[14]

THE PRESIDENTS

Presidents of this period were Ronald Reagan (1981–89, fortieth president), George H. W. Bush (1989–93, forty-first president), and William Jefferson Clinton (1993–2001, forty-second president). Ronald Wilson Reagan was beloved by whites and detested by Blacks. He stood tall, appearing to stand for the best in America, but Blacks saw in him a president trying to perpetuate the world of his childhood, in which racism and discrimination were part of the ebb and flow of life. He believed in a world of his own making, failing to acknowledge that America was not the idyllic land of peaceful harmony he imagined. He was seen as a relic from a time Blacks had fought to erase from the American landscape. His election was seen as a setback in the struggle for Black rights. Attorney Alex Berteau remarked, "Whatever momentum was there went bang, after Reagan became president. . . . What I'll never understand was how we could take a man, born in almost the first decade of the century, and get him to preside over the next to last decade, to do everything in his power to throw us back into the first decade of the century. What a rip-off."[15]

The 1980s were a transitionary decade as the country witnessed one of the most dramatic shifts in Black life within a generation. These were the best and the worst of times for Black Americans. Blacks achieved an unprecedented level of inclusion in the intimacies of American life. Racial progress was seen in the rapid increase in economic and social opportunities. A comparison with two-income white families showed that Black income rose from 73 percent (1968) to 82 percent (1986) of white income. The Black middle class increased by 107 percent between 1960 and 1970, with 27 percent earning between $25,000 and $50,000 a year. In 1984, 44 percent of Black families were homeowners.[16] Between 1970 and 1990, universities and colleges moved away from denials based on race to full admission policies. Between 1972 and 1982, if a Black student attended an integrated school, it greatly enhanced the odds that they would attend an integrated college, live in an integrated neighborhood, land a white-collar position, and earn more money than those whose experience included a segregated education.[17] Greater access to higher education increased dramatically the ranks of Black professionals. The number of Black college and university professors doubled; physicians tripled; and engineers quadrupled. The number of attorneys increased more than sixfold. [18]

The job of being president involved utilizing both a domestic and international playbook. For Reagan it was no different, as foreign affairs played a prominent role in his presidency. His foreign policy, the Reagan Doctrine, was guided by a Cold War mentality as he continued the fight against communism. With a heartless determination, he ordered military and political interventions in Grenada, El Salvador, and Nicaragua. He attempted to sidestep a congressional prohibition on providing support to the Nicaraguan Contras by misappropriating funds from Iranian weapons sales. He had foreign policy successes and failures. The world applauded in 1987 when he and Mikhail Gorbachev cosigned the Intermediate-Range Nuclear Forces Treaty to reduce both countries' nuclear arsenals. But he was embroiled in political scandal from the Iran-Contra debacle that led to the conviction of some of his cabinet members. Under his macho cowboy administration, 241 marines were murdered in a terrorist attack on a U.S. compound in Beirut.

He was completely out of touch with the American public and the global community in his approach to South African apartheid. His policy strongly resembled the position criticized by King as a "wait, progress will come" approach. His Constructive Engagement policy endorsing greater cooperation to bring about reforms was deemed noneffective. He criticized the African National Congress (ANC), calling it communist-inspired and a danger to peace. He unwaveringly supported South African President P. W. Botha even after Botha stated that the one-person vote would only lead to chaos in his country. In 1986, he vetoed the Comprehensive Apartheid Act. Reagan objected that the law would harm Black South Africans: "Punitive sanctions, I believe, are not the best course of action; they hurt the very people they are intended to help. My hope is that these punitive sanctions do not lead to more violence and more repression." He added, "It is counterproductive for one country to splash itself all over the headlines, demanding that another government do something."[19] Both houses of Congress overrode his veto, with eighty-one House Republicans siding with Democrats. The congressional Black Caucus sponsors, Representatives Bill Gray (D-PA) and Ron Dellums (D-CA), disagreed with the president. Gray defined the veto as "a moral and diplomatic wake-up call."[20] Rep. Mickey Leland (D-TX) said, "This is probably the greatest victory we've ever experienced. The American people have spoken and will be heard around the world."[21] Other countries followed suit as European nations and Japan issued their own sanctions. The new law had a devastating effect on the South African economy. Bank loans, financial investments, bank accounts, and airport landing rights were banned. Imports such as steel, iron, coal, textiles, uranium, and farm products were no longer allowed.[22] Apartheid soon ended.

The new president was the darling of conservatives. His supply-side economics, also called Reaganomics, rewarded the wealthy with tax cuts to incentivize economic investment. The result was the most severe recession since the 1930s, one that almost bankrupted the government. The federal government amassed more debt during his eight years in office than during the entirety of the country's history. The small-government, fiscal conservative oversaw an 11 percent increase in federal spending, especially military increases, that caused the national debt to balloon from $900 million to almost $2.7 trillion.[23] As a candidate he promised to remove government regulations, including those safeguarding the environment and providing consumer protections. His actions to deregulate the savings-and-loan industry proved to be disastrous when, in 1987, the stock market crashed.[24] His policies halted social and economic progress for the poor and racial minorities as Americans lost jobs, homes, businesses, and farms. African Americans suffered a 31.6 percent poverty rate, triple that of whites (10.1 percent). His administration did little to alleviate economic hardship, and his policies made life worse for the impoverished. Domestic spending was slashed by $39 billion. Federal programs that provided needed relief, such as Aid to Families with Dependent Children, Medicaid, food stamps, school lunch, and job training, received severe cuts. A million people lost their food stamps; 400,000 lost all welfare benefits, and 279,000 endured other reductions.[25]

Black scholars portrayed the Reagan presidency as white backlash against Black progress. A century of redlining and segregationist policies saw loans denied to Blacks seeking to move into white neighborhoods. Redlining drew an exclusionary line of red ink around neighborhoods of color in 239 cities, inside the borders of which mortgage loans were denied. Redlining practices of the mid-1930s to the 1950s placed Black-owned homes in poorer neighborhoods with lower financial worth.[26] A 2018 National Community Reinvestment Coalition study determined that 75 percent of Black communities redlined between 1935 and 1939 were still mired in poverty. A similar report by the Center for Investigative Reporting revealed that redlining continues as sixty-one metro areas practice discriminatory lending. Redlined communities were prone to gentrification, and residents experienced greater wealth disparity between new and long-term residents.[27] Blacks were not the only demographic targeted, as in different times in history Catholics, Jews, Asian immigrants, and southern Europeans have been considered undesirables. Utilizing census information, a study by Redfin real estate brokerage revealed that the percentage of Black families who own their homes is lower now than it was in 1934.[28] Blacks born between 1956 and 1965 were homeowners by the time they were fifty years old. Blacks born between 1966 and 1976 only achieved a 40 percent rate of home ownership, with many gains wiped out by the Great Recession. In 2020, only 44 percent of black families owned their home, while 73.7 percent of white families were homeowners. Harvard's Chris Herbert wrote, "Black homeownership rates are noticeably lower among people in their 40s and 50s because they were victims of subprime loans or saw their parents lose their homes to foreclosure in larger numbers than white people."[29] Estimates are that members of the #BlackLivesMatter Generation will have even lower rates of home ownership. The racial ownership gap in many cities is wide, with just 25 percent of Black families owning a home in Minneapolis compared with 76 percent of whites, which is the widest gap in U.S. cities with more than 1 million residents. In Washington, DC, 51 percent of Black households are homeowners, the highest rate in the country, but this is far lower than the 70 percent of white home-owning households. Blacks pay higher property taxes, higher by as much as 13 percent and higher than whites with a comparable home, due to racial segregation.[30]

As whites fled the inner city, so did jobs and businesses. Black entrepreneurs who managed to survive were those with a Black clientele: restaurants, barber and beauty shops, hair braiding, childcare, catering, mechanic shops, hair care manufacturers, and funeral homes. Once well-off communities sunk into poverty and despair: Chicago's South Side, East New York in Brooklyn, South Bronx, South Central Los Angeles, East Oakland, and most of Detroit. Predatory lending agencies charging outlandish rates of interest moved into neighborhoods. Illegal narcotics and violence began to appear in middle-class neighborhoods where previously they were nonexistent. Police targeted low-level violators who did not have the connections or resources to launder money or ship drugs into the country.[31] Sociologist Larry Bobo described a subtle yet insipid racial antagonism he termed *laissez faire racism*. He chronicled its manifestations in

> white car dealerships that charge Blacks hundreds of dollars more for automobiles than they do whites; hospitals that routinely provide substandard treatment for minorities; insurance companies that systematically charge Black consumers higher rates than whites to insure homes of identical market value; grocery store chains that transport older produce from white suburban shopping-mall markets to groceries in predominantly Black communities; the denial of employment opportunities at senior levels of management and administration in large companies and institutions.[32]

For many Blacks, Reagan represented a reversal of Black advancement. In 1966 he ran for California governor and was quoted as saying, "If an individual wants to discriminate against Negroes or others in selling or renting his house, it is his right to do so."[33] His candidacy for the presidency was announced in Neshoba County, Mississippi, where Chaney, Goodman, and Schwerner were murdered. He told a cheering crowd of whites, "I believe in state's rights." Blacks interpreted this to be slang for white supremacy. Shortly afterward, the Ku Klux Klan endorsed him. Reagan rejected this endorsement eventually, but he was criticized for his slow rejection of their support. On the campaign trail he retold the story of the "welfare queen" who ripped off the system. In the public imagination, the term "welfare queen" was meant to evoke the image of a Black woman. During a 1985 radio interview, he issued a startling analysis that segregation was a thing of the past. "They have eliminated the segregation that we once had in our own country—the type of thing where hotels and restaurants and places of entertainment and so forth were segregated—that has all been eliminated."[34] He later apologized. This despite the fact that he was publicly criticized for allowing tax breaks for segregated schools and country clubs that prohibited Black membership. Josephine Clement stated, "[W]ith Mr. Reagan, things have regressed. He gave people permission to be their worst selves. We're still dealing with that. What is it he said? He didn't know there was hunger. He didn't know there was racism. He just wrote it off and dismantled a lot of good legislation."[35] When Reagan was elected president, Republican Benjamin Hooks, president of the NAACP, called a press conference on November 22, 1980, to declare that there is a

> new hysteria that prevails in many of the Black communities of our nation following the election of the Reagan administration, and more particularly the election of a very conservative Senate and House which caused the displacement of many of the most liberal names that Blacks have come to rely upon over the years. . . . It is unfortunate, it is pathetic and tragic that once again Black people and their sympathetic white allies are called upon almost single-handedly as a group to defend the great American idea against those who hold high office who would spit on the flag, tramp on the constitution and crumble the Bill of Rights into nothingness.[36]

Reagan was not a president Blacks had confidence in. Blacks saw early evidence to support the belief that Reagan was not receptive to dismantling white supremacy because of his efforts to deconstruct federal protections barring racial discrimination. Blacks charged him with intentionally eradicating policies adopted during the civil rights era.

Blacks experienced intense frustration during his administration for his refusal to address racism in America. Race relations were polarized as the White House attempted to roll back affirmative action programs and diminish welfare programs. His disdain for anything remotely promoting racial equality disappointed and angered Black America. NAACP President Benjamin Hooks vigorously opposed the president's policies as ineffective and damaging to African Americans. The Urban Institute released a prolonged report that the administration's policies were benefiting the wealthy and creating havoc for poor Americans. The United States Commission on Civil Rights accused Reagan of being responsible for a lack of federal oversight and enforcement of civil rights in the country. A lawyers' association laid claim to the fact that the Civil Rights Division of the Justice Department had retreated from its responsibility to enforce the civil rights of Blacks. In 1988, Charlayne Hunter-Gault, on behalf of *Life* magazine, interviewed Black leaders for a special edition. When asked about then-President Reagan, June Jordan commented, "In the '60s we didn't have Ronald Reagan. I think that cannot be underestimated. I mean *him*, quite personally, and I also mean the people he represents. He has legitimized a depthless egoism and cruelty of perspective and meanness of spirit that is unprecedented in our lifetime. I think people feel encouraged now to be racist—to be base, to be big and bad and base out loud."[37] Falaka Fattah said,

> I don't think he was just Reagan. I think that he was reinforced by right-wing religious communities in terms of saying it's okay to be mean, it's okay not to care, it's okay to exercise your prejudice. You don't even have to worry about how offensive you are in terms of your bigoted words. Before the present administration came into power with the support of conservative ministers, many more Americans were trying to put forth an honest effort to avoid having two unequal societies.[38]

The president pushed back on criticisms of his administration's insensitivity to the Black community. He was consistent in his refusal to examine whether his policies had a detrimental effect on Blacks, always placing fault elsewhere. On several occasions he said the plight of Blacks was due to the failure of Johnson's Great Society programs that brought into being a welfare state that economically crippled Black Americans. He offensively stated that it introduced a modernized version of bondage. In his speech at the National Black Republican Council dinner, the president continued to blame Johnson and the Democrats for failing Black America. He charged that social programs did more harm than good and that the anwer to Black progress was in the economic sector. At the 1981 NAACP convention, Reagan blamed Blacks for their economic bondage and castigated Black voters who did not support him or his policies. "Just as the Emancipation Proclamation freed Black people 118 years ago, today we need to declare an economic emancipation."[39] The president reaffirmed his belief that progress would come from cutting taxes and an end to government regulations. Republican Hooks used one word to describe Reagan's program: "Joke."[40]

A 1982 *New York Times* article reported that Reagan sought to rebut the notion that his policies were anti-Black. Seeking to counter charges that he laid waste to departments and programs designed to eliminate discrimination, he stated, "I can assure you that with regard to any hint of discrimination that we have done more than any other generation or administration, I should say, to punish those who attempt to discriminate and to make sure that the opportunities are equal for all."[41] It was damaging to the president's position when an African American member of his administration, Samuel R. Pierce, the Secretary of Housing and Urban Development, disagreed with the rebuttal. He acknowledged that the Reagan administration did not have a healthy acquaintance with the Black community with inadequate understanding of its needs. He highlighted as evidence the decision to allow schools practicing discrimination to receive tax exemptions and the president's opposition to any enforcement of the Voting Rights Act.[42]

The question of his racial objectivity has been long debated. His slow awakening to the importance of nationalizing the birthday of Martin Luther King Jr. was a constant irritant for Black Americans. His failure to realize the importance of this act to the entire nation was demonstrated by his endorsement of North Carolina Senator Jesse Helms's theatrics to derail the vote. Reagan commented privately that he would have preferred a day of remembrance and revealed to former Republican Governor Meldrim Thomson of New Hampshire, "I have the same reservations you have, but here the perception of too many people is based on image, not reality."[43] To the infuriation of Blacks, when he was compelled to sign the bill, he held an event in the Rose Garden to appropriate the moment in 1983. "And I just have to believe that all of us, if all of us, young and old, Republicans and Democrats, do all we can to live up to those commandments, then we will see the day when Dr. King's dream comes true."[44] The question has been revisited by the release of a 1971 conversation between him and President Richard Nixon that revealed a willingness to use racist language. In discussing the United Nations, Reagan commented, "To see those, those monkeys from African countries, damn them, they're still uncomfortable wearing shoes."[45] Renee Graham wrote in a 2019 Boston Globe article, "Why Is Anyone Surprised by Reagan's Racism?"

> President Ronald Reagan was racist. In other news, the moon is high. . . . He bent one woman's story, dubbing her a "welfare queen," into a vile stereotype of black women hustling taxpayer dollars to support lavish lifestyles. Reagan then used it to attack housing benefits, aid to children in poverty, and food stamp programs. His disdain for the gay community made him ignore the ravages of AIDS, which also disproportionately affected straight black women and Haitians, for most of his presidency. Many were killed by presidential neglect, as well as the virus.[46]

While the Teflon President left office with a 70 percent approval rating among whites, Blacks perceived him as more image than substance.[47] The 1984 Nobel Peace Prize winner, Bishop Desmond Tutu, declared Reagan's policies "immoral, evil and totally un-Christian."[48] His numbers ranged from a dismal 9 percent approval in 1983 to a high of 23 percent among Blacks in 1986. Jesse Jackson stated, "As I see it, there is no room in Reagan's world for us." A *Washington Post*-ABC News poll that same year demonstrated that 56 percent of Blacks labeled him a racist and two-thirds affirmed the belief that the president's economic policies were harmful to Black America.[49]

The 1990s could be described as one of the most quixotic decades in American history as it pertains to race and society. Tiffanie Darke described the 1990s as "a decade of enormous disruption, the axis on which the old world ended and a new one began. . . . The growing power of the Internet, the scrutiny of an ever more powerful press, the rise of entertainment culture in politics and the advance of technology in collecting DNA evidence all came together in 1998."[50]

Despite gains, a sizable percentage of Blacks suffered under poverty and systemic racism. Inequities in education, wealth disparity, discrimination in employment and housing, criminal injustice, and overt racism proved barriers too high for many to overcome. The era's successes were offset by a decrease in industrial jobs as corporations moved their operations and industries overseas. Blacks working in blue-collar positions were hardest hit, as 30 million jobs were eliminated due to factory closings and relocations. The industrial prison complex imprisoned more Black men than the number of those enrolled in college. An attack on affirmative action and the 1978 *Bakke* decision that outlawed the use of quotas in hiring threatened to turn back the clock. Black uprisings in Miami (1980) and Los Angeles (1992) represented anger at the slowness of progress and the country's failure to fulfill the promises of opportunity for all.[51]

Using California as a case study, this period saw an alarming rise in Black incarceration. Reagan's War on Drugs resulted in a disproportionate increase. With a public intent to focus on crack cocaine, the real target was the Black community through racial profiling and racist bias in sentencing. By 1999, 90 percent of the 12,749 prisoners incarcerated on crack charges were Black. Studies confirmed that whites trafficked in crack cocaine at twice the rate of Blacks and used powdered cocaine at three times the Black rate. During this same time, Black incarceration rates quadrupled.[52] Professor of sociology Douglas Massey summarized to Studs Terkel,

> Everything is filtered through a system that is not racially neutral. All these things make it much worse for the Blacks. Reagan came to power because of race. . . . I don't think most whites understand what it is to be Black in the United States today. They don't even have a clue. They blame the Blacks to a large degree for their own problems. . . . Since the Kerner Report of 1968, finding two societies, separate

and unequal, it's worsened. There is more toleration of it. In 1968, as bad as the riots were, there was hope, among whites as well as Blacks, that things would get better . . . but since the mid-seventies, public investments have disappeared and the commitment to civil rights has completely gone. . . . When you create two societies, so separate, so unequal, people at the bottom half are ultimately going to lash out at the people at the top half . . . increasingly, white America has adopted private solutions to public problems . . . they demand more repressive police-state tactics to control these others. . . . I think whites have a difficult time separating race from class. They look at a Black person and the color of his skin triggers a number of assumptions about his behavior. Black skin means crime, drugs, welfare dependency, lack of work values. These perceptions make it more likely that those conditions will in fact occur . . . neither group is very good at separating race from class . . . both Black and white are trapped by race.[53]

George Herbert Walker Bush (1989–93) practiced quiet diplomacy and declared his goal to be a "kinder" and "gentler" nation.[54] He inherited a drowning economy from the previous president and allocated $166 billion to rescue savings-and-loan lending institutions. He ordered the invasion of Kuwait to oust Iraqi leader Saddam Hussein during Operation Desert Storm on January 17, 1991. He met with Russian leader Gorbachev three times in 1991. His pledge of "Read my lips: No new taxes!" came back to haunt him when he attempted to balance the budget by siding with the Democratic congressional majority by raising taxes.[55]

Bush's administration could be best described as one without an identity in its relationship to the Black community. It never presented itself as either pro-Black or antagonistic. It was a perfect one-term placeholder between the Reagan and Clinton administrations. He attempted to walk a fine line between expressing racial tolerance and acting with racial acceptance. He publicly recognized his son's biracial children of white and Mexican descent. He installed Blacks at high positions in his cabinet and granted them political appointments. Colin Powell became the first Black chairman of the Joint Chiefs of Staff. Clarence Thomas replaced Thurgood Marshall as Supreme Court justice. Dr. Louis Sullivan served as the first Black Secretary of Health and Human Services. Condoleezza Rice was appointed head of national security.[56] His legacy with the Black community is mixed, as he is considered a racial moderate with no personal racist beliefs. When first elected to Congress, he voted for the 1968 Fair Housing Act after the assassination of Martin Luther King Jr. He was tolerant in his personal views but never politically consistent concerning issues of race. In 1991 he denounced David Duke in his campaign to be elected governor of Louisiana. He felt compelled to speak out as a matter of personal integrity and principle against the candidacy of a bigot.

Jesse Jackson reflected on his life as being racially broad-minded. "He was a fundamentally fair man. He didn't block any door. He was never a demagogue on the question of race."[57] The *Washington Informer* suggested that he had a complex and mixed record with Black America during his service as the forty-first U.S. president. "He promised his administration would be less oppressive for African Americans after eight years of Reaganism, arguably the most racist presidency since the Jim Crow era. Bush, a moderately conservative Republican and Ronald Reagan's vice president, promised a 'kinder, gentler' style of governing that suggested a retreat from mean-spirited rhetoric and policies of 1981–89."[58] After police officers brutalized Rodney King and were acquitted, sparking an uprising in Los Angeles, his dual-purposed statement criticized the rioters while acknowledging racial injustice. "As your president, I guarantee you this violence will end. This is not about civil rights or the great cause of equality that all Americans must hold. It is not a message of protest. It's been the brutality of a mob, pure and simple. But beyond the urgent need to restore order is the question of justice. . . . I felt anger. I felt pain. I thought, 'How can I explain this to my grandchildren.'"

Nevertheless, President Bush made use of racial acrimony for his political advantage. He would disregard his values and become a political opportunist willing to do whatever it took to win an election, even exploiting racial prejudice. Rice University historian Douglas Brinkley commented, "Intellectually and emotionally, he was somebody who was civil rights minded. Bush wanted to see himself being a man devoid of racism. But the reality is that Bush often had to do dog whistles and appeal to less enlightened Americans on race."[59] During his presidential campaign, supporters aired the infamous Willie Horton television ad, utilizing the image of a Black man who raped and murdered a white woman while on furlough from prison. He never disavowed the commercial and was determined to attach the Horton case to his opponent, painting him as soft on crime. Rutgers University history and journalism professor David Greenberg stated that Bush struggled with choosing to do the "right thing" over that which was politically expedient. Historian Timothy Naftali defined the candidate as different from the politician. "He came from the northern Republican tradition, which was moderate and somewhat progressive on race at the time. But George Bush sometimes chose expediency in his campaigning. He didn't always have the courage of his convictions as a candidate, but more often than not, he had the courage of his convictions in office."[60]

Still, like many politicians, politics got in the way of impartial governing. He lived a life of political ambiguity throughout his career of public service. While in office he wavered on his commitment to defending Black rights and was inconsistent in his support for civil rights legislation. He consistently refused to support any version of affirmative action, catering to white fears that the racial reforms of the Civil Rights Movement went too far. During his senate campaign in Texas in 1964, he criticized his opponent for voting for the Civil Rights Act. In office he justified his vote against the 1964 Civil Rights Act by saying, "The new civil rights act was passed to protect 14 percent of the people. I'm also worried about the other 86 percent."[61] He failed to acknowledge that his support went to the 86 percent, regardless of the fact that the majority was often negligent when it came to the rights of Black Americans. Three decades later he repeated this action by vetoing the Civil Rights Act of 1990, claiming that it was a quota bill. A coalition of Blacks, unions, and women formed a chorus to criticize his use of the presidential pen. Black leaders described him as "Reagan in disguise. . . . The rhetoric may be gentler and kinder, but the policies of George Bush are no less dangerous and regressive than those of Ronald Reagan and Ed Meese."[62] Supporters of the bill included Blacks in his administration and the U.S. Civil Rights Commission, whose membership was mostly Republican. Verbal jabs in press coverage of these events accused him of trying to "out-Reagan Reagan" and acting out of "political rhetoric designed to please Jesse Helms, David Duke and their followers in the ultra-right-wing of the Republican Party."[63]

A supreme pragmatist, he recognized that the country needed relief from Reagan's sanguine demeanor and promised a "kinder, gentler nation." What he delivered was a harsher, more punitive criminal justice system. The so-called War on Drugs was a war on Blacks and the poor. He defined drug use as the number one issue in the United States and continued the escalation in tough sentencing for those convicted of illegal possession. He expanded punitive sentencing and requested $1.5 billion to enlarge federal law enforcement spending. He lobbied for the construction of prisons and jails and the hiring of judges and prosecutors to administer them. His administration orchestrated the cocaine sentencing discrepancy that mandated longer judicial sentences for the sale of crack cocaine. It caused a hike in the years Black and brown men were sentenced to prison. He racialized criminality in such a subtle manner that Black men became associated with the breaking of the law. Whites wanted to disassociate themselves from being labeled racist yet were susceptible to messages with coded racial implications. Michelle Alexander, in *The New Jim Crow*, wrote, "The War on Drugs, cloaked in race-neutral language, offered whites opposed to racial reform a unique opportunity to express their hostility toward Blacks and Black progress, without being exposed to the charge of racism."[64] There were tremendous political implications as campaigns afterward employed similar tactics. Of greater impact was the way the Democratic Party responded to Republican allegations that it was soft on crime, which led to President Bill Clinton's support for tough crime policy. Marcia Chatelain of Georgetown University said, "The reason why the Willie Horton ad is so important in the political landscape—it wasn't just about a racist ad that misrepresented the furlough process. But it also taught the Democrats that to win elections, they have to mirror some of the racially inflected language of tough on crime."[65]

The 1990s saw phenomenal achievements by Black people. For the first time in American history, Blacks had considerable influence on their projected image. Rather than being bombarded by negative, stereotypical racial caricatures designed and projected by others, a carefully crafted and marketed profile was generated by a race that was individualized yet understood communal implications. Spike Lee's commercials on the "be like Mike" campaign promoted a Black male image that was endorsed around the world. While Nike's purpose was to sell shoes, Lee wanted to sell a Black man worth emulating and a race worth admiring. Rap music went from being ostracized by the music industry to becoming a cultural empire that impacted global culture. Not only did artists produce platinum-selling CDs, but they founded record companies that handled marketing, production, and distribution. Russell Simmons and Sean "P-Diddy" Combs became major executives and style setters. Bryant Gumbel was the first Black anchor for the *Today Show*. Bill Cosby, of *The Cosby Show*, became America's TV dad. Spike Lee proved that Blacks could direct as Denzel Washington established a new generation of poise and dignity for the Black actor. Morgan Freeman, Angela Bassett, Samuel L. Jackson, Forest Whitaker, and Halle Berry acquired A-list status. Black plays from the Black perspective caught the attention of diverse audiences as August Wilson, Suzan-Lori Parks, and George Wolfe brought Black life and culture to mainstream America. Pulitzer Prizes were awarded to August Wilson (1990), Toni Morrison (1993), George Walker (1996), and Wynton Marsalis (1997). Basketball and football seized the spotlight from baseball as Michael Jordan became a celebrity with global appeal. Million-dollar contracts were subsidized by multi-million-dollar endorsement contracts. The top music entertainers were Michael Jackson and Prince. Funk bands created a new sound that captured the airwaves. Opera venues that previously denied access to Black performers opened for Jessye Norman, Leontyne Price, and Kathleen Battle. Willie O'Ree was the first Black National Hockey League player and in 1988 headed its youth diversity program. The world of golf would have its first Black superstar athlete when Tiger Woods won the Masters Tournament. Blackness became more acceptable and normalized.[66]

Black business evolved from catering to a primarily Black customer base to sitting at the head of the table of multinational corporations. Reginald

Lewis became a billionaire with his acquisition of TLC Beatrice International. Kenneth Chenault became the CEO of American Express and Richard Parsons of AOL-Time Warner.[67] Robert L. Johnson launched Black Entertainment Television in 1980 and brilliantly capitalized on MTV's refusal to broadcast Black videos by showcasing Black movies and music videos. By 1992 there were 621,000 Black-owned businesses nationwide. Those in the fields of real estate, insurance and finance increased fourfold within fifteen years.[68] It was also a time when the Black presence in politics reached significant milestones and continued to grow. In 1984 and 1988, Jesse Jackson ran for president and became a major player in Democratic Party politics. Black mayors were elected in Kansas City, Missouri; Memphis; Denver; Houston; St. Louis; Dallas; and Jackson, Mississippi. In 1991 Clarence Thomas became the second Black man appointed to the Supreme Court. Congress passed the Civil Rights Act of 1991 and the Hate Crime Enhancement Act of 1994. The Congressional Black Caucus (CBC) became the most progressive entity of the U.S. Congress due to growth from thirteen members in 1971 to thirty-eight in 2000.[69]

But there was also a downside. For African Americans, race still figured prominently in every aspect of life, as racist practices were cloaked under worded niceties and accepted behavior. Clarence Page wrote in the *Chicago Tribune* that the 1980s were a mixed bag for Black Americans. Page surmised that while individuals fared well with the sociological changes, Blacks at the bottom of the economic food chain remained there.

> Individuals like Oprah Winfrey and Bill Cosby obviously prospered. . . . The list of successful black individual achievement goes on and on, and that's encouraging. But as a group, most of black America has yet to recover from the back-to-back recessions of the late 1970s and early '80s, new data show. While the rising tide of seven years of economic recovery lifted boats in the black upper class, the black middle class actually sank a little and most of the 31 percent of black America in poverty remained stuck on the bottom. A four-month investigation reported in *Money Magazine*'s December issue found that the percentage of black families earning $25,000 to $50,000 a year, adjusted for inflation, fell from a high of 30.5 percent in 1976 to 26.7 percent in 1988, according to previously unpublished census data. This resulted in a black economic picture shaped like an hourglass: More prosperity at the top, more misery at the bottom. The black upper class (those earning $50,000 or more per year) grew from 7.7 percent to 12.6 percent during the same period, but its gains were offset by an increase in black families earning $5,000 or less, to 11.9 percent from 6.7 percent.[70]

William "Bill" Jefferson Clinton (1993–2001) won the presidency over the incumbent Bush to become the first Baby Boomer to occupy the White House. He is beloved by a generation of African Americans. The man from Hope, Arkansas, was confident, inspirational, and charming and became sardonically known as the first Black president. He always appeared to be genuinely at ease around Black people and in touch with what was important to the community, as demonstrated by his appearance on the *Arsenio Hall Show* during his first campaign. During his term he issued a presidential apology for the Tuskegee Syphilis Experiment. He directed Health and Human Services Secretary Donna Shalala to implement better service to communities of color. She granted Tuskegee University funding for a campus bioethics center.[71]

Clinton came into office with a surprising number of Black women rising to prominence in a number of fields. Carol Mosely Braun (Illinois) was elected to the U.S. Senate. M. Jocelyn Elders became the first woman and African American to serve as U.S. Surgeon General. Toni Morrison was the first African American to win a Nobel Prize in Literature.[72] Dr. Mae Jamison went into outer space aboard the shuttle Endeavor.[73] The president appointed Blacks to a record number of five cabinet positions. According to NPR, "The Clinton years were also known for a booming economy. During that time, the median household income in African American households grew by 25 percent, twice as fast as it did for all households nationwide. In addition, African American unemployment plummeted from 14.1 percent to 8.2 percent. And the administration touted its record of boosting loans to minorities."[74] During the Clinton terms, 1993 to 2000, there was a 33 percent increase in the Black family income from $27,731 to $36,939. During the same period, Black poverty decreased from 33.1 percent to 22.5 percent. These rates were the best for any race.[75] In 1993 he signed the North American Free Trade Agreement (NAFTA), which eased trade between the United States, Mexico, and Canada. In 1996 he was impeached by the House of Representatives, yet the Senate acquitted him.

There were serious downsides to his administration's policies and its negative impacts on the Black community. The Democrats were effectively propagandized by Republicans, and therefore Clinton wanted to prove that he was not soft on crime. There was a racial component to this criticism, as it inferred that he was in cahoots with Blacks. He sought to dispel these charges by equating Black poverty with a lack of personal responsibility. He promoted a bill called the Personal Responsibility and Work Opportunity Reconciliation Act of 1996. His adoption of the Republicans' welfare reform policy placed a five-year moratorium on benefits, was distributed by block grants to individual states, and harmed many impoverished Blacks. The 1994 three-strikes provision increased incarceration and caused young Black male unemployment to rise to its highest level. Black men were six times more likely than whites to be incarcerated.[76]

This policy was opposed by a multitude of Black leaders and organizations. Congressman John Conyers criticized the increase in prison construction as a simple solution to a complex problem. The Black Caucus endorsed a bill that focused on crime prevention, treatment for addiction, and job creation programs. According to Michelle Alexander, Clinton's support of these tougher policies was to win white swing voters over to the Democratic Party by proving that he was tougher on people of color than Republicans.

> Now, a new racial caste system—mass incarceration—was taking hold, as politicians of every stripe competed with each other to win the votes of poor and working-class whites, whose economic status was precarious, at best, and who felt threatened by racial reforms. . . . Clinton escalated the drug war beyond what conservatives had imagined possible a decade earlier. . . . The Clinton Administration's "tough on crime" policies resulted in the largest increases in federal and state prison inmates of any president in American history. . . . Ninety percent of those admitted to prison for drug offenses in many states were Black or Latino.[77]

According to a 2016 *New Republic* article, "Most shockingly, the total numbers of state and federal inmates grew more rapidly under Bill Clinton than under any other president, including the notorious Republican drug warriors Richard Nixon, Ronald Reagan, and George H. W. Bush."[78] Former Federal Reserve Chairman Alan Greenspan touted Bill Clinton as "the best Republican president we've had in a while."[79]

During this generation's lifetime, entrenched racism embraced disenfranchisement and mass incarceration while ignoring the crack and AIDS epidemics. Homicide became the leading cause of death for young Black men between the ages of fifteen and twenty-four, six times the rate for any other racial group. The burning of Black churches across the country reached an apex. Inner-city students were much more likely to attend schools predominantly of one color. Schools in Alabama, New Jersey, New York, Louisiana, and Texas demonstratively lacked adequate resourcing compared to white schools. America was possessed by a conservative spirit weary of discussions on race, having concluded that enough had been done to right the sins of the past. Whites claimed America was a color-blind society, but Public Enemy rapped that the KKK wore three-piece suits.[80] Graham C. Kinloch of Florida State University researched the 1980s' race relations. His analysis showed that a white, conservative power structure was much more concerned about personal economics than racial progress and was hostile to the idea of racial equity. He concluded,

Traditional white attitudes are based on the consistency of white prejudice and self-interest, resulting in conservative "adaptations" to economic decline with ideologies such as "reverse discrimination" and changing forms of institutionalized racism. These factors, in turn, serve to maintain the negative status of minorities through economic and occupational control, educational inequality, political and legal manipulation, sustained segregation, and social rejection in integrated settings. From this it is concluded that race continues to be of major rather than declining significance in the society. . . . Institutionalized racism will continue to adapt to changing conditions and hold its victims captive for decades and generations to come.[81]

During his presidency, Clinton's Black approval rating never fell below 90 percent. It reached a high of 93 percent, 4 percentage points higher than Jesse Jackson's. After impeachment, it fell to a low of 91 percent, and when he left office it was back up to 93 percent. He remains one of the most popular presidents in the history of America in the eyes of many Black Americans.[82] Later generations, however, have some harsh feelings. In 2016, presidential candidate Hillary Clinton was confronted by BLM activists and asked, "You and your family have been personally and politically responsible for policies that have caused health and human services disasters in impoverished communities of color through the domestic and international War on Drugs that you championed as First Lady, Senator and Secretary of State. And so, I just want to know how you feel about your role in that violence, and how you plan to reverse it?"[83]

SUMMARY OF THE #BLACKLIVESMATTER GENERATION

The #BlackLivesMatter Generation remains plagued with many of the same problems embedded in the African American experience. Reniqua Allen's book, *It Was All a Dream: A New Generation Confronts the Broken Promise to Black America*, examined the disillusionment of this generation through a nationwide series of interviews. "Whatever dreams we once had are in grave danger of never becoming a reality. We see versions of Black millennial success in sports, in popular culture, and in politics, yet these are the exceptions, not the rule. Success for young Black people is increasingly difficult to achieve."[84] Members of this generation have expressed dismay that society has not been inclusive but filled with old patterns of racial discrimination and exclusion. Disproportionate incarceration, inequitable schools, unaffordable housing, employment discrimination, food deserts, police brutality, over-policing, neighborhood violence, gentrification, environmental racism, healthcare, and other pertinent issues were rampant.[85] Her *New Republic* article "The Missing Black Millennial" stressed that

> The Black millennial, then, is composed of contradictions and ambiguity, her journey of tentative steps forward and horrific setbacks. In this, young Blacks are not so different from their ancestors, complicating the whole notion of generational change that we are used to ascribing to non-Black people, in which a particular cohort is perceived as being fundamentally different from its predecessors. In many ways, the story of the Black millennial is as much about consistency as it is about change—which is to say that the story of the Black millennial is the story of what it means to be Black, period.[86]

Without apology they publicly affirm, "I am Black, and this is who I am. If you don't like it, that's your problem, not mine. Deal with it!" They do not need to go on a journey to discover their racial identity; they know who they are. They affirm their total selves; they are African American, and they are Black. They creatively intertwine race, culture, and art. Everything about them, the way they dress, talk, and walk, demonstrates pride in Blackness.[87] Actor Zendaya was interviewed in *Grazia* magazine and said, "I've learned that you have to learn to love and respect yourself first and foremost. Why? Because, if you're confident within, that's the only way attacks won't be able to personally affect you. . . . Fortunately I've never had a problem with my body or the way I look, that's just not something I've had to deal with."[88]

Yet the members of this generation feel misunderstood in almost every direction. Whites perceive their unapologetic Blackness as problematic, and older Blacks don't understand their emotional frustration since society is now less discriminatory. They do not readily agree with older generations and say that racism is still an obstacle to getting ahead in America. They are much more optimistic, even in the face of their own struggles. According to a survey by the Kinder Houston Area, there is an eleven-point difference between them and the prior generation when each generation is asked if Blacks and other minorities have the same opportunities as whites in the United States today. Each succeeding generation has tended to possess lesser degrees of negative outlook about prospects for the race.[89] Attorney Alex Berteau had an interesting conversation with a colleague that reflects this reality.

> The other day I was talking to a young associate, a lawyer. . . . There are things that influenced me that he can't possibly relate to. He's Black, too. I explained to him that this date personifies a lot of things for me. Here I am, born forty-four years ago in a little Louisiana town where everything was segregated. I only went to kindergarten because my parents and other Black parents sponsored the school in

a Baptist church, under the state law at the time, only white children were allowed to go to kindergarten schools at public expense. As I spoke to this guy, it dawned on me that he never saw a bathroom that said WHITE and BLACK. When I came out of law school in 1973, this kid was ten years old. I don't think of myself as an old person, yet he was saying to me, "I can't feel what you're saying, except that I've heard about it."[90]

Members of this generation are weary of the advice of older Blacks who feel a need to provide unsolicited guidance. Simone (no last name provided), a thirty-year-old Harvard graduate, commented, "My personal take (is that members) of the civil rights generation have two models for corporate business success. They either advocate 'complete assimilation' or adopt an 'I'm successful but I'm still down' persona. Neither model works very well for those of us who don't have the . . . history of dealing with hard-core institutionalized and blatant racism."[91]

This generation could easily be called the Social Media Generation, being tech savvy and able to multitask with ease. It has mastered social media with Facebook, YouTube, and Twitter (now X) as primary social media platforms. According to a 2016 Nielsen report, "Young, Connected and Black," their presence on these platforms promotes cultural change, breaks barriers, and creates new opportunities for engagement. They are early adopters of technology and quickly master new mobile devices. Ninety percent own a smartphone and use it to create community networks, increase awareness on social issues, and browse to effect change. They spend an amazing amount of time online. Fifty-five percent spend at least one hour each day on social media sites. Another third average three hours online daily, two hours each week searching randomly, and an additional hour watching videos. Sixty-four percent regularly update their personal internet pages. All of these are at higher rates than for whites. Lower-income teens are far more likely to use Facebook than teens in other households with more income. Girls are more likely to use Snapchat while boys are more inclined to identify YouTube as their go-to platform. This generation is a rampant consumer of entertainment media. They spend thirty-three hours per week watching television shows, 12.5 times higher than comparable whites.[92] Television executives have taken note, with an increased Black presence on television shows and commercials. Between 2011 and 2015, broadcast network TV ad expenditures targeting Black audiences increased by 255 percent. Programs with predominately Black leads and supporting casts integrated the networks to a greater degree than in previous generations.[93] But their proficiency has not translated into job opportunities. The National Urban League's 2018 State of Black America report, "Save Our Cities: Powering the Digital Revolution," determined that in the tech world, Blacks are sought after as consumers but not employees. Less than 5 percent of the tech workforce is African American, with the exception of Facebook, which reported 6.1 percent.[94] Google fired artificial-intelligence computer scientist Timnit Gebru in December of 2020 from her work on facial recognition software bias. She offered a critical paper on the company's treatment of minority employees and stated that she felt "constantly dehumanized. My theory is that they had wanted me out for a while because I spoke up a lot about issues related to Black people, women, and marginalization. They wanted to have my presence, but not me exactly. They wanted to have the idea of me being at Google, but not the reality of me being at Google."[95]

Social media is this generation's primary tool for protest; they often post online about outrage over acts of individual and systemic racism. Ron Gregory, after the murder of Michael Brown in Ferguson, Missouri, spoke about the generational differences in protest methodologies to the *Washington Post*. "The difference is, in the '60s, we were disciplined. We were trained when we marched. We were taught if they spit on you, just wipe it off and continue marching. But we are dealing with a new breed of youngster. They say, 'You better not spit on me.'"[96] Denis Brown, although older at forty-eight, defended the young activists. "They have been to so many funerals. . . . They are not afraid to die. That brazen defiance is fueled by an anger a lot of older people can't comprehend."[97] An iconic picture was snapped of Ieshia Evans as she stood statuesque while being arrested by Louisiana State Police in Baton Rouge in 2016. She posted, "When the police pushed everyone off the street, I felt like they were pushing us to the side to silence our voices and diminish our presence. They were once again leveraging their strength to leave us powerless. As Africans in America, we're tired of protesting that our lives matter, it's time we stop begging for justice and take a stance for our people. It's time for us to be fearless and take our power back."[98]

They are activists with a purpose and are not their parents' generation of protesters. They are angry, confrontational, and unafraid. They are very likely to get in the face of older Blacks, challenging them to be more engaged while also criticizing white allies. When the police tell them to disperse, they walk closer to the wall of shields. When tear gas cannisters are shot in their direction, they throw them back. They reject age-old tactics such as sit-ins and even diplomacy, as nothing ever seems to change. They witnessed the murder of George Floyd, and many have had their own run-ins with police whom they felt harassed them without warrant. They have generational differences with older Blacks. Concerning policing, they tend to disagree with older Blacks but agree with young whites. Upwards of 70 percent do not feel that police should have a broad ability to search individuals or their vehicles. Older Blacks are split evenly (50 percent) in granting police broad authority when conducting a search. Young whites (63 percent) disapprove of granting the right to searches, also disagreeing with older whites. Both members of this generation (75 percent) and older African Americans (84 percent) agree that there is still much change needed for racial progress.[99]

White millennials are often described as progressive, open-minded, and tolerant of diverse points of view. They live in a rapidly changing society and a racially diverse world and struggle less than older whites with racial and sexual diversity. While this is true in comparison to other whites, compared to the #BlackLivesMatter Generation, they are not as socially progressive.[100] Research in 2017 found that racial prejudice is surprisingly present among millennials, who reflect many of their parents' prejudices, especially toward African Americans. Twenty-three percent defined BLM as "invalid racists," and over half equated the movement with white nationalism. Smaller percentages shared negative racial perceptions against other white generations, but not by much: 31 percent of millennials rate Blacks lazier than whites compared to Generation X (32 percent) and Baby Boomers (35 percent).[101] After racial incidents on the campuses of Duke, Oklahoma, and South Carolina, the *Christian Science Monitor* raised the question, "Are Millennials Racist?"[102] PBS reported that a 2012 Public Religion Institute poll revealed that "58 percent of white millennials say discrimination affects whites as much as it affects people of color. Only 39 percent of Hispanic millennials and 24 percent of Black millennials agree."[103] An MTV poll revealed that only 39 percent of white millennials believe "white people have more opportunities today than racial minority groups."[104] By contrast, 65 percent of people of color felt that whites have differential access to jobs and other opportunities. And 70 percent of millennials reported believing that "preferential treatment" should never be given to one race over another despite "historical inequalities." Obama's election, to them, proved that racial discrimination had been eliminated and that Blacks are to blame for any lack of success. Racism, if it exists, is minimal and relegated to the past.[105] Mychal Denzel Smith blames part of the problem on their parents, who tried to teach them to be color-blind in an effort to prevent the growth of racist attitudes in them. Smith states that Baby Boomers and Gen Xers, influenced by their interpretation of the lessons of the Civil Rights Movement, defined racism as an individual shortcoming. They failed to discern its infiltration into the systems and institutions that are so flawed and that continue to be influenced by their racist past. They intended to instill in their children the ability to judge a person not by the color of their skin but by their merit. But these parents failed to grasp the fact that white supremacy is the legacy of slavery and Jim Crow, and its impact goes far beyond the damage an individual can do. They learned to not see race, discuss it, or understand the complexity of eradicating racism.[106]

According to Perry Bacon Jr., factors such as age and race influence decisions. "Age matters, too, largely because voters under 30 tend to be very Democratic-leaning. As does race, mainly because of the huge difference between White voters (about 40 percent back Democrats) and Black ones (more than 80 percent support Democrats). And there is a growing diploma divide, particularly among White voters. (College graduates are increasingly Democratic, while those without degrees are more Republican.) A gender gap exists, too. (Women prefer Democrats; men, Republicans.) But it's much smaller than some of the other divides. Religion and population density often outweigh race and education in terms of how people vote. White evangelical Christians, even those with college degrees, overwhelmingly vote for Republicans. Asian Americans who are Christian are much more conservative than their non-Christian counterparts. White people without degrees who live in urban areas are significantly more liberal than those in rural areas."[107]

They share some values as their white counterparts. They insist on work-life balance and do not intend to sit in front of a computer 24/7 at the sacrifice of having a personal life. They take pride in their work but do not maintain the same work loyalty as their parents' generation. They do not define themselves by what they do professionally and are not what they do. They do not want to carry work home from the office and expect their employers to respect their time off. They do not expect work obligations to interfere with time they have set aside with family. Overall percentages of this age group reveal that larger numbers are unmarried with at least one child than previous generations. Of those who do marry, most marry later in life. Twenty-four percent of #BlackLivesMatter generationers are married, with Asians, whites, and Hispanics averaging 45 percent. Only 46 percent of Blacks live in what might be considered a traditional family unit. Almost 22 percent have a child and are unmarried, with higher numbers than other races: 16 percent of Hispanics, 9 percent of whites, and 4 percent of Asian Americans. Black women (67 percent) have the highest numbers of never having married: the numbers of Hispanics (39 percent), whites (24 percent), and Asians (11 percent) are all lower. Eleven percent live with someone and 18 percent are in an interracial marriage. Black men of this generation (23 percent) are more likely than either white or Hispanic (34 percent combined) to live with their children.[108]

#BlackLivesMatter Generation members are more religious than others within their age range, a fact that remains consistant throughout generations of Blacks. Larger percentages believe in God, report that religion is important to them, pray, and attend worship services. Compared to white Millennials, they express stronger beliefs about heaven and are more likely to read Scripture. Sixty-one percent feel a deeper sense of spiritual peace and well-being compared to 50 percent of white Millennials. More than half (61 percent) report that they pray daily, compared to 39 percent of white Millennials. Thirty-eight percent say they attend religious services weekly, while 25 percent of white Millennials go to worship. Interestingly enough, they are less likely to do so than Blacks as a whole. Compared to older generations, they pray less often, read Scripture less, and attend fewer weekly services.[109] They are less likely to maintain membership in a Black congregation, as only 27 percent attend a Black church. Nine percent attend a white congregation and 14 percent a multiracial church. Almost half, 49 percent, seldom or never attend church services.[110]

The #BlackLivesMatter Generation continues to be a protest generation. They grew up with more positive images on television, in politics, and in sports than any previous generation. But they also experienced continuing discrimination, segregation, and inequality in the distribution of resources. Their response was to hit the streets to say, "No more!" They are less concerned with prosperity and want a work-life balance. They love their parents and forebears but reject their advice to accept unfair treatment as the price for success. They are angered by the success of a few while the majority of Black people are suffering in modern-day ghettos in dilapidated housing. They continue to challenge the status quo and are vocal in standing up for what is right.

6

Obama Generation (Generation Z)

1997–2020

As I watched with amazement the crowd at Grant Park in Chicago the night President Barack Obama made his acceptance speech, the one thing that struck out to me was the diversity of faces in the crowd. I would guess that people from every ethnic background imaginable were in the crowd, some cheering, many crying, still smiling or just savoring the moment. For me it signaled the beginning of a new America. The realization that we had blurred the edges of the color line in a huge way was not taking place just in Chicago, it was taking place all over the world. My oldest son, a junior at Yale, together with some 200 Black students, had marched from the Afro American Cultural Center to Old Campus. . . . There they were joined by another 500 students. At first the African American students were going to sing "Life Every Voice And Sing," popularly known as the Black National Anthem. But then, looking around at the various races and ethnicities of the students who had joined in on the celebration, and realizing that Obama's victory was not only for African-Americans, but rather for *all* Americans, they began to sing "The Star-Spangled Banner." This new America includes all of us.[1]

—Rodney J. Reynolds

The Obama Generation is among the most racially and ethnically diverse in American history. In 2020, Pew Research Center defined the members of this generation as between the ages of six and twenty-one, with 48 percent being of a mixed racial background. This percentage is much higher than Millennials (39 percent) and double that of Baby Boomers. Pew estimates that one in four Black people are found within this generation. The Great Recession greatly decreased immigration and therefore this generation has fewer members who were born in another country. Yet smaller percentages of this generation self-identify as Black; the percentage has decreased from 93 percent (2000) to 87 percent (2019). More identify themselves as biracial, most often with Black and white biological lineage. Regardless, 25 percent are Latinx (Hispanic); Asian Americans increased from 4 percent to 6 percent; and African Americans are at 14 percent. Pew Research Center analyzed in 2021,

> The Black population of the United States is diverse. Its members have varied histories in the nation—many are descendants of enslaved people, while others are recently arrived immigrants. The Black population also has nuanced ethnic and racial identities reflecting intermarriage and international migration. As a result, there are key distinctions in demographic and economic characteristics between different parts of the national Black population, highlighting its diverse multitude of backgrounds.[2]

This generation received its name from the forty-fourth president of the United States, Barack Hussein Obama Jr. He was the son of Kenyan Barack Hussein Obama and Ann Dunham, a white woman born in Wichita, Kansas. Their biracial son was born in Honolulu, Hawaii, on August 4, 1961. He was a Black child raised by white grandparents who provided him with a loving home. During his 2008 presidential campaign, he delivered a speech on March 18, 2008. He described his life:

> I am the son of a Black man from Kenya and a white woman from Kansas. I was raised with the help of a white grandfather who survived a Depression to serve in Patton's Army during World War II and a white grandmother who worked on a bomber assembly line at Fort Leavenworth while he was overseas. I've gone to some of the best schools in America and lived in one of the world's poorest nations. I am married to a Black American who carries within her the blood of slaves and slaveowners—an inheritance we pass on to our two precious daughters. I have brothers, sisters, nieces, nephews, uncles and cousins, of every race and every hue, scattered across three continents. . . . I will never forget . . . the idea that this nation is more than the sum of its parts—that out of many, we are truly one.[3]

The United States has experienced the demographic changes that social scientists predicted, and there have been major shifts in the racial makeup of the country. According to Brookings, racial diversification increased at a more rapid rate than previously anticipated. Remarkable growth was witnessed in racial-ethnic demographics. The year 2019 marked the first time that a majority of the nation's youth were of color or of an ethnic identity other than white. Black and Latinx youth accounted for 40 percent of the increase.[4]

According to Pew Research Center, the U.S. Census Bureau, and the National Bureau of Economic Research, there were 46.8 million people in the United States who self-identified as Black in 2019. In 1980, Blacks constituted 11.5 percent of the population; by 2000, the number had risen to 12.1 percent. Between 2004 and 2014, the Black population grew by 21 percent, with predictions that by 2060 Blacks will represent 17.9 percent of the population.[5] In 2021, 14 percent of the U.S. population was Black; 60 percent was non-Hispanic white; 18 percent was Hispanic; 7 percent was Asian American; and 2 percent was American Indian or Alaska Native. Incredibly, this accounted for a 29 percent increase since 2000, when the numbers totaled around 36.2 million. Ten percent were born outside of the country, totaling 4.6 million. Eight percent defined themselves as biracial, mostly from a union of Black and white parents. Five percent (2.4 million) defined themselves as "Black Hispanic."[6]

Projections indicate that American racial diversity will continue to increase in the coming decades. Between 2000 and 2010, the Latinx community experienced a phenomenal rate of growth,with total birth rates of infants of color outnumbering white babies. The Census Bureau reported that July 1, 2015, triggered a demographic shift when a slight majority of children born were of color and for the first time most preschool students were of color. A 2018 Pew Research study, "Post Millennials," revealed that almost half of six- to twenty-one-year-olds were Hispanic, African American, or Asian. They successfully integrated the American school system, and there is no longer a white majority. A regional survey of southern and western schools revealed that no single racial-ethnic demographic dominated; western schools are 40 percent white, 40 percent Hispanic, 9 percent Asian, 5 percent Black, and 7 percent other.[7]

This is the generation in which a rigid racial categorization will prove much more difficult, as these young Americans have a diverse racial lineage. Racial identity has been made much more complicated as the number of children born of biracial parents dramatically increased. Future discourses will have to examine the impact of Blackness on men and women who identify as biracial. Members born into both worlds have faced levels of denial of inclusion from both Blacks and whites, which impacts their sense of identity. According to 2017 Census Bureau statistics, 68 million young people constitute the youngest, most educated, and most politically active generation in American history. An astonishing number self-identify as being mixed race, or biracial. This generation of African Americans will be willing to define themselves through a multitude of racial identities.[8] They consider themselves the norm rather than the other and readily adopt a variety of racial identities without shame. Their greater racial diversity will have a profoundly positive impact, resulting in a nation less divided along racial lines. This generation will bring about tremendous racial change, as they are less restrained by past racial stereotyping and intolerance. Actor Matthew McConaughey shared in *AARP the Magazine* his observation of his biracial children: "The next generation gets it. It's beautiful when Camila and I overhear our children talk about a friend, and then the friend shows up and that friend has darker skin—but we didn't know because they never said, 'Oh, my friend who's Black.' It's not even in their context of how to define someone."[9]

With the growth of these "new minorities," Hispanics, Asians, and multiracial persons, America is experiencing a cultural resurgence that is transforming the nation demographically. The movement of diverse groups will decrease neighborhood segregation, increase interracial marriage, and produce generational change. The Brookings Institute's William Frey, in *Diversity Explosion*, revealed that this racial shift will have an unimaginable impact:

> America reached an important milestone in 2011. That occurred when, for the first time in the history of the country, more minority babies than white babies were born in a year. Soon, most children will be racial minorities: Hispanics, blacks, Asians, and other nonwhite races. And, in about three decades, whites will constitute a minority of all Americans. This milestone signals the beginning of a transformation from the mostly white baby boom culture that dominated the nation during the last half of the twentieth century to the more globalized, multiracial country that the United States is becoming.[10]

Black America in the twenty-first century is young, vibrant, and demonstrating demographic growth, with a whopping 58 percent of the total U.S. population (329.5 million) being thirty-eight years or younger. Blacks maintain an average age of 31.6 years, 14 percentage points younger than the population as a whole; whites have an average age of 39 years. Almost a third of Blacks (30 percent) are below the age of twenty while only 11 percent are over sixty-five years old.[11] The Census Bureau reported that between 2010 and 2020, whites as a racial group declined in population for the first time in the country's history. In just one decade, the racial majority shifted toward people of color while white growth slowed tremendously. Not only are white Americans decreasing in numerical strength, they are also getting older as American youth become increasingly racially diverse. Whites were the only group to experience no growth but actually decreased in population. They had fewer births and a higher death rate.[12]

Blacks populate every region of the country, but in 2020 the majority lived in the South (54 percent). The Northeast and Midwest contained equal numbers, at 19 percent, while 10 percent resided in the West. No section of the

United States is more indicative of the change in racial demographics than the Midwest. Migrants of color have resettled westward with a higher birthrate. Even agricultural communities in Iowa have grown disproportionately as racial-ethnic youth population outpaced the population of older whites. Since 2010, in eighty-four out of Iowa's ninety-nine counties, young people of color had greater growth rates. In 151 counties across the country, Blacks or Hispanics were the dominant racial demographic in 2018, an increase of forty-one counties. Blacks were the largest demographic in seventy-two municipalities in the South and Southwest, up from sixty-five in 2000. The major cause was Black migration from northern cities to southern suburbs. Demographic changes occurred in fifteen counties that were not majority Black in 2000. Mississippi (seven), Alabama (two), and Virginia (one) had the greatest increases.[13] Several cities have huge concentrations including New York City (3.8 million), Atlanta (2.2 million), and Washington, DC (1.7 million).[14] Twenty-nine percent reside in urban communities (Washington, DC, metro region, San Francisco, Atlanta, New York, Boston, and Los Angeles). Fifty-nine percent of Black youth live in cities. Five states contain the largest Black populations (37 percent): Texas (3.9 million), Florida (3.8), Georgia (3.6), New York (3.4), and California (2.8).[15] Ten states contain 58 percent of the Black population: Texas, Georgia, Florida, New York, North Carolina, California, Illinois, Maryland, Virginia, and Louisiana.[16]

This generation witnessed some of the most significant events in American history. Several were the most memorable for those born in this generation. The Smithsonian National Museum of African American History and Culture opened on the national mall in Washington, DC. As memorable as the 2001 terrorist attack on the World Trade Center towers was,[17] COVID-19, the killing of George Floyd, and the Trump presidency have also been imprinted on this generation's minds. Joe Biden selected Kamala Harris as his vice president, the first Black and Asian woman to hold the position. But for many, of greater significance was the election of the first African American president, and, correspondingly, the first Black family to live in the White House. Seventy-one million stayed up to watch returns on the night of his election. In Chicago almost a quarter of a million people stood arm-in-arm in nervous anticipation, with Jesse Jackson in attendance. Older adults who had experienced Jim Crow segregation were moved to tears. The late Congressman John Lewis commented to NPR, "And it's what Dr. King was talking about. That day will come when we will forget about race and color and see people as people, as human beings. And it's going to be amazing for me, and I'm going to do everything possible not to shed tears of joy. I know Dr. King and others are looking down, and they're probably saying hallelujah, hallelujah."[18]

Former president George W. Bush remarked that Obama's election represented "a triumph of the American story. . . . Many of our citizens thought they would never live to see that day."[19] The *Atlantic* conducted a series of interviews with pre-teens in 2016 to inquire about the impact of the election of Barack Obama, asking whether their generation's perception of their country has been impacted and how they themselves were impacted. The students, between the ages of eleven and thirteen, were racially diverse and provided their opinions and impressions on the election. They all commented that anyone could be elected president, regardless of race, gender, or sexual identity. Statements included, "If someone Black could be president after it forever being white presidents, maybe a woman can be president. Or we can have a gay president. None of that even matters anymore. . . . That's progress. We didn't discriminate by race; he was judged by his ability. We used to think that just because someone was a different color, that they were inferior, but this election shows we can all be judged the same. . . . When Obama became president, suddenly people thought, oh, the barrier is gone. Now we can climb. That's what his presidency meant to me. It's like I have a chance now." They also commented on the candidacy of Donald Trump and their impressions: "The next president should work to unify our country and help us unify with other countries. I hear that Donald Trump was being really racist to other countries."[20]

A major part of this generation's experience has been living within the contradictions of life in America. Racial discrimination continued to produce inequity in education, healthcare, and wealth gaps. At the same time, there were advances in educational achievement, health coverage, the middle class, and police prosecution for abuses. Frederick Joseph spoke of the Black experience as being composed of both positive and negative components while citing evidence of change.

> Being Black in 2020 is an amalgamation of all of the oppressive forces that we've been talking about happening at one time. But I do think that we are on the verge of change. . . . [O]ne chant in particular I've never heard before was "white silence is violence." That's a brand new one I've never heard in my entire life. But I think it was a testament to white people waking up and being activated to the fact that, the very nature of the systems in America are disproportionately impacting and destroying black and brown lives.[21]

They experienced moments of celebration concerning the Black narrative. Many Americans view Blacks as residing in inner-city, impoverished, crime-ridden, public housing neighborhoods. A 1991 Gallup poll revealed that Blacks and whites equally shared this perception that three out of four African

Americans were impoverished urban residents. According to Brookings, however, 40 percent of African Americans list their economic category as middle class. The percentages provide evidentiary proof as middle-class Blacks greatly outnumber those living below the poverty line.[22] A Nielsen report, "Increasingly Affluent, Educated and Diverse: African-American Consumers—The Untold Story," reported a drop in the rate of Black poverty. Between 2004 and 2014, Black families living in poverty with annual incomes below $25,000 dropped from 43 percent to a low of 37 percent. Those with higher incomes ($50,000–$75,000) increased by 18 percent, while households making over $100,000 increased by 95 percent.[23] According to Pew Research Center, 47.9 million Black people in the United States made up 14.4 percent of the nation's population. Household incomes were in the range of under $50,000 for 49 percent of the population, while 51 percent earned at least $50,000. One-third were in the $75,000 range including 22 percent who earned over $100,000. Married couples presided over 39 percent of Black households; females were the head-of-household for 31 percent; males were over 5 percent of households.[24] Seventy-five percent of Black married couples are homeowners. Almost a third of Black families live in the suburbs, which, over the past thirty years, contain the greatest racial and ethnic diversity growth due to lower rental and mortgage costs.

This generation made gains in education as well. Pew Research Center reported that 87 percent of Black students earned a high school diploma. In 2020, 24 percent of both Blacks and whites enrolled in either undergraduate or post-graduate programs completed four years of college. In 2019, 23 percent of Black Americans aged twenty-five and older had a bachelor's degree or higher, up from 12 percent in 1989. That same year, 33 percent of all Americans older than twenty-five held degrees. According to Pew, "In 2022, 26.1% of Black adults ages 25 and older—7.8 million people—had earned at least a bachelor's degree. That was up from 14.5% in 2000."[25] A greater number of Black women have high school and college degrees. Black women aged twenty-five or older increased their college enrollment from 57 percent to 59 percent in 2013. While 33 percent of all American women have a bachelor's degree or higher, 24 percent of Black women hold similar degrees. Nineteen percent of Black men have bachelor's degrees.[26] The Bureau of Justice Statistics (BJS) released statistics that in 2020 Black incarceration fell to its lowest levels since 2006 with a 34 percent decrease. Between 2000 and 2015, overall incarceration fell by 24 percent; for Black women, it declined by 50 percent.[27]

There is still much that needs to be overcome. Despite the fact that the country has become more racially diverse, this generation remains the most segregated in American society. The most partitioned cities are those with the largest Black populations: Washington, DC (Anacostia), Chicago (South and

West), and Detroit have large concentrations of Blacks and significant levels of racial isolation.[28] During the first decade of the twenty-first century, American schools were segregated along racial, ethnic, and economic lines in a manner that benefited whites and disadvantaged people of color. This period saw the resegregation of the American school system in every region of the country. A growing percentage of Black and Latino children were in minority major-ity schools, as 40 percent attended schools that were 90 percent racial eth-nic. More private schools were created as parents exercised school choice and placed their children in isolated academic silos. Adequately funded financially and materially, well-equipped teachers in these schools taught smaller classes. Even in integrated school settings, the education received differed by race. School tracking placed Black students in vocational programs while whites took college preparatory courses.[29] Economic Policy Institute determined in 2022, "Districts in high-poverty areas, which serve larger shares of stu-dents of color, get less funding per student than districts in low-poverty areas, which predominantly serve white students, highlighting the system's inequity. School districts in general—but especially those in high-poverty areas—are not spending enough to achieve national average test scores, which is an estab-lished benchmark for assessing adequacy. Efforts states make to invest in edu-cation vary significantly. And the system is ill-prepared to adapt to unexpected emergencies."[30]

THE PRESIDENTS

Presidents and their policies continued to impact the lives of African Ameri-cans disproportionately. This generation's elected presidents were George W. Bush (2001–9, forty-third president), Barack Obama (2009–17, forty-fourth president), and Donald J. Trump (2017–20, forty-fifth president). These three presidential elections were of utmost importance to their lives.

George W. Bush (2002–9) was elected the forty-third president under con-troversy. Politics have always been an extremely volatile issue during this gen-eration's lifetime. Bush was declared the winner of the November 7, 2000, presidential election between Al Gore and George Bush. The Supreme Court decided the victor by ending the counting of ballots, handing Bush a victory by only six hundred votes.[31] Blacks had voted overwhelmingly for Al Gore, the Democratic candidate. Thousands were disenfranchised in several states, especially Florida, where Black votes were discarded at ten times the rate of those of whites. The *Washington Post* determined that of the 175,000 legal bal-lots cast in Florida that were discounted, the vast majority were from Black voters. A count of 136 ballots out of every 1,000 were discarded, three times the rate for discarded white votes. In Gadsden County, Blacks constituted 60 percent of the population and were the highest percentage of voters. They also had the highest percentage of rejected ballots (2,085), as one in every eight votes were not counted. In Jefferson County, a former Black-belt county, 571 ballots were discarded.[32] In 2021 *Rolling Stone* reported,

> Back in 2000, 12,000 eligible voters—a number twenty-two times larger than George W. Bush's 537 vote triumph over Al Gore—were wrongly identified as convicted felons and purged from the voting rolls in Florida, according to the Brennan Center for Justice. African Americans, who favored Gore over Bush by 86 points, accounted for 11 percent of the state's electorate but 41 percent of those purged. . . . A Republican governor in a crucial battleground state instructs his secretary of state to purge the voting rolls of hundreds of thousands of allegedly ineligible voters. The move disenfranchises thousands of legally registered voters, who happen to be overwhelmingly Black and Hispanic Democrats. The number of voters prevented from casting a ballot exceeds the margin of victory in the razor-thin election, which ends up determining the next President of the United States.[33]

The Florida debacle started a trend in Republican politics: the scrubbing of legally enrolled Black voters from the voting rolls. The court's decision did not sit well with the Black community. Following the election ruling, Gallup reported that 68 percent of Blacks responded that they felt "cheated," with 37 percent reporting feeling "bitter and angry."[34] Their response did not result in violence or conspiracy theories that created a distrust in American democracy. Instead, it was an especially calm response of political acceptance by a people used to disappointment who had a legitimate cause for distrust considering the centuries of disenfranchisement they had experienced. This is especially remarkable when their response is compared to the violent response to the results of the 2020 election, in which Trump supporters invaded the U.S. Capitol.

The newly elected president made a rallying cry of his desire to bring the nation together. Fifty-eight percent of Blacks responded that they would accept the new president and wanted him to be fair in the wake of the chaos his election produced. They were willing to give him a chance. Bush responded by appointing several Blacks to his cabinet: Colin L. Powell (Secretary of State), Rod Paige (Secretary of Education), and Condoleezza Rice (Secretary of State). Powell and Rice were the first African American male and female to serve in their posts.

After refusing previous invitations, his speech at the 2000 NAACP convention on July 10 was performed with two intentions. He attempted to grow his popularity with the Black community and increase the number of votes cast

for Republican candidates in the upcoming midterm elections. He recounted
his support of HBCUs, appointments of Blacks, and the renewal of the Voting Rights Act. He promoted the No Child Left Behind Act (NCLBA) as a
promise of quality education for Black children. It rewarded schools producing quality education and offered vouchers for parents to choose a school of
their choice.[35]

> Under my vision, all students must be measured. We must test to
> know. And low-performing schools, those schools that won't teach and
> won't change, will have three years to produce results, three years to
> meet standards, three years to make sure the very faces of our future
> are not mired in mediocrity. And if they're not able to do so, the
> resources must go to the parents so that parents can make a different
> choice. You see, no child—no child should be left behind in America.
> . . . See every child can learn. . . . Education helps the young. . . . I'll
> lift the regulations that hamper private and faith-based programs. I'll
> involve them in after-school programs and maternity group homes,
> drug treatment programs and prison ministries. And I have laid out
> specific incentives to encourage an outpouring of giving in America.[36]

The speech was politely received but did little to convince Black voters. This
was partly in consideration of the fact that his educational policies failed to
produce any significant benefit to Black students. In reality, NCLBA normalized standardized testing and cut funding to low performing schools, penalizing
disproportionately schools with large African American student populations.
His administration placed a financial freeze on Pell Grant increases and made
qualifying more difficult; Blacks constituted 27 percent of all recipients. The
budget of the Department of Education had its funding cut by $3.1 billion,
causing the elimination of forty-two programs. He cut programs that provided
support to racial-ethnic and poor students such as Upward Bound, Gear Up,
Talent Search, and the Thurgood Marshall Legal Educational Opportunity
Program. Congress denied his request to cut the Perkins college loan program
for low-income students by $65 million. He was an ardent opponent of affir-
mative action programs. In 2003, he chose MLK Day to announce the administration's support for a case against the University of Michigan's affirmative
action admissions.[37]

Several of his appointees were highly controversial and opposed vigorously
by the civil rights community. He nominated two candidates to the Supreme
Court, John Roberts and Samuel Alito, who opposed any application of affirmative action programs. The NAACP and the National Urban League cited
Attorney General John Ashcroft's opposition to affirmative action, school
desegregation, and gay rights. Their concerns were correct, as the Justice
Department under Bush greatly decreased its enforcement of civil rights cases.

Rod Paige was an enemy of affirmative action and left questions about his competency. A 2004 report by the U.S. Commission on Civil Rights (Office of Civil Rights Evaluation) stated:

> This report finds that President Bush has neither exhibited leadership on pressing civil rights issues, nor taken actions that matched his words. . . . President Bush has not defined a clear agenda nor made civil rights a priority. . . . (He) seldom speaks about civil rights, and when he does, it is to carry out official duties, not to promote initiatives or plans for improving opportunity. Even when he publicly discusses existing barriers to equality and efforts to overcome them, the administration's words and deeds often conflict. . . . Despite promising to unite the nation and improve its election system, the President failed to act swiftly toward election reform. . . . No Child Left Behind Act (NCLB) has flaws that will inhibit equal educational opportunity and limit its ability to close the achievement gap. . . . The President's stance on affirmative action is equivocal at best. President Bush has tried to please both supporters and opponents, a tactic that has resulted in a misleading and vague position. He has not exhibited strong leadership on this issue where leadership is vital. . . . These examples offer evidence that the President has not assembled an administration committed to civil rights enforcement. Instead, he has placed into high positions individuals who, although racially and ethnically diverse, share his narrow interpretation of civil rights. . . . President Bush redefines civil rights, at times by promoting unrelated initiatives under a civil rights banner.[38]

Two of the most significant events in the country's history occurred during his presidency. The September 11, 2001 (9/11) attacks on the twin towers of the World Trade Center in New York City and the Pentagon in Washington, DC, shook the entire country. On September 20, President Bush declared a global "War on Terror" and announced, "Every nation in every region now has a decision to make. Either you are with us, or you are with the terrorists." His approval rating surged to 90 percent.[39] Four years later, Hurricane Katrina flooded New Orleans, a city that was 67 percent Black and 30 percent poor. Even after the National Weather Service issued dire warnings for the Gulf Coast, Bush stayed on his ranch for twenty-nine consecutive days of vacation. He visited weeks after the devastation and said, "Poverty has roots in a history of racial discrimination, which cut off generations from the opportunity of America. We have a duty to confront this poverty with bold action."[40] He proposed to Congress the creation of several programs to offer job training, education, childcare, business investment, and land for homes. Neither the worker recovery accounts, Urban Homesteading Act, nor the Gulf Enterprise Zone ever came into fruition. During his 2007 State of the Union address, he

made no mention of Katrina, poverty, or racial justice.[41] Under both catastrophes, Bush was considered to have been negligent. His approval rating
with Black Americans was a dismal 2 percent. His inaction led rapper Kanye
West to retort on live television, "George Bush doesn't care about Black
people."[42]

An underlying current in the disruption of Bush's relationship with the
Black community was his treatment of Colin Powell, his Secretary of State.
Powell was revered as the "most trusted man in America"[43] at the time of
his joining the Bush cabinet. The president tried to take advantage of his
popularity with the American public by hiring him as Secretary of State. His
stoic, reserved nature was nonthreatening to whites and appealing to Blacks
as a highly visible representation of a competent Black man. Vernon Jordan
said, "It's very fortunate that Colin has done such an outstanding job. It says,
'Folks, given the chance we (Blacks) can do anything, and that includes being
president." Powell himself responded, "Surprisingly, most Black Americans
I talk to are proud of the fact that I have this job."[44] Bush's hiring of him
was a relatively positive move, as Blacks considered him to be a fair, balanced
Republican who supported affirmative action. He was an experienced member of several presidential cabinets, and his advice was widely respected. All
of that was squandered by his presence in the Bush administration. Serving
only one term, Powell was isolated between Vice President Dick Cheney and
Defense Secretary Donald Rumsfeld's more hawkish posturing, and his positions were rarely followed by the president. Bush sent him to testify before
the United Nations Security Council with faulty and incorrect information.
The Secretary did his job, and overnight a majority of the public, for the first
time, supported an invasion of Iraq. But even his family were unnerved by
the way he was being handled. According to the *Washington Post*, "His wife,
Alma, had a sense of foreboding; her husband, she thought, was being used
by the White House. Powell's daughter Linda, who had listened to the speech
on the radio, had found his performance unsettling. His voice was strained,
she thought, as if he were trying to inject passion into the dry words through
the sheer force of his will."[45] After a year of war, the fallout began, and Powell was even more isolated from the White House. He fumed in frustration,
"There are people who would like to take me down. It's been the case since I
was appointed. By take down, I mean 'keep him in his place.'"[46] By the time
he was forced to resign in November of 2004, his political credibility and
career were over.

Powell had his critics in the Black community, as some considered him a
compromising figure without the strength of his convictions. They felt that his
image of a Black moderate was undeserved, and he never went out on a limb
as an advocate for racial justice while a member of any cabinet. Jesse Jackson
commented in the late 1990s that Powell could never have a great deal of

popularity among Blacks. He said in an article written by Henry Louis Gates Jr. for the *New Yorker*,

> We do know that very right-wing white people can trust him. They can trust him to drop bombs. We know that Reagan could trust him. Historically, there's been this search—whites always want to create the black of their choice as our leader. So for the white people this nice, clean-cut black military guy becomes something really worth selling and promoting. But have we ever seen him on a picket line? Is he for unions? Or for civil rights? Or for *anything*?[47]

Bush has become much more popular with the Black community since leaving office. One of the least talked about but significant achievements of his administration was his December 16, 2003, signing of H.R. 3491, which created the African American Museum of History and Life in Washington, DC. This effort was initiated in 1929 by Black veterans seeking to have land in the nation's capital set aside for such a museum. Many are amused by the loving relationship he has with Michelle Obama. He delivered his strongest anti-racism statement ever when George Floyd was murdered in June 2020:

> "It remains a shocking failure that many African Americans, especially young African American men, are harassed and threatened in their own country. . . . The doctrine and habits of racial superiority, which once nearly split our country, still threaten our Union. . . . This tragedy—in a long series of similar tragedies—raises a long overdue question: How do we end systemic racism in our society? . . . Many doubt the justice of our country, and with good reason. Black people see the repeated violation of their rights without an urgent and adequate response from American institutions."[48]

The election of Barack H. Obama (2009–17) was momentous in so many ways. His election as president of the United States was unforgettable for most. His administration passed the Patient Protection and Affordable Care Act, Obamacare, and guaranteed healthcare for all Americans despite preexisting conditions. He was elected as the first African American president of the United States. He won 53 percent of the popular vote with a total of 365 electoral votes, and his inauguration was witnessed by 1.8 million people, a record. For many, the unbelievable dream came true, a Black person was elected president of the United States. Juanita Abernathy (wife of Ralph Abernathy) said,

> I vividly remember when Barack Obama spoke at the 2004 Democratic national convention, a young, virtually unknown state senator from Illinois. I said to my family, "This young man could become president." There was a special aura about him. Then, as he began his trek toward the nomination, the only concern was his need for

financial and organizational support. Both of which, to the amazement of many, proved professionally orchestrated, managed with great precision, and funded beyond one's wildest dreams. Each accomplishment was a testament to this man's leadership. There was never any doubt in my mind, as I watched Obama maneuver through the political machinations, that he would be elected president. In fact, during my many speeches across the country over the past two years, I lifted my voice and sang Obama's praises. Now President, Obama's time has come to deliver to the world a new America and an enlightened image of democracy. I believe that God Almighty has brought him to this point for such a time as this.[49]

Even before being elected, for many Blacks, his behavior was perceived as presidential. When Hurricane Katrina wreaked its havoc, then-Senator Obama reflected, "I hope we realize that the people of New Orleans weren't just abandoned during the hurricane. They were abandoned long ago—to murder and mayhem in the streets, to substandard schools, to dilapidated housing, to inadequate health care, to a pervasive sense of hopelessness."[50]

The 2008 candidacy of Barack Obama increased Black political participation. In the 2012 election, Blacks held the highest voter registration and turnout percentage of any racial group. In the 2016 election, Black women demonstrated a disproportionate turnout and determined several key races. In 2018, Black women won elections deemed impossible, even by 2012 standards. In the 2020 election, an all-time record high of 30 million Blacks were eligible to vote. More than one-third were residents in nine states and greatly impacted the outcome in elections in Arizona, Florida, Georgia, Iowa, Michigan, North Carolina, Ohio, Pennsylvania, and Wisconsin. Sixty-three percent polled said that they were highly motivated to vote. More than half of eligible voters who are Black have some college education (54 percent).[51]

Chris Todd, in *The Stranger*, described what awaited Obama as he entered into the White House.

> Barack Obama inherited a country going through its most turbulent period since the Great Depression, when the national economy underwent a similar transition from rural, agrarian dependence to an urban, industrialized core. . . . Obama came into office in the midst of two failing wars, the threat of continued terrorist attacks, a rising China, a reasserted Russia, North Korean nuclear bullying, and an Iran busily spinning its own centrifuges, among other foreign policy challenges.[52]

When he entered the White House, the country was fighting two foreign wars, in Iraq and Afghanistan. He demanded the closure of the Deepwater

Horizon oil leak located offshore of Louisiana. He endorsed the Arab Spring as a "moment of opportunity." He ordered the assassination of Osama bin Laden in Pakistan and had his body buried at sea. He signed the Iran Nuclear Deal and restored diplomatic relations with Cuba. He signed the Paris Climate Change Agreement to curb carbon pollution. He placed sanctions on Russia and expelled thirty-five Russian diplomats in response to the cyberattack against the Democratic National Committee. He won the 2009 Nobel Peace Prize at the beginning of his presidency. As a candidate he promised to close Guantanamo Bay and end the war in Iraq, and he participated in the G20 Summit in London.[53]

When he took office, the nation was experiencing its worst financial crisis since the Great Depression of the 1930s: the Great Recession. One of his first official acts was the signing of the Lilly Ledbetter Fair Pay Act of 2009, which provided protection and equal pay for women. This was an understated issue for many Black women, who make less money than men or white women. Under his administration, the Black unemployment rate had its largest decline in American history.[54] The Obama Justice Department issued more consent decrees against police departments than at any other time. On March 23, 2010, he signed into law the Affordable Care Act, also called Obamacare, which mandated healthcare coverage and eliminated exclusions for preexisting conditions. When Trayvon Martin was murdered, he announced that if he had a son he would resemble Trayvon. The Black Lives Matter movement was born when Michael Brown was murdered. He endorsed gay marriage and sensible gun legislation after the killing of children at Sandy Hook Elementary School in Newtown, Connecticut. He called Donald Trump unfit for the presidency during the 2016 campaign.

He never wanted to be the Black president but a president who was Black. Throughout his campaign and presidency, race was a central topic of conversation. Barack and Michelle were drawn as terrorist cartoons. Rush Limbaugh called him, on air, "Barack the Magic Negro." Michelle was not off limits. Roger Stone circulated a rumor that Michelle uttered the word *whitey*, which had racist overtones. In West Virginia, one-fifth of white voters admitted that race influenced their vote. A 2015 poll revealed that 54 percent of GOP voters thought Obama was a Muslim, and only 29 percent believe that he was born in America.[55] Protesters at his speeches carried pictures of him in racial stereotypes, such as portraying him as a witch doctor with a bone stuck in his nose. Many carried automatic weapons to anti-Obama rallies. He was hung in effigy, or lynched, from a tree on the campus of the University of Kentucky. A member of the police commission in Wolfeboro, New Hampshire, was forced to resign after he called the president a "n*****." He acknowledged it and refused to apologize by saying, "I believe I did use the 'N' word in reference

to the current occupant of the White House. For this, I do not apologize—
he meets and exceeds my criteria for such."[56] As president, when Professor
Henry Louis Gates was arrested for going into his own home and Obama
said that the policeman had acted stupidly, the uproar caused him to hold the
Beer Summit between Gates and the policeman. His statement that Trayvon
could have been his son was delivered during the eulogy he gave at the funeral
of a Georgia state senator who was the victim of a racist massacre at a Black
church in Charleston, South Carolina. During the September 2009 speech to
a joint session of Congress on healthcare, Senator Joe Wilson (SC) shouted
out, "You lie"[57] during his address. Oprah Winfrey commented to the BBC,
"There is a level of disrespect for the office that occurs. And that occurs, in
some cases, and maybe even many cases because he's African American."[58]

There were Black critics of the president. None were more strident or
vicious than Cornel West. He called the president a "white man with Black
skin," a "Rockefeller Republican in blackface," a "Brown-faced Clinton," and
a "neoliberal opportunist."[59] LZ Granderson, writing for CNN, accused Tavis
Smiley of being a bitter Obama Twitter troll. Smiley complained in 2011 that
Obama was the first president to not invite him to the White House and that
when the president spoke on race, his comments were without substance or
commitment to racial justice. He faulted the Black community for not taking
the president to task for his lack of economic improvement. West and Smiley's
complaints engendered some lobbed at them. Granderson said, "Smiley and
West appear to be two egocentric men who believe they are the face of Black
intellectualism. And any Black talking heads who don't side with them have,
in West's words, 'sold their souls.' It feels that West and Smiley are more upset
that Obama didn't kiss their rings before he walked through the door than
about anything he's done since he got inside."[60]

During the campaign, he was compelled to deliver a speech on race after
slices of sermons by his former pastor, the Reverend Jeremiah Wright, were
played repeatedly on CNN as the pastor railed against American racism.
Obama delivered the clearest analysis of the persistent and damaging impacts
of race on the country and Blacks. But he also challenged Blacks to do more
by taking control of their destinies, giving in is never an option. Many Blacks
wanted to know what he thought they had been doing throughout American
history. Keeanga-Yamahtta Taylor wrote in *The Guardian* that that dual call
to responsibility through speeches rendered with "dubious even-handedness,
even in response to events that required decisive action on behalf of the racially
aggrieved. . . . His unwillingness to address the effects of structural inequality
eroded younger African Americans' confidence in the transformative capacity
of his presidency."[61] In 2016 he invited a group of Black leaders to meet with
him at the White House; members of Black Lives Matter declined the invite.

He said publicly, "You can't refuse to meet because that might compromise the purity of your position. The value of social movements and activism is to get you at the table, get you in the room, and then start trying to figure out how is this problem going to be solved. You then have a responsibility to prepare an agenda that is achievable—that can institutionalize the changes you seek— and to engage the other side."[62]

Throughout it all, Black America had his back. His polling numbers, according to Gallup, fluctuated between 84 and 92 percent approval and stayed 40 points higher than the American public's as a whole. It was lowest, 80 percent, among young Blacks between eighteen and twenty-nine years of age.[63] During his reelection race in 2012, the Black turnout was the highest for any presidential campaign. When he was first elected in 2008, the Black rate amassed a 21 percent increase in voting strength, the highest ever. For the first time, it was larger than the percentage of whites who voted, 69.1 percent to 65.2 percent.[64]

The president left office with high approval rates among Black Americans. It could be argued, however, that the popularity of his wife demolished that of the president, as she was popular among Black and white women, and men as well. Her speeches move hearts with catchphrases uttered long after the speech is over, such as, "When they go low, we go high."

Donald John Trump was elected the forty-fifth president on November 8, 2016. Donald Trump has been viewed as the new and even more hate-filled version of Reagan who dares to say publicly what Reagan would only think but never say. He even recycled Reagan's 1980s slogan, "Make America Great Again." The Black community worked tirelessly to make him a one-term president. On January 27, 2017, he signed an executive order ending refugee resettlement for the next 120 days. It also banned any travel from seven Muslim countries for ninety days, with anyone from Syria prohibited from entry. During his first foreign trip, he withdrew the United States from the Paris Climate Accord and also from the Trans-Pacific Partnership. He met with Russian President Vladimir Putin in Hamburg, Germany, during the G20 summit. He created a racial controversy when he refused to oppose Nazi rioters as racists and instead said that there were "fine people" on both sides. Within a year he had fired FBI Director James Comey and Secretary of State Rex Tillerson. He announced a zero tolerance policy for refugees and instituted family separations in which children were housed in animal cages. He presided over the longest partial government shutdown in United States history, from December 22, 2018, until January 25, 2019. He called Haiti and African nations "shithole countries" and told Representatives Alexandria Ocasio-Cortez, Rashida Tlaib, Ilhan Omar, and Ayanna Pressley to "go back to their home countries"[65] despite the fact that all four women were

United States citizens. He dissolved the North American Free Trade Agreement (NAFTA) and replaced it with the United States Mexico-Canada Agreement (USMCA). During protests in the wake of the murder of George Floyd, protesters were cleared from the streets around the White House with tear gas. The president walked across the street from the White House to take a picture holding an upside-down Bible in front of St. John's Episcopal Church.

Before being elected, he attempted to coerce Blacks into voting for him by asking quizzically about what they have to lose. African American ministers gathered in May of 2017 to answer his question. Pastors of some of the most prominent Black churches and well-known ministers such as Cynthia Hale, Teressa Hord-Owens, Freddie Hayes, Jimmie R. Hawkins, and others did a press conference on the steps of the United Methodist Building and strongly denounced the president's public policy to counter his attempt to entice the Black voter with false platitudes. The Reverends Raphael Warnock, Leslie Copeland Tune, Aundreia Alexander, and others were arrested in the Senate Hart Building as a part of the protest.

In addition to politics, this generation has been thoroughly impacted by the world of technology. Facebook, Twitter, the iPhone, iPad, Instagram, and the internet combined to impact communication, business, and even personal relationships. The use of social media is highest among Black Americans, with a disproportionate number using it as a form of political engagement and protest. This sort of engagement reached an all-time high with the murder of George Floyd, but it actually goes as far back as 2014 with its use after the murders of Eric Garner in New York City and Freddie Gray in Baltimore. Twitter (now X) is the platform readily available to gather and distribute information. Black Twitter has created its own highly effective community that dispatches information at a rapid-fire pace. While social media is a tool utilized by all ages, Black youth (48 percent) use it at higher levels to post pictures and engage with others in political protest. Seventy-nine percent of Blacks between the ages of eighteen and forty-nine admitted to such usage of social media, while 59 percent of those fifty or older reported the same type of usage. Sixty percent of all Blacks reported that they use social media to find like-minded people and ways to get involved in political activism. Fifty-one percent see social media as a means to increase their level of engagement. Seventy percent define media platforms as an effective tool to influence others politically. Researchers have affirmed that social media is useful in leveling the playing field for marginalized communities in their efforts to effect social change. After the murder of Michael Brown, the hashtag #BlackLivesMatter was tweeted almost 8.8 million times. Such a high number of tweets captures the attention of media and increases national and even global coverage.[66] In 2020, almost a quarter (23 percent) of social media users reported that their opinion was influenced by something they saw or read on social media. In 2018 the number reporting such an influence was 17 percent. Many had their opinion of Black Lives Matter positively influenced while they formed negative opinions about police violence. Blacks and Asian Americans reported the highest level of being influenced (29 percent and 28 percent) respectively.[67] In 2018, 10 percent of Black children aged three to eighteen did not have internet access at home. In comparison, 6 percent of all American children lacked the internet at home.

Under Trump's lack of leadership, 8 million Americans were infected with the coronavirus and 600,000 died. He ended the Pandemic Response Unit and shut down the Social and Behavioral Sciences Team. The COVID-19 pandemic had a devastating impact on the Black community on two fronts: health and economy. In terms of the death rate, the majority of deaths were of Black and brown people. Blacks died at twice the rate of whites from the virus and constituted 21 percent of U.S. deaths. According to the *New York Times*,

> In Illinois, 43 percent of people who have died from the disease and 28 percent of those who have tested positive are African Americans, a group that makes up just 15 percent of the state's population. African Americans, who account for a third of positive tests in Michigan, represent 40 percent of deaths in that state even though they make up 14 percent of the population. In Louisiana, about 70 percent of the people who have died are black, though only a third of that state's population is. North Carolina and South Carolina reported a ratio of black residents to white residents who have tested positive for the virus that well exceeds the general population ratio. Black people are overrepresented among those infected in the Las Vegas area and among people who have tested positive for the virus in Connecticut. In Minnesota, black people have been infected with the coronavirus at rates roughly proportionate to their percentage of the state's population.

Dr. Arline Geronimus at the University of Michigan diagnosed the impact of "weathering" as a major factor in the disproportionately high death rate. She believed that Blacks suffered from the combination of exposure to toxins, sleep deprivation, and extreme stress as complicating factors.[68]

Economically the pandemic devastated the American economy. Before the pandemic, the 2019 Black median income was $44,000, with 54 percent making less than $50,000 annually. There were three levels of attainment. Those making less than $25,000 constituted 29 percent; 25 percent earned between $25,000 and $49,999. Less than 20 percent earned $50,000, while 10 percent earned less than $75,000 and 18 percent more than $100,000.[69] In 2020 unemployment increased tremendously from 6.2 million (February) to 20.5

million (May), causing 13 percent of the Black population to lose jobs. Black men were the only racial demographic who suffered a lower increase in unemployment than during the Great Recession. Their percentage topped 15.8 percent but was less than the percentage of 21.2 percent due to the type of jobs lost.[70] A 2021 Pew poll revealed that while 34 percent of Blacks state that their financial situation is excellent or good, 66 percent report it as being only fair or in poor shape. Of the former, 49 percent have a college degree and 30 percent do not. Tremendous job losses have impacted the ability of Black people to continue to save money in a financial institution. Of those with a history of accumulating savings, 44 percent struggled to save less than they had before COVID. Some have managed to increase the amount saved, as 33 percent of those with a college degree do so, and 18 percent of those without.[71]

As a result of COVID-19, Black businesses were devastated, reducing available financial resources and complicating their ability to meet expenses. When the country experienced its first lockdown in the spring of 2020, 52 percent of Black adults endured unemployment. The hardest hit were the service industries that employed disproportionately Black and brown employees (48.8 percent). Low-wage workers, especially Black females, were impacted in devastating ways, with fewer having savings or accumulated wealth.[72] Black businesses were stalled by the stay-at-home orders that shuttered many doors. Two out of every five Black businesses closed permanently, twice that of white companies. Black employers received fewer loans from the $660 billion Paycheck Protection Program (PPP), as three-quarters of loans over $150,000 were granted to white-owned businesses. The Small Business Administration charged that congressional guidelines to increase grants to minority-owned businesses and underserved borrowers were not adhered to, according to an SBA inspector general's report. Ninety percent of Black businesses were denied loans and 40 percent closed their doors. While reports circulated that wage losses were mostly recovered, this was only true for Asian, Hispanic, and white workers. The recovery income of Blacks was $2,000 less than it was before 2000. Gentrification has always followed periods of economic depression, as Black-owned properties are purchased at lower prices because their owners are offered lower bids. The Black Lives Matter Movement issued a call to corporate America to support Black businesses. Some small businesses received catering orders to feed employees and first responders. Greg Dulan, owner of Crenshaw Soul Food Kitchen, responded to the uncertainty: "If we're going to have a strong African American business community which helps to uplift African American neighborhoods, then some of these things that are happening have to continue long-term. . . . The only way African American businesses are going to survive is we have to own our own stuff."[73]

After mishandling the COVID-19 epidemic, Trump refused to wear a mask and later announced that he had the virus. It also infected his wife, Melania, son Byron, and members of the White House staff. Less than a week later he was back on the campaign trail holding rallies and not practicing social distancing or mask wearing. All of this occurred before the end of his first term. Also during this term, the House of Representatives voted to impeach Donald Trump. The Senate voted to acquit on February 5, 2020. He is the only American president to have been impeached by the House twice, with the second time coming after the January 6, 2021, insurrection at the Capitol.

Trump constantly bragged that he had done more for Blacks than anyone, but his administration was devastating for the Black community. According to Brookings, Blacks were stuck in low-paying jobs without benefits. Economic inequalities had created a wide financial gap between white and Black families, a gap that in 2020 was as wide as the one that existed in 1968. Research indicates that where one starts on the wealth spectrum can determine where one ends up. According to a 2017 study by Demos that compared the wealth of single-parent white families to the wealth accumulated by dual-parent Black and Latino families, "White families build and accumulate more wealth more quickly than Black and brown families do."[74] Black wealth and holdings have fluctuated while white wealth has skyrocketed. Median white family wealth is ten times that of Black families, with Blacks possessing only 10 cents for every dollar owned by a white family. To equal the economic wealth of one white family, the net worth of 11.5 Black families would have to be combined. According to a 2019 Federal Reserve Survey of Consumer Finances, Black household median incomes average $24,100, compared to $188,200 for white households.[75]

Black two-parent families earn 13 percent less than white families. Less than 2 percent of Black families have a net worth of a million dollars, equating to one out of every fifty Black families. One out of every seven white families hold that status, a number that has held firm since 1992.[76] Education level usually impacts income, except in the Black community. This study refutes the premise put forth by Daniel Patrick Moynihan's 1965 report, "The Negro Family," that the reasons for Black economic struggles are disruptions in the Black family structure, single-mother headed households, lack of personal responsibility, and social respectability. Demos pointed out that "family structure does not drive racial inequity, and racial inequity persists regardless of family structure. The benefits of intergenerational wealth transfers and other aspects of white privilege . . . benefit white single mothers, enabling them to build significantly more wealth than married parents of color."[77] Black and white families with a high school diploma demonstrate the disparate worth as the white family maintains control of ten times the amount of wealth. A

Black head of household with a college degree still does not equal the wealth of a white family head with only a high school degree.[78] Measurements of wealth include home ownership, real estate holdings, boats, cars, jewelry, stocks, bonds, and other financial assets. During the past two decades, which included a recession, white financial worth doubled in value. Less than half of Black families own one home, and their homes tend to have lower property values. White home values increase while Blacks tend to lose their homes or retain the same property values. Whites are up to thirty times more likely than Blacks to have been bequeathed a home and other forms of inheritance; only 10 percent of Blacks inherit a home from parents. According to economist Darrick Hamilton, "It is wealth that begets more wealth. . . . We can find instances in our history in which, even when Black people were able to acquire those assets, they were subject to confiscation, fraud and theft because we remain politically vulnerable."[79]

Trump failed to acknowledge the presence of systemic racism, ended racial sensitivity and critical race theory training in federal agencies and declared all efforts to be racist. There was no benefit other than teaching Americans to hate their own country. In 2016 hate crimes increased by 200 percent in areas where he held campaign rallies. The virus killed twice as many Blacks as whites in raw numbers.[80] Southern states like Texas mirrored their actions to discriminate against families seeking to use housing vouchers such as Section 8. The Trump administration used racist justification to reverse the Obama 2015 Affirmatively Furthering Fair Housing regulation that sought to eliminate racial disparities in the suburbs. HUD Secretary Ben Carson determined that the policy was unnecessary and noneffective as local communites were best equipped to meet the needs of residents. Washington should leave the work to those most equipped to handle their own problems. Trump tweeted that he was preserving the neighborhoods of "suburban housewives of America" and keeping them safe from crime. But the Black community saw this as a coded reference to keeping Blacks out of white neighborhoods.[81] The *New York Times* released a much acclaimed series of critical historical articles called the 1619 Project that focused on enslavement as it related to U.S. history. This project was disavowed by state Republican lawmakers in Missouri and Iowa who acted to remove federal funding from local school districts that included it in their curriculum. A primary point of contention centered around the project's determination that 1619 was a year of greater significance than 1776 as a marker for the nation's founding. The former marked the year that enslaved Africans first set foot on American shores. Trump became so riled that he set up his own commission, The 1776 Commission, that declared that it was not hypocritical that the founding fathers were slave owners while they issued a call for freedom.[82]

Trump lost the 2020 election to Democratic candidate Joe Biden, due in large part to the Black vote going to the Democrats. In a 2020 preelection Nationscape survey, Democratic presidential candidate Joe Biden led the incumbent among Black men (76 percent) and Black women (87 percent).[83] The response of Trump voters, primarily white Americans, was radically different from the response of the Black Gore voters in the 1993 election. Rather than accept the election results, they complained loudly, angrily, and violently. Throughout the Biden administration there were cries that he was not the legally elected president, with yard signs and banners reading, "F*** Joe Biden." Conspiracy theories were spread daily by conservative radio commentators and television personalities. On January 6, 2021, President Trump riled up a crowd of protesters by stating that the election was stolen, and he urged them to march down to the Capitol to disrupt the congressional certification of the election. Thousands marched to the Hill, surrounded the building, and climbed the walls. Capitol police attempted to prevent the crowd from mounting the steps leading to the doors but were overwhelmed by the sheer numbers. After battling with the police, hundreds smashed windows, battered doors, and entered the building, with many shouting, "Hang Mike Pence!" Members of Congress were quarantined inside the building and were ushered out secretly, barely escaping. This remarkable episode was in stark contrast to the peaceful complaints of the Black community when George W. Bush was elected. The Biden administration subsequently endured constant accusations that the election had been stolen.

SUMMARY OF THE OBAMA GENERATION

The Obama Generation, for all its uniqueness, in one very important way is a throwback generation. For the first time since the Great Migration generated a demographic movement from South to North, this generation finds itself back home in the South, as did the New Negro Generation. Pew states that in 2019, 56 percent of Blacks lived in the South. Seventeen percent were located in the Midwest and Northeast while 10 percent were in the West. This is the result of the reverse migration of the previous generation (#BlackLivesMatter Generation). Five states contain 37 percent of the Black population: Texas (3.9 million), Florida (3.8 million), Georgia (3.6 million), New York (3.4 million), and California (2.8 million). Blacks who self-identify as Black only are found in larger percentages in Texas, Georgia, Florida, New York, and North Carolina. Biracial Blacks are found proportionately in California, Texas, Florida, Ohio, and New York. The largest Black Hispanic population is found in New York.[84]

For members of the Obama Generation, in the midst of greater racial diversity, the key to their identity is identifying as African American. According to a 2021 BET survey among those eleven to twenty-two years of age, most are not ashamed to be labeled as Black or African American. As many as 72 percent proudly claim their racial heritage of Blackness. They demonstrate an interest in a wide variety of hobbies, many not traditionally associated with Black culture. They are intentionally expanding on what it means to be Black in America.[85] Olympian gymnast Simone Biles has spoken openly of her desire to be a role model to young African Americans and declared that she had done so. She shared her earlier insecurity over being one of a few persons of color in a sport with a white majority of athletes and fans. She was trolled constantly on her appearance, with people stating that she didn't meet certain standards of beauty. She teamed with other Olympic athletes and SK-II to promote self-love and internalized appreciation for one's appearance. "I have gotten a lot of comments over the past couple of years about how my hair looks, how my calves are too big, my arms are too big, I don't look like the average girl in today's age, I have too many muscles. All of those things were pretty hurtful. . . . You feel uncomfortable with your body and then you have everybody online saying this is what you should or shouldn't look like." [86]

This generation has the ability to openly share and receive opinions on a variety of controversial subjects without discomfort. Unlike previous generations, they are extremely comfortable with not being locked into set patterns of what is the norm. Intersectionality of life appeals to them, as one's sense of identity is not permanent but changeable. They stress that a person should have the right to define who they are. Members of this generation have matured in a society where same-sex marriage and the nation's first African American president were normalized. They will not be locked into prior definitions of race or sexual identity. Actor Yara Shahidi speaks openly of her intercultural experience being raised in Minneapolis as the daughter of an African American mother and an Iranian father. Her activism was inspired by her maternal grandfather, a former member of the Black Panthers. She shared in a 2019 interview with *Town & Country*,

> Because of my family's background, I understand how interconnected cultures are. Traditions may be different, but in terms of shared values they're transcontinental. My love of history, or even being socially engaged, stems from having, firsthand, people to care about around the globe and at a young age expanding my community beyond these fake borders we put on each other. . . . I think it's normal now to be on the cusp of many different emerging identities, which makes it more important not only to advocate for the things you're familiar with but to intentionally educate yourself and expand.[87]

Inwardly members of this generation share a quality possessed by previous generations: strength in perspective. They want more out of life than just work, and they strive for life-work balance, with the emphasis on life. More than previous generations, they desire to live a blended life without becoming workaholics. They were raised by parents who taught them to be independent thinkers and raise questions. They are less intimidated by authority and willing to challenge rules and norms with which they disagree. In 2015, seventeen-year-old singer Coco Jones walked away from a relationship with Disney. She shared that they "weren't as compatible together. Some things just don't work together. . . . I just wanted to go somewhere else with my voice. We just agreed to part ways, but now being independent, it gives me time to be who I want to be and sing what I want to sing."[88] They have less brand loyalty in the midst of rapidly changing cultural trends. Their response to stimuli greatly impacts voting patterns, as loyalty to political parties does not matter as much as loyalty to what they believe and value. Sasha Obama said in her mother Michelle's Netflix documentary, *Becoming*, "I'm excited for her to be proud of what she's done, because I think that that's the most important thing for a human to do, is be proud of themselves."[89]

They are natural-born advocates who speak out quickly and often. They are protective of Black culture and challenge cultural appropriation. Almost half (47 percent) are against cultural appropriation and are on the alert when fashion, hairstyles, and language thefts occur. Over half want more respect from corporations when businesses seek to entice them as consumers by appropriating Black trends.[90] When they joined the leadership of the Parkland School-led March for Our Lives, they educated the young activists about how gun violence terrorizes their community. They are much more willing to question authority and critique the systems of government. They speak publicly about their belief that adults have left them a legacy of injustice and seem unwilling to implement change. They are appalled that their parents have not resolved the issues of racial injustice the country has struggled with for so long. Racial injustice is intolerable to them. They say thoughts and prayers are not enough. Zac Nuzum, a seventeen-year-old African American father of biracial twins, proclaimed, "We are saying there is a lot of unconscious bias, and there is still a lot of racial, racist tolerances that one generation has passed down to the next. We are saying the buck stops here."[91] Seventeen-year-old Malak Silmi, after the election of Donald Trump, invited former NBA player Mahmoud Abdul-Rauf to her mosque during Black History Month in 2018. Silmi, who is Palestinian, hasn't stood for the Pledge of Allegiance at Dearborn High since her freshman year. She commented, "He strongly believed in a thing, and he strongly defended it. . . . It just makes me think that we actually are a powerful population, a powerful minority in America."[92]

The marches against gun violence were just the beginning. In 2020 there was an avalanche of protests in numbers not seen since the days of the Civil Rights Movement. The protesters also demonstrated the diversity of the nation, as every demographic was present. Black Lives Matter signs dominated, and it was shouted from coast-to-coast. Xavier Brown, a freshman at the University of California, voiced a widely felt sentiment. "We were just trying to inspire other youth that anyone can organize, anyone can protest, so to begin a revolution in your own way. . . . I just hope that it shows that the Black community will never give up what they believe in."[93] Pollster Kristen Soltis Anderson said of this generation that they prefer "the idea of rather than having to adapt to the tough world that they're facing, they're just going to change that world. They're going to speak out about what they want to see differently, and they're going to push for change."[94]

There are political differences between Blacks of this generation and older Blacks. Older Blacks are much more partisan. They are more supportive of the Democratic Party and its leadership and strongly strident in their disapproval of the GOP. According to a HIT survey, 75 percent of Black registered voters aged fifty and older viewed congressional Democrats favorably, while only 22 percent thought congressional Democrats failed in responding to Black needs. A little over half (54 percent) under the age of fifty approved of congressional Democrats, with 36 percent voicing disapproval. Black voters under fifty years (57 percent) polled were in agreement with the statement, "The Democratic Party takes Black people for granted." Only 40 percent of older voters agreed.[95] The 2020 election continued to demonstrate the strength of the Black vote but also signaled a greater sense of political splintering. Donald Trump won a larger percentage of the vote from people of color than any Republican since 1960. No politician since 1996 won as large a percentage of the Black vote as Trump did in 2020. Twelve percent of Blacks voted for him, and he garnered 35 percent of the Muslim vote. Throughout his term, he bragged that only President Abraham Lincoln had done more for Black Americans.

Overall, there has been an increase in people in this age range who have been forced to return home and move in with their parents, the major causes being the coronavirus pandemic and its economic fallout that has led to job loss and high unemployment rates. This increase was witnessed by every racial demographic, all genders, in cities and rural areas as well as throughout the country. Young adults between the ages of eighteen and twenty-four were impacted the most. In the past, young Blacks and Hispanics were more likely to live in their parents' homes than were whites. In the 2020s, this trend reversed. For African Americans, there was a 55 percent increase in the number of Black youths of this generation who moved back home, with the majority being young men from the South. The most commonly cited reasons for this were the closure of college dorm rooms (23 percent) or job loss (18 percent). These percentages are the highest since the Great Depression.[96]

There are some alarming trends present in this generation. Members are dying by suicide in unprecedented numbers. For young adults between ten and thirty-four years of age, suicide is the second leading cause of death. The suicide rate for Black youth is growing in frightening numbers. In 2016 and 2018, Black children demonstrated the highest rates of suicide among U.S. children five to eleven years old. The rates have been steadily climbing as between 2003–7, fifty-four children ended their lives; between 2008–12 the number grew to fifty-nine. Psychology professor Rheeda Walker blames the myth that suicide is a "white thing" and the hesitation from Black youth to confide their pain. She challenged the use of conventional methods over means of spiritual coping techniques.[97] The causes are complex and many. Many exist in perpetual states of fear, apprehension, and lack of hope that life will ever get better. One young Black preteen from Illinois stated in a PBS documentary called *A Day in the Life of America,* "I'm scared of gunshots, because when I hear them, my heart starts racing and I run. I seen people get shot. I seen the bullet fly past me."[98]

They exhibit two conflicting attributes at the same time: tremendous confidence and anxiety. They are driven to succeed. They are proud of what they have accomplished as a race but also think that there is too much focus on the past. They are committed to not just survive but seek to thrive. They revere the past but want a more contemporary celebration of Black life through uplifting the positive side of the Black experience. According to a BET study, "They want to reframe stories of historical resilience and look to more future–focused narratives of Black excellence—highlighting modern–day trailblazers, celebrating Black achievements, promoting Black culture in school, and immortalizing Black heroics."[99] While walking the road untraveled, they also experience the nervousness of youth. They understand that the path ahead is filled with uncertainty as economic stability is becoming more difficult to achieve. They are nervous that by the time they reach adulthood, they might not have acquired the necessary skills to compete. They fear that their schools and colleges are not preparing them for life in the real world. They feel that they are resourced to a greater degree, finding information and opportunities via social media. It is through social media that inspiration is found, as 42 percent learn from social media what others are achieving and thus can explore different ways to make money. As many as 62 percent want to create their own businesses and believe that working online offers greater financial opportunities (42 percent) to create something that is profitable and belongs to them.[100]

Spirituality is important to the Obama Generation, but their spirituality does not follow traditional patterns. They overwhelmingly identity themselves as Christian (67 percent).[101] Among those who are church members, 53 percent attend Black congregations while 25 percent worship in a predominantly white church. They are more informed about other religions and open to learning from different faiths. They don't affiliate with a religion simply because it is the belief of their parents or community. They demonstrate an interest in what it is that speaks to them, even combining the attributes of more than one into a spiritual worldview. They seek wellness and will practice faiths that enable a sense of wholeness. They practice different disciplines combining prayer, Scripture reading, meditation, and traditional Christian worship. It is their faith that makes them tolerant of different lifestyles, especially concerning gender and sexuality. They don't relate to the conservatism of American Christians who spend more time condemning than loving others.[102] Shaylen Hardy, national director of Black Campus Ministries for InterVarsity Christian Fellowship, commented in *Christianity Today*, "Black young adults have become cynical about the gospel's credibility because of the persistence of racial injustice and white supremacy. They reject the silence (and complicity) they find in some church communities. As a result, they may be likely to view the church's entire belief system as uncredible and untrustworthy."[103] The Reverend Kelli W. Taylor, chaplain at Methodist University, affirmed that Black students are invested in prayer and Scripture but have grown exhausted with churches that don't apply their faith's teachings. "They are weary of prayer without action and scripture study that ignores the central message of the gospel that says you cannot say you love God and hate your brother or sister. They want to engage the message of the biblical prophets who were social critics."[104]

The Obama Generation is rapidly introducing change into America. Their perspective about race is contrary to that of both Blacks and whites who were born before them. They identify as Black but have problems with the narrowness of racial categories. This generation values the freedom to choose and then expand one's identity beyond traditional definitions. They witnessed the murder of George Floyd and joined with their white and Latino brothers and sisters to march in almost every state in the country. They have experienced racial divides in their high schools, but they have also experienced growing acceptance of people of color across the country in a variety of fields and locations. They are determined to establish a new identity for the nation where race does not produce negativity or exclusion in American life. For them, there's no going back to yesterday, only pressing forward.

Conclusion

This book is about identity and its importance to each one of us. Identity is shaped by physical, mental, social, familial, societal, and interpersonal factors that affect one early in life and continue throughout one's lifespan. Our values, relationships, perspectives, and even our behavior can be determined by who we believe ourselves to be and who we are not. In many ways, our identities are shaped at an early age, but they are also reshaped as we make decisions in different periods in our lives.

Our parents are major influencers from early in life. The absence of either can have lifelong impacts, delaying a sense of knowing oneself. Our identity, while shared with others within our different alliances, is also unique to each one of us. Our personality, in combination with the innate gifts we possess, is manifested in our outer appearance, our interests, and our commitments.

We can develop a sense of unity based on our biological connections with family and extended family. So much of our knowledge of self is based on family history and the tales of the heroics of ancestors who bravely ventured forth to seek opportunity for advancement. Economic, educational, and employment opportunities have provided us with further information that in turn helps shape our sense of self.

The Black community has had a sense of urgency about establishing a sense of self in order to promote self-awareness and communal uplift. Generations have helped to pass on the stories of family that have helped many to know who they are and thus equipped the community with a sense of belonging. Because the United States is a nation obsessed with race, with varying societal values placed on being Black in America, being Black and American has alternately generated a sense of pride and also dismay at discriminatory treatment.

All of this is to say that these elements have been important to African Americans, but also to all Americans, and people everywhere. We cannot go forward unless we have a history to rely upon. A healthy life is found when we discover ourselves, either early or late in life. We all need something that serves as an anchor that helps keep us stable and emotionally secure. If we go through life with feelings of insecurity, we will lack the confidence to engage with others in manners that are productive and wholesome.

Going forward, the Black community is determined to develop an even greater cohesion based on an identity that enables all who self-identify as Black to have a sense of love and affirmation of self. A sizable portion of young adults struggle with low self-esteem, live in impoverished communities, and feel unsupported. The formation of an identity associated with family and social institutions can help. Even in a diminished capacity, the church remains a place where values are instilled and community is established. For many, sports provide opportunities for teamwork and a sense of belonging in solidarity with others.

For people of faith, our religious beliefs play a major role in how we identify ourselves. African Americans are the most religious Americans and have settled into different church bodies that provide solace and a sense of belonging. Our church family can provide a more intimate relationship than we share with members of our biological family. In the end, we all need to feel that we have a strong and independent sense of identity and awareness. This helps us to define who we are to others and feel a sense of love and emotional security within.

Notes

Introduction

1. Reniqua Allen, *It Was All a Dream: A New Generation Confronts the Broken Promise to Black America* (New York: Nation Books, 2019), 9.
2. Carolyn A. Liebler and Meghan Zacher, "History, Place, and Racial Self-Representation in 21st Century America," *Social Science Research* 57 (2016): 211–32, https://www.ncbi.nlm.nih.gov/pmc/articles/PMC5651049/.
3. Amanda Barroso, "Most Black Adults Say Race Is Central to Their Identity and Feel Connected to a Broader Black Community," Pew Research Center, February 5, 2020, https://www.pewresearch.org/fact-tank/2020/02/05/most-black-adults-say-race-is-central-to-their-identity-and-feel-connected-to-a-broader-black-community/.
4. Angelica Quintero, "America's Love-Hate Relationship with Immigrants," *Los Angeles Times*, August 2, 2017, https://www.latimes.com/projects/la-na-immigration-trends/.
5. Ohimai Amaize, "The 'Social Distance' between African and African-Americans," *JSTOR Daily*, July 14, 2021, https://daily.jstor.org/the-social-distance-between-africa-and-african-americans/.
6. Juliana Menasce Horowitz, Kim Parker, Anna Brown, and Kiana Cox, "Amid Racial Reckoning, Americans Divided on Whether Increased Focusing on Race Will Lead to Major Policy Change," Pew Research Center, October 6, 2020, https://www.pewresearch.org/social-trends/2020/10/06/acknowledgments-47/.
7. Juliana Menasce Horowitz, Anna Brown, and Kiana Cox, "Race in America 2019," Pew Research Center, April 9, 2019, https://www.pewsocialtrends.org/2019/04/09/race-in-america-2019/.
8. Anna Brown, "Key Findings on Americans' Views of Race in 2019," Pew Research Center, April 9, 2019, https://www.pewresearch.org/fact-tank/2019/04/09/key-findings-on-americans-views-of-race-in-2019/.
9. Claudia Deane, Maeve Duggan, and Rich Morin, "Americans Name the 10 Most Significant Historic Events of Their Lifetimes," Pew Research Center, December 15, 2016, https://www.pewresearch.org/politics/2016/12/15/americans-name-the-10-most-significant-historic-events-of-their-lifetimes/.
10. Christine Tamir, Abby Budiman, Luis Noe-Bustamante, and Lauren Mora, "Facts about the U.S. Black Population," Pew Research Center, March 25, 2021, https://www.pewresearch.org/social-trends/fact-sheet/facts-about-the-us-black-population/.

11. Kim Parker, "How Pew Research Center Will Report on Generations Moving Forward," Pew Research Center, May 22, 2023, https://www.pewresearch.org/short-reads/2023/05/22/how-pew-research-center-will-report-on-generations-moving-forward/.

12. Sally Hicks, "Talking 'bout My Generation," *Duke Magazine*, May–June 2005, https://alumni.duke.edu/magazine/articles/talking-bout-my-generation.

13. Beverly Mahone, "When Will African American Baby Boomers Be Counted," *HuffPost*, August 20, 2012, https://www.huffpost.com/entry/black-baby-boomer-health_b_1793662.

14. Akin Bruce, "Generational Differences among African Americans in Their Perceptions of Economic Opportunity," *Urban Edge*, Rice University Kinder Institute for Urban Research, July 4, 2018, https://kinder.rice.edu/2018/07/04/generational-differences-among-african-americans-their-perceptions-economic-opportunity (italics added).

15. Denise G. Yull, "Race Has Always Mattered: An Intergeneration Look at Race, Space, Place, and Educational Experiences of Blacks," *Education Research International*, October 1, 2014, https://www.hindawi.com/journals/edri/2014/683035/.

16. Ellis Cose, *The End of Anger* (New York: HarperCollins, 2011), 66, 134.

17. Ellis Cose, "The Black Generation Gap," *The Root*, https://www.theroot.com/the-black-generation-gap-1790864171.

18. Bakari Kitwana, *The Hip-Hop Generation: Young Blacks and the Crisis in African-American Culture* (New York: Civitas Books, 2002), 5.

19. M. K. Asante Jr., *It's Bigger Than Hip Hop: The Rise of the Post-Hip-Hop Generation* (New York: St. Martin's Griffin, 2008), 7–11.

20. Nelson George, *Buppies, B-Boys, Baps, and Bohos: Notes on Post-Soul Black Culture* (Cambridge, MA: Da Capo Press, 1992), 2.

21. Allen, *It Was All a Dream*, 3–4.

22. Lindsay M. Chervinsky, "The Outsized Role of the President in Race Relations," *Smithsonian Magazine*, October 8, 2020, https://www.smithsonianmag.com/history/outsized-role-president-race-relations-180976022/.

23. Jeremy Hobson, "Teddy Roosevelt's Complicated Legacy 100 Years after His Death," WBUR, March 21, 2019, https://www.wbur.org/hereandnow/2019/03/21/teddy-roosevelt-legacy-100-years.

24. Ronald Walters, "How Do African-American Scholars Rank Presidents?," History News Network, https://historynewsnetwork.org/article/450.

25. Alvin B. Tillery Jr. and Hanes Walton Jr., "Presidential Greatness in the Black Press: Ranking the Modern Presidents on Civil Rights Policy and Race Relations, 1900–2016," Academia, 2017, https://www.academia.edu/30300231/Presidential_Greatness_in_the_Black_Press_Ranking_the_Modern_Presidents_on_Civil_Rights_Policy_and_Race_Relations_1900_2016. Tillery also wrote a *Washington Post* article addressing this issue, "Here's How Black Newspapers Rank the U.S. Presidents," *Washington Post*, February 21, 2017, https://www.washingtonpost.com/news/monkey-cage/wp/2017/02/21/heres-how-black-newspapers-rank-the-u-s-presidents/.

Chapter 1: New Negro Generation

1. Alaine Locke, "Alan Locke on 'The New Negro' (1925)," *The American Yawp Reader*, https://www.americanyawp.com/reader/22-the-new-era/alain-locke-on-the-new-negro-1925.

2. Norman Coombs, *The Black Experience in America: The Immigrant Heritage of America* (Twayne, 1972), available at https://rucore.libraries.rutgers.edu/rutgers-lib/2152 /PDF/1/play/.

3. Alain Locke, *Voices of the Harlem Renaissance* (Old Saybrook, CT: Konecky & Konecky, 2019), 3, 7, 8, 13.

4. James Tolbert-Rouchaleau, *James Weldon Johnson* (New York: Chelsea House Publishers, 1988), 81.

5. Baratunde Thurston, *How to Be Black* (New York: HarperCollins, 2013), 31–32.

6. David Cecelski, "Hattie Brown: A Freedom Story," *News & Observer*, August 9, 1998, https://www.ncpedia.org/listening-to-history/brown-hattie.

7. Charles Reagan Wilson and William Ferris, eds., *Encyclopedia of Southern Culture: Volume 1* (Chapel Hill: University of North Carolina Press, 1989), 320–21.

8. "A Sampling of Jim Crow Laws," *Anchor: A North Carolina History Online Resource*, https://www.ncpedia.org/anchor/sampling-jim-crow-laws.

9. Len Lear, "Lifelong Northwest Philly Resident and Oldest Man in City, Russell A. Harvey, Dies at 105," *Chestnut Hill Local*, February 3, 2021, https://www .chestnuthilllocal.com/stories/lifelong-northwest-philly-resident-and-oldest-man -in-city-russell-a-harvey-dies-at-105,16418.

10. "The State of African Americans in the South," Digital History, 2021, https://www .digitalhistory.uh.edu/disp_textbook.cfm?smtid=2&psid=3177.

11. David Cecelski, "Joyce Justice Williams: Farm Days," *News & Observer*, June 8, 2008, https://www.ncpedia.org/listening-to-history/williams-joyce.

12. B. Grunder, M. Heinz, G. McCall, A. Bishop, and T. Finchum, "Evaluating the Oral Narratives of Minority Centenarians: A Case Study in Social Justice," *Innovation in Aging* 2, issue supplement 1 (2018): 643, https://academic.oup.com /innovateage/article/2/suppl_1/643/5169815.

13. Alfred Edmond Jr., "#Fridayreads: World Record-Holding Centenarian Reveals Why She Runs," *Black Enterprise*, December 15, 2017, https://www.blackenterprise .com/fridayreads-world-record-holding-centenarian-reveals-why-she-runs/.

14. James Sullivan, "Vermont Centenarian Embodied a Rare History," *Boston Globe*, July 14, 2015, https://www.bostonglobe.com/arts/books/2015/07/13 /centenarian-daisy-turner-became-narrator-sweeping-african-american-family -tale/npQHoPH1YG7AdmIuZcMXqJ/story.html.

15. Joy Hakim, *An Age of Extremes* (Oxford: Oxford University Press, 1994), 141.

16. August Meier and Elliott Rudwick, *From Plantation to Ghetto* (New York: Hill and Wang, 1976), 192.

17. Theodore Roosevelt, "Theodore Roosevelt on Race," *Negro Digest* 12, no. 1 (November 1961): 49, https://books.google.com/books?id=g7MDAAAAMBAJ &printsec=frontcover&source=gbs_ge_summary_r&cad=0#v= onepage&q&f=true.

18. Edmund Morris, *Theodore Rex* (New York: Modern Library Paperbacks, 2002), 52–53.

19. Locke, *Voices of the Harlem Renaissance*, 333, 340.

20. David Cecelski, "Dorcas E. Carter: The Great Fire of '22," *News & Observer*, January 14, 2001, https://www.ncpedia.org/listening-to-history/carter-dorcas.

21. Willard B. Gatewood Jr., "Aristocrats of Color: South and North: The Black Elite, 1880–1920," *Journal of Southern History* 54, no. 1 (February 1988): 6–7, 20, https://www.jstor.org/stable/2208518.

22. Coombs, *The Black Experience in America.*

23. Ronda Racha Penrice, *African American History for Dummies* (Hoboken, NJ: Wiley Publishing, 2007), 133–37.

24. Toluse Olorunnipa and Griff Witte, "George Floyd's America: Born with Two Strikes: How Systemic Racism Shaped Floyd's Life and Hobbled His Ambition," *Washington Post*, October 8, 2020, https://www.washingtonpost.com /graphics/2020/national/george-floyd-america/systemic-racism/.

25. Russell G. Brooker, "The Rosenwald Schools: An Impressive Legacy of Black-Jewish Collaboration for Negro Education," America's Black Holocaust Museum, https://www.abhmuseum.org/the-rosenwald-schools-an-impressive-legacy-of -black-jewish-collaboration-for-negro-education/.

26. David Cecelski, "Alethea Williams-King: The Widow's Mite," *News & Observer*, April 9, 2006, https://www.ncpedia.org/listening-to-history/williams-king.

27. Wilson and Ferris, *Encyclopedia of Southern Culture*, 237–39.

28. "Major Landmarks in the Progress of African Americans in Higher Education," *Journal of Blacks in Higher Education*, https://www.jbhe.com/chronology/.

29. Femi Lewis, "African-American History Timeline: 1910–1919," ThoughtCo., https://www.thoughtco.com/african-american-history-timeline-1910-1919-45426.

30. "Booker T. Washington Delivers the 1895 Atlanta Compromise Speech," History Matters, http://historymatters.gmu.edu/d/39/.

31. Lerone Bennett Jr., *Before the Mayflower: A History of Black America* (New York: Penguin Books, 1982), 231.

32. Penrice, *African American History for Dummies*, 139–40.

33. Marcia A. Smith, *Black America: A Photographic Journey* (New York: Fall River Press, 2009), 164, 166.

34. Bennett, *Before the Mayflower*, 327–28.

35. Meier and Rudwick, *From Plantation to Ghetto*, 204–5.

36. Benjamin Quarles, *The Negro in the Making of America* (New York: A Touchstone Book, 1969), 171.

37. Quarles, 434–35.

38. Meier and Rudwick, *From Plantation to Ghetto*, 204–5.

39. James M. McPherson, *"To the Best of My Ability": The American Presidents* (New York: Dorling Kindersley, 2000), 180–87.

40. Lerone Bennett Jr., in *Ebony: Pictorial History of Black America, Volume III: Civil Rights Movement to Black Revolution* (Nashville: The Southwestern Company, 1971), 162.

41. Morris, *Theodore Rex*, 54–55.

42. Morris, 54–55.

43. John Hope Franklin, *From Slavery to Freedom: A History of Negro Americans* (New York: Vantage Books, 1969), 422–23.

44. Michael J. Klarman, *Unfinished Business: Racial Equality in American History* (Oxford: Oxford University Press, 2007), 98.

45. Klarman, 98.

46. Morris, *Theodore Rex*, 455.

47. Stephanie Christensen, "Niagara Movement (1905–1909)," Black Past, December 16, 2017, https://www.blackpast.org/african-american-history/niagara -movement-1905-1909/.

48. Susan Bragg, "The National Association for the Advancement of Colored People and the Long Struggle for Civil Rights in the United States," Black Past, January 19, 2009, https://www.blackpast.org/african-american-history/national -association-advancement-colored-people-and-long-struggle-civil-rights-united-s/.

49. McPherson, *"To the Best of My Ability,"* 188–94.

50. "William Howard Taft: The 27th President of the United States," WhiteHouse .gov, https://www.whitehouse.gov/about-the-white-house/presidents/william -howard-taft/.

51. Klarman, *Unfinished Business*, 87.
52. Klarman, 97.
53. Klarman, 87.
54. McPherson, *"To the Best of My Ability,"* 188–95.
55. "President William Howard Taft Expels Black Soldiers from San Antonio for Protesting Jim Crow," Equal Justice Initiative, https://calendar.eji.org/racial-injustice/apr/03.
56. "Aug. 13, 1910: Ministers Appeal to President Taft after Slocum Massacre," Zinn Education Project, https://www.zinnedproject.org/news/tdih/ministers-taft-slocum-massacre/.
57. "The Best Option," ehistory, The Ohio State University, https://ehistory.osu.edu/exhibitions/1912/race/trvs.
58. McPherson, *"To the Best of My Ability,"* 196–205.
59. Franklin, *From Slavery to Freedom*, 453.
60. "The Transformation of the Racial Views of Harry Truman," *Journal of Blacks in Higher Education*, no. 26 (Winter, 1999–2000): 28, https://www.jstor.org/stable/2999133.
61. David Pietrusza, *1920: The Year of the Six Presidents* (New York: Carroll & Graf Publishers, 2007), 355.
62. Wilson and Ferris, *Encyclopedia of Southern Culture*, 243–44.
63. Bennett, *Before the Mayflower*, 295.
64. "Standing Up for the Race," PBS, https://www.pbs.org/blackpress/educate_event/standing.html.
65. Bennett, *Before the Mayflower*, 342.
66. "Woodrow Wilson and Race in America," PBS, American Experience, https://www.pbs.org/wgbh/americanexperience/features/wilson-and-race-relations/.
67. Pietrusza, *1920*, 355.
68. Herbert G. Ruffin II, "William Monroe Trotter (1872–1934)," Black Past, January 23, 2007, https://www.blackpast.org/african-american-history/trotter-william-monroe-1872-1934/.
69. Franklin, *From Slavery to Freedom*, 454.
70. Sydney Trent, "The Black Sorority That Faced Racism in the Suffrage Movement but Refused to Walk Away," *Washington Post*, August 8, 2020, https://www.washingtonpost.com/graphics/2020/local/history/suffrage-racism-black-deltas-parade-washington/.
71. Locke, *Voices of the Harlem Renaissance*, 382.
72. Isabel Wilkerson, *The Warmth of Other Suns: The Epic Story of America's Great Migration* (New York: Vintage Books, 2010), 8–9.
73. Smith, *Black America*, 118.
74. Time-Life Books, eds., *African American Voices of Triumph: Perseverance* (New York: Time-Life Custom Publishing, 1993), 156–57.
75. Nathan Miller, *Star-Spangled Men: America's Ten Worst Presidents* (New York: Touchstone Books, 1998), 192.
76. Miller, 207–10.
77. Pietrusza, *1920*, 364–65.
78. McPherson, *"To the Best of My Ability,"* 194–95, 206–11.
79. Robert Shogan, *Harry Truman and the Struggle for Racial Justice* (Lawrence: University Press of Kansas, 2013), 9.
80. Miller, *Star-Spangled Men*, 205.
81. "Lynching," Digital History, 2021, https://www.digitalhistory.uh.edu/disp_textbook.cfm?smtid=2&psid=3178.

82. David R. Colburn, "Rosewood and America in the Early Twentieth Century," *Florida Historical Quarterly* 76, no. 2 (Fall 1997), https://www.jstor.org/stable/30146345.

83. Penrice, *African American History for Dummies*, 125–28.

84. Jeffrey S. Adler, "Less Crime, More Punishment: Violence, Race, and Criminal Justice in Early Twentieth-Century America," *Journal of American History* 102, issue 1 (June 2015), http//academic.oup.com/jah/article/102/1/34/686429.

85. Jeffrey S. Adler, "'We've Got a Right to Fight; We're Married': Domestic Homicide in Chicago, 1975–1920," *Journal of Interdisciplinary History* 34, no. 1 (Summer, 2003), https://www.jstor.org/stable/3656706.

86. Miller, *Star-Spangled Men*, 195.

87. Pietrusza, *1920*, 369–76.

88. Brian Gorman, "Party Loyalty for What?," *Medium*, November 2, 2020, https://bgorman357.medium.com/may-god-write-us-down-as-asses-if-ever-again-we-are-found-putting-our-trust-in-either-the-53fd8a5ecfd2.

89. Shogan, *Harry Truman and the Struggle for Racial Justice*, 9.

90. The New England Centenarian Study by the BU School of Medicine, "Why Study Centenarians? An Overview," January 1, 2023, https://www.bumc.bu.edu/centenarian/statistics/#:~:text.

91. "2017 Profile of African Americans Age 65 and Over," Administration for Community Living and Administration on Aging, U.S. Department of Health and Human Services, https://acl.gov/sites/default/files/Aging%20and%20Disability%20in%20America/2017OAProfileAfAm508.pdf.

92. "2019 Profile of Older Americans," Administration for Community Living, U.S. Department of Health and Human Services, May 2020, https://acl.gov/sites/default/files/Aging%20and%20Disability%20in%20America/2019Profile OlderAmericans508.pdf.

93. "America's Centenarians: Data from the 1980 Census," National Institutes of Health, National Library of Medicine, September 1987, https://pubmed.ncbi.nlm.nih.gov/12341602/.

94. Adam Davey, Merril F. Elias, Ilene C. Seigler, Uday Lele, and Peter Martin, "Cognitive Function, Physical Performance, Health, and Disease: Norms from the Georgia Centenarian Study," Digital Commons at the University of Maine, 2010, https://core.ac.uk/download/pdf/217067086.pdf.

95. Robert Douglas Young, "African American Longevity Advantage: Myth or Reality? A Racial Comparison of Supercentenarian Data," July 21, 2008, https://scholarworks.gsu.edu/gerontology_theses/10/, 14–17, 157, 160.

96. Thomas T. Perls, "Male Centenarians: How and Why Are They Different from Their Female Counterparts?," *Journal of the American Geriatrics Society*, June 6, 2017, https://agsjournals.onlinelibrary.wiley.com/doi/full/10.1111/jgs.14978.

97. Juan Williams, *Thurgood Marshall: American Revolutionary* (New York: Random House, 1998), 15.

98. Langston Hughes, "My Most Humiliating Jim Crow Experience," *Negro Digest* 3.7 (May 1945): 33–34, https://www.cde.state.co.us/cophysicaleducation/mymosthumiliatingjimcrowexperiencepdf.

99. S. E. Williams, "Telling Their Stories & Honoring Our Centenarians," *Voice* 50, March 16, 2017, https://theievoice.com/telling-their-stories-honoring-our-centenarians/.

100. Scott Simon and Andrew Craig, "Hester Ford, Oldest Living American, Dies at 115 (Or 116)," NPR, April 24, 2021, https://www.npr.org/2021/04/24/990505023/hester-ford-oldest-living-american-dies-at-115-or-116.

101. "This Black Woman with More than 200 Descendants Is Celebrating Her 116th Birthday as the Oldest Living American," Because of Them We Can, August 21, 2020, https://www.becauseofthemwecan.com/blogs/the-feels/oldest -living-american-with-more-than-200-descendants-celebrates-116th-birthday.

102. Alijean Harmetz, "Lena Horne, Singer and Actress, Dies at 92," *New York Times*, May 10, 2010, https://www.nytimes.com/2010/05/10/arts/music/10horne .html.

103. Erin Hoover Barnett, "Centenarian's Wisdom Remains a Lesson Today," Oregon Health & Science University News, March 24, 2020, https://news.ohsu .edu/2020/03/24/centenarians-wisdom-remains-a-lesson-today.

104. Frederick N. Rasmussen, "Edna L. Middleton, a Centenarian Who Worked as a Wartime Shipyard Riveter and Supported Civil and Women's Rights, Dies," *Baltimore Sun*, March 25, 2021, https://www.baltimoresun.com/obituaries/bs-md -ob-edna-middleton-20210325-rzacduxdgzcu7jbzlurmmxoo5i-story.html.

105. Sarah L. Delany and A. Elizabeth Delany with Amy Hill Hearth, *Having Our Say: The Delany Sisters' First 100 Years* (New York: Dell, 1994), 5.

106. Chelsea Brasted, "America's Oldest Living WWII Veteran Faced Hostility Abroad—and at Home," *National Geographic*, May 11, 2020, https://www.national geographic.com/history/article/americas-oldest-living-wwii-veteran-faced -hostility-abroad-home.

107. Brasted, "America's Oldest Living WWII Veteran."

108. Clifton L. Talbert, *When We Were Colored* (New York: Penguin Books, 1989), 4–5.

109. Thomas N. Maloney, "African Americans in the Twentieth Century," Economic History Association, https://eh.net/encyclopedia/african-americans-in-the -twentieth-century/.

110. Talbert, *When We Were Colored*, 643.

111. Paige Frank, "A Life of Work: Audrey James," University of Nevada, Las Vegas New Center, October 26, 2023, https://www.unlv.edu/news/article/life-work.

112. Barnett, "Centenarian's Wisdom Remains a Lesson Today."

113. Time-Life Books, eds., *African American Voices of Triumph*, 153.

114. Yagana Shah, "Meet the 5 Oldest People in the World and Learn Their Secrets to a Long Life," *HuffPost*, updated December 6, 2017, https://www.huffpost .com/entry/worlds-oldest-people-1800s-secrets-to-long-life_n_6655570. See also https://www.usatoday.com/story/news/world/2014/09/05/six-people-still -alive-who-were-born-in-the-19th-century/15122367/.

115. Sydney Page, "She Was Forbidden as a Young Woman From Trying On Her Dream Wedding Gown Because She's Black. Now, at 94, She Finally Did It," *Washington Post*, July 19, 2021, https://www.washingtonpost.com/lifestyle /2021/07/19/wedding-dress-black-bride-segregation/.

116. Harm Venhuizen, "Oldest Living WWII Veteran Celebrates 111th Birthday," *Military Times*, September 12, 2020, https://www.militarytimes.com/news /your-army/2020/09/12/oldest-living-wwii-veteran-celebrates-111th-birthday/.

117. Phillip Kish and Christopher Buchanan, "Georgia's Oldest Living Person Turns 114," *Alive*, December 8, 2018, https://www.11alive.com/article/life/family /seniors/georgias-oldest-living-person-turns-114/85-42d80f6f-5b0d-42a9-a402 -dc651e6974dc.

118. Rasmussen, "Edna L. Middleton."

119. "Solano County Centenarians to Be Honored at 5th Annual Commemoration on Oct. 4," Solano County, California, August 26, 2011, https://www .solanocounty.com/news/displaynews.asp? NewsID=453&TargetID=1.

120. Brasted, "America's Oldest Living WWII Veteran."

121. Deborah Bayliss, "Twelve African American Centenarians Honored," *Citizen Weekly*, October 3, 2013, https://citizennewspapergroup.com/news/2013 /oct/03/twelve-african-american-centenarians-honored/.

122. Shirley J. Carlson, "Black Ideals of Womanhood in the Late Victorian Era," *Journal of Negro History* 77, no. 2 (Spring 1992), 62, https://www.jstor.org/stable/3031483.

123. Michael Cunningham and Craig Marberry, *Crowns: A Brief History of Church Hats* (New York: Doubleday, 2000).

124. Ben Dickinson, "Cicely Tyson on Rejection, Her Mother, and Choosing the Right Roles," *Elle*, January 28, 2021, https://www.elle.com/culture/movies-tv /a13793949/cicely-tyson-women-in-hollywood-november-2017/.

125. Simon and Craig, "Hester Ford."

126. D. Wilson, "African-American Woman Jeralean Talley Is Now the World's Oldest Person," The Grio, April 7, 2015, https://thegrio.com/2015/04/07/african -american-is-world-oldest-person/.

127. David Cecelski, "Capt. Eugene W. Gore: The Smell of Money," *News & Observer*, June 9, 2002, https://www.ncpedia.org/listening-to-history/gore-eugene-w.

128. Nadia Neophytou, "Remembering Ida Keeling, Who Set Track Records into Her 100s," *Runner's World*, September 15, 2021, https://www.runnersworld .com/runners-stories/a37611220/remembering-ida-keeling/.

129. Jo Kwon, "At 106, Orange County's Oldest African American Is Still Going," Spectrum News 1, January 8, 2020, https://spectrumnews1.com/ca/la-west /human-interest/2020/01/08/at-106--orange-county-s-oldest-african-american -is-still-going.

130. Kwon, "Orange County's Oldest African American."

Chapter 2: Motown Generation

1. Nelson George, *Buppies, B-Boys, Baps, and Bohos: Notes on Post-Soul Black Culture* (Cambridge, MA: Da Capo Press, 1992), 182–83.

2. "The Roaring Twenties," History.com, March 28, 2023, https://www.history .com/topics/roaring-twenties/roaring-twenties-history.

3. Charles Reagan Wilson and William Ferris, eds., *Encyclopedia of Southern Culture: Volume 1* (Chapel Hill: University of North Carolina Press, 1989), 231.

4. "Black History Milestones: Timeline," History.com, January 24, 2024, https:// www.history.com/topics/black-history/black-history-milestones.

5. Lisa Robinson, "It Happened in Hitsville," *Vanity Fair*, December 13, 2008, https://www.vanityfair.com/culture/2008/12/motown200812.

6. *Hitsville: The Making of Motown*, directed by Ben and Gabe Turner (Los Angeles: Capitol Music Group, 2019).

7. Christina Pomoni, "The Social Impact of Motown Music in American Culture," Dr. Robert Muller—1960s Psychedelic Hippie Culture, blog, https://psychedelichippie music.blogspot.com/2009/10/social-impact-of-motown-music-on.html.

8. Arwa Haider, "Motown: The Music That Changed America," BBC, January 9, 2019, https://www.bbc.com/culture/article/20190109-motown-the-music-that -changed-america.

9. Ibram X. Kendi, "The 11 Most Racist U.S. Presidents," *HuffPost*, May 27, 2016, https://www.huffpost.com/entry/would-a-president-trump-m_b_10135836.

10. *Ebony Pictorial History of Black America, Volume II: Reconstruction to Supreme Court Decision 1954* (Nashville: Southwestern Company, 1971), 104.

11. Wilson and Ferris, *Encyclopedia of Southern Culture*, 299.

12. Wilson and Ferris, 307.

13. "Negroes Still Going North," *Jet* 1, no. 2 (November 8, 1951): 10, https:// books.google.com/books?id=I0MDAAAAMBAJ&printsec=frontcover& source=gbs_ge_summary_r&cad=0.

14. Marcia A. Smith, *Black America: A Photographic Journey* (New York: Fall River Press, 2009), 116–17.

15. "Founder and Editor of the *Chicago Defender*," Library of Congress, https:// www.loc.gov/exhibits/african/afam009.html#obj4.

16. Alain Locke, *Voices of the Harlem Renaissance* (Old Saybrook, CT: Konecky & Konecky, 2019), 279.

17. Wilson and Ferris, *Encyclopedia of Southern Culture*, 308, 319.

18. *Ebony Pictorial History of Black America, Volume II*, 111–12.

19. Smith, *Black America*, 167.

20. David Driskell, David Levering Lewis, and Deborah Willis Ryan, *Harlem Renaissance: Art of Black America* (New York: Harry N. Abrams, 1987), 53–55.

21. Thomas N. Maloney, "African Americans in the Twentieth Century," Economic History Association, https://eh.net/encyclopedia/african-americans-in-the -twentieth-century/.

22. Maloney, "African Americans in the Twentieth Century."

23. Smith, *Black America*, 164–65.

24. Smith, 117.

25. Wilson and Ferris, *Encyclopedia of Southern Culture*, 259–60.

26. Nathan Miller, *Star-Spangled Men: America's Ten Worst Presidents* (New York: Touchstone Books, 1998), 106.

27. David Pietrusza, *1920: The Year of the Six Presidents* (New York: Carroll & Graf Publishers, 2007), 363.

28. Kurt Schmoke, "The Little Known History of Coolidge and Civil Rights," *Coolidge Quarterly* 1, no. 3 (November 2016), https://coolidgefoundation.org /wp-content/uploads/2016/12/Coolidge-Quarterly_Vol-1-Issue-3.pdf.

29. "The Transformation of the Racial Views of Harry Truman," *Journal of Blacks in Higher Education*, no. 26 (Winter, 1999–2000): 28, https://www.jstor.org /stable/2999133.

30. Maceo Crenshaw Dailey Jr., "Calvin Coolidge's Afro-American Connection," *Contributions in Black Studies* 8, article 7 (1986), https://scholarworks.umass.edu /cgi/viewcontent.cgi?article=1055&context=cibs.

31. Smith, *Black America*, 200.

32. Wilson and Ferris, *Encyclopedia of Southern Culture*, 321.

33. Wilson and Ferris, 294–95.

34. James M. McPherson, *"To the Best of My Ability": The American Presidents* (New York: Dorling Kindersley, 2000), 221.

35. "Great Depression History," History.com, October 20, 2023, https://www .history.com/topics/great-depression/great-depression-history.

36. David Cecelski, "Sheila Kingsberry-Burt: The Undercrust of Living Dust," *News & Observer*, April 8, 2001, https://www.ncpedia.org/listening-to-history /kingsberry-burt-sheila.

37. George F. Garcia, "Herbert Hoover and the Issue of Race," *The Annals of Iowa* (1979), https://pubs.lib.uiowa.edu/annals-of-iowa/article/3996/galley/112895/view/.

38. Jeffrey S. Adler, "Less Crime, More Punishment: Violence, Race, and Criminal Justice in Early Twentieth-Century America," *Journal of American History* 102, issue 1 (June 2015), https://academic.oup.com/jah/article/102/1/34/686429.

39. Cecelski, "Kingsberry-Burt"; Emily Langer, "Lucille Bridges, Who Stood by Daughter Ruby through School Desegregation, Dies at 86," *Washington Post*, November 11, 2020, https://www.washingtonpost.com/local/obituaries/lucille -bridges-who-stood-by-daughter-ruby-through-school-desegregation-dies-at-86 /2020/11/11/ab37a36e-241d-11eb-952e-0c475972cfc0_story.html.

40. Peter Irons, "Jim Crow's Schools," American Federation of Teachers (AFT), 2002, https://www.aft.org/periodical/american-educator/summer-2004 /jim-crows-schools.

41. Sonya Ramsey, "The Troubled History of American Education after the Brown Decision," Organization of American Historians, https://www.oah.org/tah /issues/2017/february/the-troubled-history-of-american-education-after -the-brown-decision/.

42. Carter G. Woodson, *The Mis-Education of the Negro* (Washington, DC: Associated Publishers, 1933).

43. Smith, *Black America*, 191–93.

44. Michael Fultz, "Teacher Training and African American Education in the South, 1900–1940," *Journal of Negro Education* 65, no. 2 (Spring 1995).

45. "Major Landmarks in the Progress of African Americans in Higher Education," *Journal of Blacks in Higher Education*, https://www.jbhe.com/chronology/.

46. Petula Dvorak, "The 10 Worst Presidents: Besides Trump, Whom Do Scholars Scorn the Most?," *Washington Post*, February 20, 2018, https://www.washington post.com/news/retropolis/wp/2018/02/20/the-10-worst-presidents-besides -trump-who-do-scholars-scorn-the-most/.

47. Olivia B. Waxman, "5 Reasons Why Supreme Court Nominations Have Failed," *Time*, July 10, 2018, https://time.com/5333778/supreme-court-nominee -rejections/.

48. Benjamin Quarles, *The Negro in the Making of America* (New York: A Touchstone Book, 1969), 207–8.

49. Shirlee Taylor Haizlip, *The Sweeter the Juice: A Family Memoir in Black and White* (New York: Simon & Schuster, 1994), 21.

50. McPherson, "*To the Best of My Ability*," 230.

51. Smith, *Black America*, 201.

52. "Dirty Linen of the Week," *Jet* 1, no. 1 (November 1, 1951): 16, https://books .google.com/books?id=JEMDAAAAMBAJ&printsec=frontcover&source=gbs _ge_summary_r&cad=0.

53. "FDR and the New Deal," PBS, *Slavery by Another Name*, https://www.pbs.org /tpt/slavery-by-another-name/themes/fdr/.

54. "African Americans and the New Deal," Digital History, 2021, https://www.digital history.uh.edu/disp_textbook.cfm?smtID=2&psid=3447.

55. Ronda Racha Penrice, *African American History for Dummies* (Hoboken, NJ: Wiley Publishing, 2007), 143.

56. John Hope Franklin, *From Slavery to Freedom: A History of Negro Americans* (New York: Vintage Books, 1969), 527, 531.

57. "Joint Address to Congress Leading to a Declaration of War against Japan (1941)," National Archives, https://www.archives.gov/milestone-documents /joint-address-to-congress-declaration-of-war-against-japan.

58. Smith, *Black America*, 202.

59. Quarles, *The Negro in the Making of America*, 217–18.

60. McPherson, "*To the Best of My Ability*," 227, 231.

61. Quarles, *The Negro in the Making of America*, 155.

62. Smith, *Black America*, 202, 242–43, 246.

63. Smith, 231–34.

64. Sarah Fling, "Running against the World: Jesse Owens and the 1936 Berlin Olympics," White House Historical Association, https://www.whitehousehistory .org/running-against-the-world.

65. Smith, *Black America*, 203, 250–51.

66. Megan Rosenfeld, "Brokaw's 'Generation' Veneration," *Washington Post*, January 15, 1999, https://www.washingtonpost.com/archive/lifestyle/1999/01/15 /brokaws-generation-veneration/92b53c10-24d7-4c95-8abf-7490b3c81adf/.

67. Howard Zinn, "The Greatest Generation?," *The Progressive*, August 1, 2001, https://www.howardzinn.org/collection/the-greatest-generation/#:~:text.

68. Franklin, *From Slavery to Freedom*, 601.

69. "Baptist Hit for KKK Lethargy," *Jet* 1, no. 4 (November 22, 1951): 65, https:// books.google.com/books?id=IUMDAAAAMBAJ&source=gbs_all_issues_r&cad=1 .

70. "2019 Profile of Older Americans," Administration for Community Living, U.S. Department of Health and Human Services, May 2020, https://acl.gov /sites/default/files/Aging%20and%20Disability%20in%20America/2019Profile OlderAmericans508.pdf.

71. "2017 Profile of African Americans Age 65 and Over," Administration for Community Living and Administration on Aging, U.S. Department of Health and Human Services, https://acl.gov/sites/default/files/Aging%20and%20 Disability%20in%20America/2017OAProfileAfAm508.pdf.

72. "2018 Profile of African Americans Age 65 and Over," Administration for Community Living, U.S. Department of Health and Human Services, October 2019, https://acl.gov/sites/default/files/Aging%20and%20Disability%20in% 20America/ 2018AA_OAProfile.pdf

73. David Cecelski, "Joe Lewis: We Weren't Afraid," *News & Observer*, June 8, 2003, https://www.ncpedia.org/listening-to-history/lewis-joe.

74. Ellis Cose, *The End of Anger* (New York: HarperCollins, 2011), 109.

75. Christopher "Flood the Drummer" Norris, "At a Cable Television Taping, Black Journalism History Made," The Good Men Project, October 3, 2015, https://goodmenproject.com/featured-content/at-a-cable-television-taping -black-journalism-history-made-cnorris/.

76. Kyle Feldscher, "Harry Belafonte Says Greed Corrupting American Society, Tells Supporters 'We Blinked,'" Michigan Live, April 3, 2019, https://www .mlive.com/lansing-news/2015/02/harry_belafonte_says_greed_cor.html.

77. "Daughter of a Sharecropper Interview: Frankye Adams-Johnson," D.C. Everest Oral History Project, 2012, https://www.crmvet.org/nars/faj12.htm.

78. "WSSU Alumnus to Become First African American Mayor of Ahoskie," Winston-Salem State University News, November 18, 2019, https://www.wssu.edu /about/news/articles/2019/11/wssu-alumnus-to-become-first-african-american -mayor-of-ahoskie.html.

79. "People: The Younger Generation," *Time*, November 5, 1951, http://content .time.com/time/subscriber/article/0,33009,856950-1,00.html.

80. David Cecelski, "Elizabeth Ohree: Waiting Is Hard," *News & Observer*, November 11, 2001, https://www.ncpedia.org/listening-to-history/ohree-elizabeth.

81. Jennifer Dunning, *Alvin Ailey: A Life in Dance* (Reading, MA: Addison-Wesley Publishing, 1996), 6.

82. David Cecelski, "Bunny Sanders: Serpents and Doves," *News & Observer*, May 16, 2004, https://www.ncpedia.org/listening-to-history/sanders-bunny.

83. Andrew Young, *A Way Out of No Way: The Spiritual Memoirs of Andrew Young* (Nashville: Thomas Nelson Publishers, 1994), 16.

84. David Cecelski, "Don Stith: The Smoke Eaters of Warrenton," *News & Observer*, February 10, 2002, https://www.ncpedia.org/listening-to-history/stith-don.

85. Cose, *End of Anger*, 113.

86. Alana Semuels, "Segregation Had to Be Invented," *Atlantic*, February 17, 2017, https://www.theatlantic.com/business/archive/2017/02/segregation-invented/517158/.

87. Cecelski, "Sheila Kingsberry-Burt."

88. Toluse Olorunnipa and Griff Witte, "George Floyd's America: Born with Two Strikes: How Systemic Racism Shaped Floyd's Life and Hobbled His Ambition," *Washington Post*, October 8, 2020, https://www.washingtonpost.com/graphics /2020/national/george-floyd-america/systemic-racism/.

89. Cose, *End of Anger*, 108.

90. Stephanie McCrummen, "The Keeper of the Secret," *Washington Post*, March 30, 2019, https://www.washingtonpost.com/national/the-keeper-of-the-secret /2019/03/30/bc1294aa-4fe4-11e9-88a1-ed346f0ec94f_story.html.

91. "Adults in the Silent Generation Who Identify as Black," Pew Research Center, 2014, https://www.pewforum.org/religious-landscape-study/racial-and-ethnic -composition/black/generational-cohort/silent/.

Chapter 3: Black Power Generation

1. Ellis Cose, *The End of Anger* (New York: HarperCollins, 2011), 13.

2. Sheeri Mitchell, "The Colored People of the 1950s: Black History from the Pages of *Ebony*," *Ebony*, February 17, 2020, https://www.ebony.com/exclusive/bhm -ebony-colored-people-1950s/.

3. Mitchell, "The Colored People of the 1950s."

4. Cose, *End of Anger*, 119.

5. David Cecelski, "Rev. David Forbes: The Birth of SNCC (Student Non-Violent Coordinating Committee)," *News & Observer*, April 9, 2000, https://www .ncpedia.org/listening-to-history/forbes-david.

6. David Cecelski, "Willis Williams: Life and Death at Devils Gut," *News & Observer*, June 13, 1999, https://www.ncpedia.org/listening-to-history/williams-willis.

7. *America in Color*, episode 4, "The 1950s," directed by Tom Brisley, aired on June 2, 2017, Smithsonian channel, available on Amazon Prime Video.

8. William A. Nolan, "Communism Versus the Negro," *Jet* 1, no. 2 (November 8, 1951): 54, https://books.google.com/books?id=I0MDAAAAMBAJ&printsec =frontcover&source=gbs_ge_summary_r&cad=0.

9. "Words of the Week," *Jet* 1, no. 3 (November 15, 1951): 20, https://books.google .com/books?id=IkMDAAAAMBAJ&printsec=frontcover.

10. "The 1950s," History.com, June 17, 2010, https://www.history.com/topics /cold-war/1950s.

11. "Census Shows Negroes Are Quitting South," *Jet* 1, no. 5 (November 29, 1951): 6, https://books.google.com/books?id=IEMDAAAAMBAJ&printsec=frontcover#v.

12. Studs Terkel, *Race: How Blacks & Whites Think & Feel About The American Obsession* (New York: The New Press, 1992), 101.

13. "Census Shows Negroes Are Quitting South," 6.

14. "Census Shows Negroes Are Quitting South," 6.

15. Thomas N. Maloney, "African Americans in the Twentieth Century," Economic History Association, https://eh.net/encyclopedia/african-americans-in-the -twentieth-century/.

16. "Negro Police Successful in South," *Jet* 1, no. 3 (November 15, 1951): 8–9, https://books.google.com/books?id=IkMDAAAAMBAJ&printsec=front cover#v.
17. Robert Shogan, *Harry Truman and the Struggle for Racial Justice* (Lawrence: University Press of Kansas, 2013), 2.
18. DeNeen L. Brown, "How Harry S. Truman Went from Being a Racist to Desegregating the Military," *Washington Post*, July 26, 2018, https://www .washingtonpost.com/news/retropolis/wp/2018/07/26/how-harry-s-truman -went-from-being-a-racist-to-desegregating-the-military/.
19. Shogan, *Harry Truman and the Struggle for Racial Justice*, 6.
20. Shogan, 12.
21. Ronda Racha Penrice, *African American History for Dummies* (Hoboken, NJ: Wiley Publishing, 2007), 151–62.
22. Farrell Evans, "Why Harry Truman Ended Segregation in the U.S. Military in 1948," History.com, November 5, 2020, https://www.history.com/news /harry-truman-executive-order-9981-desegration-military-1948.
23. "'Race' Causes Democratic Dissension," *Jet* 1, no. 2 (November 8, 1951): 5, https://books.google.com/books?id=I0MDAAAAMBAJ&printsec =frontcover&source=gbs_ge_summary_r&cad=0#v.
24. "Segregation Impairs Mental Health," *Jet* 1, no. 2 (November 8, 1951): 20, https://books.google.com/books?id=I0MDAAAAMBAJ&printsec=front cover&source=gbs_ge_summary_r&cad=0.
25. Shogan, *Harry Truman and the Struggle for Racial Justice*, 12.
26. "Harry S. Truman and Civil Rights," National Park Service: Harry S. Truman National Historic Site, https://www.nps.gov/articles/000/harry-s-truman-and -civil-rights.htm.
27. "The Transformation of the Racial Views of Harry Truman," *Journal of Blacks in Higher Education*, no. 26 (Winter, 1999–2000): 28, https://www.jstor.org /stable/2999133.
28. Shogan, *Harry Truman and the Struggle for Racial Justice*, 6.
29. Brown, "How Harry S. Truman."
30. "The Transformation of the Racial Views of Harry Truman," 28.
31. Brown, "How Harry S. Truman."
32. James M. McPherson, *"To the Best of My Ability": The American Presidents* (New York: Dorling Kindersley, 2000), 234–40.
33. Richard Wormser, "Harry S. Truman Supports Civil Rights (1947–1948)," The Rise and Fall of Jim Crow, https://www.thirteen.org/wnet/jimcrow/stories _events_truman.html.
34. Carl T. Rowan, "Harry Truman and the Negro: Was He Our Greatest Civil Rights President?," *Ebony*, November 1959, 50, https://books.google.com/books ?id=7oo5tbhLPgoC&printsec=frontcover&source=gbs_ge_ summary_r&cad=0.
35. Michael J. Klarman, *Unfinished Business: Racial Equality in American History* (Oxford: Oxford University Press, 2007), 140.
36. Rowan, "Harry Truman and the Negro," 46.
37. William E. Leuchtenburg, "The Conversion of Harry Truman," *American Heritage* 42, issue 7 (November 1991), https://www.americanheritage.com/conversion -harry-truman#.
38. Rowan, "Harry Truman and the Negro," 46.
39. Rowan, 48.
40. "Harry S. Truman and Civil Rights."

41. "New Civil Rights Fight Looms," *Jet* 1, no. 3 (November 15, 1951): 3, https://books.google.com/books?id=IkMDAAAAMBAJ&printsec=frontcover#v=onepage&q&f=false.

42. Klarman, *Unfinished Business,* 134.

43. Brown, "How Harry S. Truman."

44. Rowan, "Harry Truman and the Negro," 48.

45. Leuchtenburg, "The Conversion of Harry Truman."

46. "President Truman and Civil Rights," White House Historical Association, https://www.whitehousehistory.org/president-truman-and-civil-rights.

47. Rowan, "Harry Truman and the Negro," 46.

48. C. N. Trueman, "Harry Truman and Civil Rights," History Learning Site, March 27, 2015, https://www.historylearningsite.co.uk/the-civil-rights-movement-in-america-1945-to-1968/harry-truman-and-civil-rights/.

49. Rowan, "Harry Truman and the Negro," 46.

50. "Remarks to the Directors of the National Newspaper Publishers Association," The American Presidency Project, November 14, 1952, https://www.presidency.ucsb.edu/documents/remarks-the-directors-the-national-newspaper-publishers-association.

51. Rowan, "Harry Truman and the Negro," 44.

52. Rowan, 44.

53. Rowan, 50.

54. "Harry S. Truman and Civil Rights."

55. "'Race' Causes Democratic Dissension," *Jet* 1, no. 2 (November 8, 1951): 5, https://books.google.com/books?id=I0MDAAAAMBAJ&printsec=frontcover&source=gbs_ge_summary_r&cad=0#v=onepage&q&f=false.

56. Lerone Bennett Jr., "What Sit-Downs Mean to America: Call to Conscience Sparks National Soul-Searching," *Ebony,* June 1960, 37, https://books.google.com/books?id=3kOsUZgXbjMC&printsec=frontcover&source= gbs_ge_summary_r&cad=0.

57. "Harry S. Truman," Stanford University: The Martin Luther King, Jr. Research and Education Institute, https://kinginstitute.stanford.edu/encyclopedia/truman-harry-s.

58. Brody Shields, "The Civil Rights Presidents: FDR to Nixon," University of Montana, undergraduate research (2015), https://digitalcommons.mtech.edu/urp_aug_2015/2.

59. "Words of the Week," *Jet* 1, no. 5 (November 29, 1951): 26, https://books.google.com/books?id=IEMDAAAAMBAJ&printsec=frontcover#v=onepage&q&f=true.

60. "The Christian Century," *Jet* 1, no. 5 (November 29, 1951): 44, https://books.google.com/books?id=IEMDAAAAMBAJ&printsec=frontcover#v=onepage&q&f=true.

61. Ibram X. Kendi, "The 11 Most Racist U.S. Presidents," *HuffPost*, May 27, 2016, https://www.huffpost.com/entry/would-a-president-trump-m_b_10135836.

62. "The Struggle for Civil Rights," University of Virginia: Miller Center, https://millercenter.org/the-presidency/educational-resources/age-of-eisenhower/struggle-civil-rights.

63. Adam Serwer, "Why Don't We Remember Ike as a Civil Rights Hero?," MSNBC, May 17, 2014, https://www.msnbc.com/msnbc/why-dont-we-ike-civil-rights-msna329796.

64. Klarman, *Unfinished Business*, 157.

65. Serwer, "Why Don't We Remember Ike."

66. Penrice, *African American History for Dummies*, 145–51.
67. "141,000,000 for Segregation," *Jet* 1, no. 1 (November 1, 1951): 28, https://books.google.com/books?id=JEMDAAAAMBAJ&printsec=frontcover&source=gbs_ge_summary_r&cad=0#v=onepage&q&f=false.
68. Marcia A. Smith, *Black America: A Photographic Journey* (New York: Fall River Press, 2009), 278–79.
69. Charles Reagan Wilson and William Ferris, eds., *Encyclopedia of Southern Culture: Volume 1* (Chapel Hill: University of North Carolina Press, 1989), 267–70.
70. "Kenneth and Mamie Clark Doll," National Park Service: Brown v. Board of Education, https://www.nps.gov/brvb/learn/historyculture/clarkdoll.htm.
71. Sheeri Mitchell, "The Blacks of the 1960s: Black History from the Pages of *Ebony*," *Ebony*, February 17, 2020, https://www.ebony.com/black-history/bhm-ebony-blacks-1960s/.
72. Serwer, "Why Don't We Remember Ike."
73. "Harry S. Truman," Stanford University.
74. McPherson, *"To the Best of My Ability,"* 242–48.
75. David A. Nichols, *A Matter of Justice: Eisenhower and the Beginning of the Civil Rights Revolution* (New York: Simon & Schuster, 2007), 1.
76. "The Struggle for Civil Rights," Miller Center.
77. Val J. Washington to the Republican National Committee, July 18, 1957, Eisenhower Library, https://www.eisenhowerlibrary.gov/sites/default/files/research/online-documents/civil-rights-act/1957-07-18-washington-to-dde.pdf.
78. "New Civil Rights Fight Looms," *Jet* 1, no. 3 (November 15, 1951): 3, https://books.google.com/books?id=IkMDAAAAMBAJ&printsec=frontcover#v=onepage&q&f=true.
79. "Negro College Booming," *Jet* 1, no. 1 (November 1, 1951): 27, https://books.google.com/books?id=JEMDAAAAMBAJ&printsec=frontcover&source=gbs_ge_summary_r&cad=0#v=onepage&q&f=false.
80. "49 Colleges Okay Anti-Bias Program," *Jet* 1, no. 3 (November 15, 1951): 22, https://books.google.com/books?id=IkMDAAAAMBAJ&printsec=frontcover#v=onepage&q&f=true.
81. "U. of Louisville Gets 270 Negro Students," *Jet* 1, no. 6 (December 6, 1951): 17, https://books.google.com/books?id=H0MDAAAAMBAJ&printsec=frontcover&source=gbs_ge_summary_r&cad=0#v=onepage&q&f=false.
82. "N. C. Public School Ends Discrimination," *Jet* 1, no. 1 (November 1, 1957): 28, https://books.google.com/books?id=JEMDAAAAMBAJ&printsec=frontcover&source=gbs_ge_summary_r&cad=0#v=onepage&q&f=false.
83. Trueman, "Education and Civil Rights."
84. "South's Private Schools Relax Bias," *Jet* 1, no. 2 (November 8, 1951): 56–57, https://books.google.com/books?id=I0MDAAAAMBAJ&printsec=frontcover&source=gbs_ge_summary_r&cad=0#v=onepage&q&f=false.
85. "Keep High Standards, Colleges Warned," *Jet* 1, no. 1 (November 1, 1951): 28, https://books.google.com/books?id=JEMDAAAAMBAJ&printsec=frontcover&source=gbs_ge_summary_r&cad=0#v=onepage&q&f=false.
86. Bennett, "What Sit-Downs Mean to America."
87. Penrice, *African American History for Dummies*, 175–80.
88. Lerone Bennett Jr., *Ebony: Pictorial History of Black America, Volume III: Civil Rights Movement to Black Revolution* (Nashville: Southwestern Company, 1971), 122, 124.
89. Penrice, *African American History for Dummies*, 181.

90. "What the Candidates Promise Negroes," *Jet* 19, no. 3 (November 10, 1960): 14, https://books.google.com/books?id=8K4DAAAAMBAJ&printsec =frontcover&source=gbs_ge_summary_r&cad=0#v=onepage&q&f=false.
91. McPherson, *"To the Best of My Ability,"* 250–56.
92. "The 1960s History," History.com, June 26, 2020, https://www.history.com /topics/1960s/1960s-history.
93. "Eight Days in Ga. Jails Leave Rev. King Unbowed," *Jet* 19, no. 3 (November 10, 1960): 4, https://books.google.com/books?id=8K4DAAAAMBAJ&printsec=front cover&source=gbs_ge_summary_r&cad=0#v=onepage&q&f=false.
94. Steven Levingston, *Kennedy and King: The President, The Pastor, and the Battle over Civil Rights* (New York: Hachette Books, 2017), 88–91, 95, 98, 101, 114.
95. Penrice, *African American History for Dummies,*168.
96. Jonathan Capehart, "Children 'Stripped of Innocence' during the Civil Rights Movement: 'Voices of the Movement' Episode 2 Transcript," *Washington Post*, April 11, 2019, https://www.washingtonpost.com/opinions/2019/04/11/children -stripped-innocence-during-civil-rights-movement-voices-movement-episode/.
97. Capehart, "Children."
98. "The Modern Civil Rights Movement and the Kennedy Administration," John F. Kennedy Presidential Library and Museum, https://www.jfklibrary.org/learn /about-jfk/jfk-in-history/civil-rights-movement.
99. Levingston, *Kennedy and King*, 120–21.
100. Levingston, 170.
101. Levingston, 135–38, 175–84.
102. Levingston, 268–76, 397–99.
103. Patrick J. Sloyan, *The Politics of Deception: JFK's Secret Decisions on Vietnam, Civil Rights, and Cuba* (New York: Thomas Dunn Books, 2015), 95–98.
104. Levingston, *Kennedy and King*, 56, 66, 257, 290–93, 405, 432.
105. McPherson, *"To the Best of My Ability,"* 250–56; and Levingston, *Kennedy and King*, 224–23.
106. Levingston, *Kennedy and King*, 400–401.
107. "Televised Address to the Nation on Civil Rights," John F. Kennedy Presidential Library and Museum, June 11, 1963, https://www.jfklibrary.org/learn /about-jfk/historic-speeches/televised-address-to-the-nation-on-civil-rights.
108. Levingston, *Kennedy and King*, 399–407.
109. "November 22, 1963: Death of the President," John F. Kennedy Presidential Library and Museum, https://www.jfklibrary.org/learn/about-jfk/jfk-in-history /november-22-1963-death-of-the-president.
110. "First 'True'Colored Doll," *Jet* 1, no. 2 (November 8, 1951): 27, https://books .google.com/books?id=I0MDAAAAMBAJ&printsec=frontcover&source =gbs_ge_summary_r&cad=0#v=onepage&q&f=false.
111. "Negro College Booming," 48.
112. J. Fred MacDonald, "The Golden Age of Blacks in Television: The Late 1960s" in *Blacks and White TV: Afro-Americans in Television since 1948* (Chicago: Nelson-Hall Publishers, 1983), 107–30.
113. Curtis Bunn, "Sidney Portier Changed Blackness in the Eyes of a Generation of Black People," NBC News, January 8, 2022, https://www.nbcnews.com/news /nbcblk/sidney-poitier-changed-blackness-eyes-generation-black-people-rcna11375.
114. David Cecelski, "George Graham: Fried Shad on Blue Monday," *News & Observer*, April 13, 2003, https://www.ncpedia.org/listening-to-history/graham -george.

115. Terkel, *Race*, 197–99.

116. David Cecelski, "Judith Shaw: Railroad Street," *News & Observer*, April 10, 2005, https://www.ncpedia.org/listening-to-history/shaw-judith.

117. David Cecelski, "Kenny Davis: It's Like Being at War," *News & Observer*, December 13, 1998, https://www.ncpedia.org/listening-to-history/davis-kenny.

118. *By Any Means Necessary: The Times of Godfather of Harlem*, episode 1, "Mecca," directed by Keith McQuirter, Epix, 2020.

119. David Cecelski, "Eddie McCoy: Write-Off Kids," *News & Observer*, December 12, 2004, https://www.ncpedia.org/listening-to-history/mccoy-eddie.

120. "Nonviolent Philosophy and Self Defense," Library of Congress, https://www.loc.gov/collections/civil-rights-history-project/articles-and-essays/nonviolent-philosophy-and-self-defense/.

121. Ibram X. Kendi, ed., *Four Hundred Souls: A Community History of African America, 1619–2019* (New York: One World, 2021), 330–31.

122. Maura Cheeks, "American Wealth Is Broken," *Atlantic*, July 31, 2019, https://www.theatlantic.com/family/archive/2019/07/the-wealth-gap-taints-americas-success-stories/593719/.

123. David Cecelski, "Gary Grant: A Boy Scout Jamboree to Remember," *News & Observer*, April 14, 2002, https://www.ncpedia.org/listening-to-history/grant-gary.

124. Kathleen Ronayne, "Harris Pays Tribute to Black Women in 1st Speech as VP-Elect," *Washington Post*, November 7, 2020, https://www.washingtonpost.com/politics/harris-pays-tribute-to-black-women-in-1st-speech-as-vp-elect/2020/11/07/9f627aea-216c-11eb-ad53-4c1fda49907d_story.html.

125. David Cecelski, "Dr. James Slade: People That Do Right," *News & Observer*, February 11, 2001, https://www.ncpedia.org/listening-to-history/slade-james.

126. Ed Gordon and Melinda Chateauvert, "Blacks Face Challenges as Boomers Turn 60," NPR, April 26, 2006, https://www.npr.org/templates/story/story.php?storyId=5363453.

127. Meredith Conroy and Perry Bacon Jr., "The Partisan, Gender and Generational Differences among Black Voters Heading into Election Day," ABC News: FiveThirtyEight, September 23, 2020, https://fivethirtyeight.com/features/the-partisan-gender-and-generational-differences-among-black-voters-heading-into-election-day/.

128. David Cecelski, "Karen Bethea-Shields: In Joan Little's Cell," *News & Observer*, January 12, 2003, https://www.ncpedia.org/listening-to-history/bethea-shields.

129. Cheeks, "American Wealth Is Broken."

130. Charlie Nelms, "Ten Things That Worry Me Most as an African American Baby Boomer," *HuffPost*, October 17, 2017, https://www.huffpost.com/entry/ten-things-that-worry-me-most-as-an-african-american_b_59e628b1e4b04e9111a3e534.

131. Shirl Spicer, "Golden A. Frinks," *Tar Heel Junior Historian*, Fall 2004, https://www.ncpedia.org/biography/frinks-golden.

132. Sheiresa Ngo, "AARP Releases Survey of African American Baby Boomers," *Black Enterprise*, June 11, 2014, https://www.blackenterprise.com/aarp-releases-survey-of-african-american-baby-boomers/.

133. David Cecelski, "Bessie Mizell: We Are All in This Together," *News & Observer*, August 11, 2002, https://www.ncpedia.org/listening-to-history/mizell-bessie.

134. Allison Klein, "Billionaire Robert F. Smith Pledges to Pay Off Morehouse College Class of 2019's Student Loans," *Washington Post*, May 19, 2019, https://www.washingtonpost.com/lifestyle/2019/05/19/billionaire-robert-f-smith-pledges-pay-off-morehouse-college-class-s-student-loans/.

135. Sally Hicks, "Talking 'bout My Generation," *Duke Magazine*, May–June 2005, https://alumni.duke.edu/magazine/articles/talking-bout-my-generation.
136. Gordon and Chateauvert, "Blacks Face Challenges."
137. Cyd Hoskinson, "African American Baby Boomers and Retirement," WJCT News, May 16, 2013, https://news.wjct.org/post/african-american-baby -boomers-and-retirement.
138. Dan Murphy, Richard W. Johnson, and Gordon B. T. Mermin, "Racial Differences in Baby Boomers' Retirement Expectations," *Older Americans' Economic Security*, no. 13 (May 2007), https://www.urban.org/research/publication /racial-differences-baby-boomers-retirement-expectations.

Chapter 4: Hip-Hop Generation

1. Bakari Kitwana, *The Hip-Hop Generation: Young Blacks and the Crisis in African-American Culture* (New York: Civitas Books, 2002), 4.
2. "Generations X, Y, Z and the Others," W J Schroer Company, http://social marketing.org/archives/generations-xy-z-and-the-others/.
3. Vena Moore, "The Invisible Black Gen-Xer," Medium, November 8, 2019, https://medium.com/the-forgotten-generation/the-invisible-black-gen-xer -80fd7a420c40.
4. Robert Siegel and Bakari Kitwana, "The Hip-Hop Generation," NPR: All Things Considered, July 2, 2002, https://www.npr.org/templates/story/story .php?storyId=1146009.
5. Siegel and Kitwana, "The Hip-Hop Generation."
6. Kitwana, *Hip-Hop Generation*, 13
7. Kitwana, 13–14.
8. Moore, "The Invisible Black Gen-Xer."
9. Brian Jones, "Growing Up Black in America: Here's My Story of Everyday Racism," *Guardian*, June 6, 2018, https://www.theguardian.com/us-news/2018 /jun/06/growing-up-black-in-america-racism-education.
10. AARP, "High Anxiety: New York City African American and Black Gen X and Boomers Struggle with Stress, Savings and Security," 2015 survey, https://www .aarp.org/content/dam/aarp/research/surveys_statistics/econ/2015/2015 -NYC-AAB-Survey-GenX-Boomer-Voters-res-econ-us.pdf.
11. Baratunde Thurston, *How to Be Black* (New York: HarperCollins, 2013), 80.
12. Thurston, 38–39.
13. Studs Terkel, *Race: How Blacks & Whites Think & Feel about the American Obsession* (New York: The New Press, 1992), 160.
14. Erin Currier, "How Generation X Could Change the American Dream," Pew, January 26, 2018, https://www.pewtrusts.org/en/trend/archive/winter-2018 /how-generation-x-could-change-the-american-dream.
15. Adam Serwer, "Lyndon Johnson Was a Civil Rights Hero. But Also a Racist," MSNBC, April 11, 2014, https://www.msnbc.com/msnbc/lyndon-johnson -civil-rights-racism-msna305591.
16. Monroe Billington, "Lyndon B. Johnson and Blacks: The Early Years," *Journal of Negro History* 62, no. 1 (January 1977), https://www.jstor.org/stable/2717189.
17. Billington, "Lyndon B. Johnson and Blacks."
18. Billington, "Lyndon B. Johnson and Blacks."
19. "The 1960s History," History.com, June 26, 2020, https://www.history.com /topics/1960s/1960s-history.
20. DeNeen L. Brown, "Shoot Them for What? How Muhammad Ali Won His Greatest Fight," *Washington Post*, June 16, 2018, https://www.washingtonpost

.com/news/retropolis/wp/2018/06/15/shoot-them-for-what-how-muhammad
-ali-won-his-greatest-fight/.

21. "The Four Days in 1968 That Reshaped D.C.," *Washington Post*, March 27, 2018, https://www.washingtonpost.com/graphics/2018/local/dc-riots-1968/.

22. Michael E. Ruane, "Fifty Years Ago Some Called D.C. 'the Colored Man's Paradise.' The Paradise Erupted," *Washington Post*, March 26, 2018, https://www.washington post.com/local/fifty-years-ago-some-called-dc-the-colored-mans-paradise-then -paradise-erupted/2018/03/22/6ae9ec1c-208e-11e8-94da-ebf9d112159c_story.html.

23. Billington, "Lyndon B. Johnson and Blacks."

24. Michael J. Klarman, *Unfinished Business: Racial Equality in American History* (Oxford: Oxford University Press, 2007), 176.

25. Ronda Racha Penrice, *African American History for Dummies* (Hoboken, NJ: Wiley Publishing, 2007), 169–74.

26. Marcia A. Smith, *Black America: A Photographic Journey* (New York: Fall River Press, 2009), 280.

27. James M. McPherson, *"To the Best of My Ability": The American Presidents* (New York: Dorling Kindersley, 2000), 258–64.

28. Alice George, "The 1968 Kerner Commission Got It Right, but Nobody Listened," *Smithsonian Magazine*, March 1, 2018, https://www.smithsonianmag .com/smithsonian-institution/1968-kerner-commission-got-it-right-nobody -listened-180968318/.

29. "Quick with the Revolver," University of Virginia: Miller Center, Presidential Recordings Digital Edition, June 1, 2020, https://millercenter.org/the-presidency /educational-resources/quick-revolver.

30. Kent B. Germany, "Lyndon B. Johnson and Civil Rights," https://prde.upress .virginia.edu/content/CivilRights.

31. Ted Gittinger and Allen Fisher, "LBJ Champions the Civil Rights Act of 1964," *Prologue Magazine* 36, no. 2 (Summer 2004), https://www.archives.gov/publications /prologue/2004/summer/civil-rights-act-1.html.

32. "The Other Gettysburg Addresses: Presidential Orations at Gettysburg–Part 3," From the Fields of Gettysburg: The Blog of Gettysburg National Military Park, https://npsgnmp.wordpress.com/2016/02/20/the-other-gettysburg-addresses -presidential-orations-at-gettysburg-part-3/.

33. David M. Shribman, "L.B.J.'s Gettysburg Address," *New York Times*, May 24, 2013, https://www.nytimes.com/2013/05/26/sunday-review/at-gettysburg -johnson-marked-memorial-day-and-the-future.html.

34. Colleen Shogan, "'We Shall Overcome': Lyndon Johnson and the 1965 Voting Rights Act," The White House Historical Association, https://www.whitehouse history.org/we-shall-overcome-lbj-voting-rights.

35. Shogan, "'We Shall Overcome.'"

36. Billington, "Lyndon B. Johnson and Blacks."

37. Serwer, "Lyndon Johnson Was a Civil Rights Hero."

38. Sheeri Mitchell, "The Blacks of the 1960s: Black History from the Pages of *Ebony*," *Ebony*, February 27, 2020, https://www.ebony.com/black-history /bhm-ebony-blacks-1960s/.

39. Mitchell, "The Blacks of the 1960s."

40. "Richard Nixon: 37th President of the United States: 1969–1974. Remarks in New York City Accepting Election as the 37th President of the United States," The American Presidency Project, November 6, 1968, https://www.presidency .ucsb.edu/documents/remarks-new-york-city-accepting-election-the-37th-president -the-united-states.

41. "Negro in Cabinet 'Positive': Jackie Robinson," *Jet* 19, no. 3 (November 10, 1960): 7, https://books.google.com/books?id=8K4DAAAAMBAJ&printsec =frontcover#v=onepage&q&f=false.

42. "Nixon, Richard Milhous," Stanford: The Martin Luther King, Jr. Research and Education Institute, https://kinginstitute.stanford.edu/encyclopedia /nixon-richard-milhous.

43. "Nixon, Richard Milhous."

44. Tim Weiner, "Richard Nixon: The Most Dangerous Man in America," *In These Times*, July 14, 2015, https://inthesetimes.com/article/richard-nixon-tim-weiner.

45. "Nixon, Richard Milhous."

46. Tim Naftali, "Ronald Reagan's Long-Hidden Racist Conversation with Richard Nixon," *Atlantic*, July 30, 2019, https://www.theatlantic.com/ideas /archive/2019/07/ronald-reagans-racist-conversation-richard-nixon/595102/.

47. "Nixon, Richard Milhous."

48. Naftali, "Ronald Reagan's Long-Hidden Racist Conversation."

49. Naftali, "Ronald Reagan's Long-Hidden Racist Conversation."

50. "Racial Tension in the 1970s," The White House Historical Association, https://www.whitehousehistory.org/racial-tension-in-the-1970s.

51. "Nixon's Record on Civil Rights," Richard Nixon Foundation, August 4, 2017, https://www.nixonfoundation.org/2017/08/nixons-record-civil-rights-2/.

52. "Congressional Black Caucus (CBC)," National Archives: African American Heritage, https://www.archives.gov/research/african-americans/black-power /cbc.

53. Robert E. Weems Jr. and Lewis A. Randolph, "The National Response to Richard M. Nixon's Black Capitalism Initiative: The Success of Domestic Détente," *Journal of Black Studies* 32, no. 1 (September 2001), https://www.jstor .org/stable/2668015.

54. German Lopez, "Was Nixon's War on Drugs a Racially Motivated Crusade? It's a Bit More Complicated," Vox, March 29, 2016, https://www.vox.com/2016 /3/29/11325750/nixon-war-on-drugs.

55. Dan Baum, "Legalize It All: How to Win the War on Drugs," *Harper's Magazine*, April 2016, https://harpers.org/archive/2016/04/legalize-it-all/, and Mark J. Perry, "The Shocking Story behind Richard Nixon's 'War on Drugs' That Targeted Blacks and Anti-War Activists," American Enterprise Institute, June 14, 2018, https://www.aei.org/carpe-diem/the-shocking-and-sickening-story -behind-nixons-war-on-drugs-that-targeted-blacks-and-anti-war-activists/.

56. Scott Laderman, "How Richard Nixon Captured White Rage—and Laid the Groundwork for Donald Trump," *Washington Post*, November 3, 2019, https://www.washingtonpost.com/outlook/2019/11/03/how-richard-nixon -captured-white-rage-laid-groundwork-donald-trump/.

57. Michelle Alexander, *The New Jim Crow: Mass Incarceration in the Age of Colorblindness* (New York: The New Press, 2012), 143.

58. Brody Shields, "The Civil Rights Presidents: FDR to Nixon," University of Montana, undergraduate research (2015), https://digitalcommons.mtech.edu /urp_aug_2015/2.

59. McPherson, *"To the Best of My Ability,"* 266–72.

60. Toluse Olorunnipa and Griff Witte, "George Floyd's America: Born with Two Strikes: How Systemic Racism Shaped Floyd's Life and Hobbled His Ambition," *Washington Post*, October 8, 2020, https://www.washingtonpost.com/graphics /2020/national/george-floyd-america/systemic-racism/.

61. Don Gonyea, "The Civil Rights Stand of a Young Gerald Ford," NPR, July 14, 2013, https://www.npr.org/2013/07/14/201946977/the-civil-rights-stand-of-a -young-gerald-ford.

62. Earl Ofari Hutchinson, "Ford: The Conflicted President on Civil Rights," *HuffPost*, May 25, 2011, https://www.huffpost.com/entry/ford-the-conflicted -presi_b_37279.

63. Thomas N. Maloney, "African Americans in the Twentieth Century," Economic History Association, https://eh.net/encyclopedia/african-americans-in-the -twentieth-century/.

64. Sheeri Mitchell, "The Afro-Americans of the 1970s: Black History from the Pages of *Ebony*," *Ebony*, February 25, 2020, https://www.ebony.com/black -history/bhm-ebony-afro-americans-1970s/.

65. Linda Darling-Hammond, "Unequal Opportunity: Race and Education," Brookings, March 1, 1998, https://www.brookings.edu/articles/unequal -opportunity-race-and-education/.

66. "School Desegregation," Encyclopedia.com, October 3, 2020, https://www .encyclopedia.com/social-sciences-and-law/law/law/school-integration.

67. Nathan Miller, *Star-Spangled Men: America's Ten Worst Presidents* (New York: Touch-stone Books, 1998), 27.

68. Robert A. Strong, "Jimmy Carter: Life before the Presidency," University of Virginia: Miller Center, https://millercenter.org/president/carter/life-before -the-presidency.

69. Miller, *Star-Spangled Men*, 33.

70. Strong, "Jimmy Carter."

71. Chuck Stone, "Black Political Power in the Carter Era," *Black Scholar* 8, no. 4 (January–February 1977): 6.

72. Robert Reinhold, "Poll Shows Blacks Decisive for Carter in Lead over Ford," *New York Times*, June 2, 1976, https://www.nytimes.com/1976/06/02/archives /poll-shows-blacks-decisive-for-carter-in-lead-over-ford-blacks.html.

73. Nadra Nareem Nittle, "President Jimmy Carter's Record on Civil Rights and Race Relations," ThoughtCo., January 16, 2018, https://www.thoughtco.com /president-jimmy-carters-civil-rights-record-2834612.

74. Bakari Kitwana, "The State of the Hip-Hop Generation: How Hip-Hop's Cultural Movement Is Evolving into Political Power," *Diogenes* 51, issue 3, https:// journals.sagepub.com/doi/pdf/10.1177/0392192104043662.

75. Ed Gordon and Russell Simmons, "Hip Hop Action Summit," NPR, July 13, 2006, https://www.npr.org/templates/story/story.php?storyId=5554608.

76. Kitwana, *Hip-Hop Generation*, 12–13.

77. Troy Smith, "Chelsea Handler Says Rapper 50 Cent Can't Support Trump 'Because He's Black,'" *Slingshop News*, June 7, 2024, https://slingshot.news /chelsea-handler-says-rapper-50-cent-cant-support-trump-because-hes-black/.

78. Gil Kaufman, "50 Cent Backtracks on His Donald Trump Endorsement: 'I Never Liked Him,'" *Billboard*, October 26, 2020, https://www.billboard .com/articles/columns/hip-hop/9472990/50-cent-reverses-donald-trump -endorsement.

79. Gene Demby, "Harry Belafonte, Jay Z and Intergenerational Beef," NPR: Code Switch, July 30, 2013, https://www.npr.org/sections /codeswitch/2013/07/30/207068455/harry-belafonte-jay-z-and-inter -generational-beef.

80. Kitwana, *Hip-Hop Generation*, 85–119.

81. Ronald E. Franklin, "Should Parents Give Their Children Distinctively 'Black' Names?," We Have Kids, November 12, 2019, https://wehavekids.com /parenting/Should-Parents-Give-Their-Children-Distinctively-Black-Names.

82. Roland G. Fryer Jr. and Steven D. Levitt, "The Causes and Consequences of Distinctively Black Names," *Quarterly Journal of Economics*, August 2004, 767, 770, 786, 801.

83. Fryer and Levitt, "The Causes and Consequences of Distinctively Black Names."

Chapter 5: #BlackLivesMatter Generation

1. M. K. Asante Jr., *It's Bigger Than Hip Hop: The Rise of the Post-Hip-Hop Generation* (New York: St. Martin's Griffin, 2008), 18.

2. Monica Anderson, Skye Toor, Lee Rainie, and Aaron Smith, "An Analysis of #BlackLivesMatter and Other Twitter Hashtags Related to Political or Social Issues," Pew Research Center, https://www.pewresearch.org/internet/2018 /07/11/an-analysis-of-blacklivesmatter-and-other-twitter-hashtags-related-to -political-or-social-issues/.

3. Asante, *It's Bigger Than Hip Hop*, 7.

4. Jenny Jarvie, "Why the Gap between Old and New Black Civil Rights Activists Is Widening," *Los Angeles Times*, July 28, 2016, https://www.latimes.com/nation /la-na-civil-rights-generation-gap-20160713-snap-story.html.

5. Tom Exter, "A Portrait of African American Millennials," Ebony Marketing Systems, January 5, 2016, https://www.ebonysystems.com/a-portrait-of-african -american-millennials/

6. Jill N. Filipovic, "Boomers Are the Real Reason Millennials Won't Be Buying Homes Anytime Soon," New America, August 13, 2020, https://www.new america.org/weekly/boomers-are-the-real-reason-millenials-wont-be-buying -homes-anytime-soon/, excerpted from her book *OK Boomer, Let's Talk* (New York: One Signal/Atria Books, 2020).

7. "Increasingly Affluent, Educated and Diverse: African-American Consumers," Nielsen, September 2015, https://www.nielsen.com/us/en/insights/report /2015/increasingly-affluent-educated-and-diverse-african-american-consumers/.

8. Jon C. Rogowski and Cathy J. Cohen, "Black Millennials in America: Document-ing the Experiences, Voices and Political Future of Young Black Americans," Black Youth Project, https://blackyouthproject.com/wp-content/uploads /2015/11/BYP-millenials-report-10-27-15-FINAL.pdf.

9. Abby Budiman, "Key Facts about Black Eligible Voters in 2020 Battleground States," Pew Research Center, October 21, 2020, https://www.pewresearch .org/fact-tank/2020/10/21/key-facts-about-black-eligible-voter-in-2020 -battleground-states/.

10. Reniqua Allen, "The Missing Black Millennial," *Al Jazeera*, February 20, 2019, https://newrepublic.com/article/153122/missing-black-millennial.

11. Exter, "African American Millennials."

12. Hillary Hoffower, "Black Millennial Households Earn About 60% of What Their White Counterparts Make, and It Highlights Just How Much Worse the Generational Wealth Gap Is along Racial Lines," *Business Insider*, July 23, 2020, https://www.businessinsider.com/black-millennials-student-debt-earnings -wealth-2020-7.

13. Leslie Hunter-Gadsden, "Why People of Color Feel the Loneliest at Work," Next Avenue, May 18, 2020, https://www.nextavenue.org/people-of-color -loneliest-at-work/.

14. "Being Black in Corporate America: An Intersectional Exploration," Coequal (formerly CTI), https://coqual.org/wp-content/uploads/2020/09/Coqual BeingBlackinCorporateAmerica090720-1.pdf.

15. Studs Terkel, *Race: How Blacks & Whites Think & Feel About The American Obsession* (New York: The New Press, 1992), 295.

16. Charlayne Hunter-Gault, "Special Issue Life: The Dream Then and Now," *Life Magazine*, Spring 1988, 46.

17. Hunter-Gault, "Special Issue Life," 46.

18. Abigall Thernstrom and Stephan Thernstrom, "Black Progress: How Far We've Come, and How Far We Have To Go," Brookings, March 1, 1998, https://www .brookings.edu/articles/black-progress-how-far-weve-come-and-how-far-we-have -to-go/.

19. Justin Elliott, "Reagan's Embrace of Apartheid South Africa," Salon, February 5, 2011, https://www.salon.com/2011/02/05/ronald_reagan_apartheid _south_africa/.

20. Andrew Glass, "House Overrides Reagan Apartheid Veto, September 29, 1986," Politico, September 9, 2017, https://www.politico.com/story/2017/09 /29/house-overrides-reagan-apartheid-veto-sept-29-1986-243169.

21. Glass, "House Overrides Reagan."

22. Glass, "House Overrides Reagan."

23. "The 1980s," History.com, April 23, 2018, https://www.history.com/topics /1980s/1980s.

24. James M. McPherson, *"To the Best of My Ability": The American Presidents* (New York: Dorling Kindersley, 2000), 288–94.

25. "African American Life in Reagan's America," College Sidekick, https:// courses.lumenlearning.com/ushistory2ay/chapter /african-american-life-in -reagans-america-2/.

26. Michele Lerner, "One Home, a Lifetime of Impact," *Washington Post*, July 23, 2020, https://www.washingtonpost.com/business/2020/07/23/black -homeownership-gap/?arc404=true.

27. Tracy Jan, "Redlining Was Banned 50 Years Ago. It's Still Hurting Minorities Today," *Washington Post*, March 28, 2018, https://www.washingtonpost.com/news /wonk/wp/2018/03/28/redlining-was-banned-50-years-ago-its-still-hurting -minorities-today/.

28. Christine Tamir, Abby Budiman, Luis Noe-Bustamante, and Lauren Mora, "Facts about the U.S. Black Population," Pew Research Center, January 18, 2024, https://www.pewresearch.org/social-trends/fact-sheet/facts-about-the-us-black -population/.

29. Lerner, "One Home."

30. Lerner, "One Home."

31. "Social and Economic Issues of the 1980s and 1990s," Amistad Digital Resource, https://www.amistadresource.org/the_future_in_the_present/social_and _economic_issues.html.

32. "Social and Economic Issues."

33. "Ronald Reagan: No Defence for 'Monkeys' Remark, Says Daughter," BBC News, August 2, 2019, https://www.bbc.com/news/world-us-canada-49207451.

34. Bernard Weinraub, "Reagan Apologizes for Asserting That Pretoria Segregation Is Over," *New York Times*, September 7, 1985, https://www.nytimes.com/1985 /09/07/world/reagan-apologizes-for-asserting-that-pretoria-segregation-is-over .html.

35. Terkel, *Race*, 356.

36. Eugene Scott, "The New Reagan Tapes Are Ugly, but Not Surprising, to a Lot of Black Americans," *Washington Post*, July 31, 2019, https://www.washingtonpost .com/politics/2019/07/31/new-reagan-tapes-are-ugly-not-surprising-lot -black-americans/.

37. Hunter-Gault, "Special Issue Life," 44.

38. Hunter-Gault, "Special Issue Life," 44.

39. William C. Love, "Benjamin Hooks, Ronald Reagan and Economic Inequality," The University of Memphis: Benjamin Lawson Hooks Papers, https://www .memphis.edu/hookspapers/topics/blh_reagan.php.

40. Love, "Benjamin Hooks, Ronald Reagan and Economic Inequality."

41. "Remembering President Reagan's Civil Rights Legacy," NPR: Tell Me More, February 4, 2011, https://www.npr.org/2011/02/04/133497430/Remembering -Presidents-Reagan-Civil-Rights-Legacy.

42. Steven R. Weisman, "Reagan Says Blacks Were Hurt by Works of the Great Society," *New York Times*, September 16, 1982, https://www.nytimes.com/1982 /09/16/us/reagan-says-blacks-were-hurt-by-works-of-the-great-society.html.

43. George J. Church, "A National Holiday for King: But Not Without Rancor," *Time*, October 31, 1983, https://time.com/vault/issue/1983-10-31/page/38/.

44. "Remembering President Reagan's Civil Rights Legacy."

45. "Reagan, Nixon and Race," University of Virginia: Miller Center, https:// millercenter.org/the-presidency/educational-resources/reagan-nixon-and-race.

46. Renee Graham, "Why Is Anyone Surprised by Reagan's Racism?," *Boston Globe*, August 2, 2019, https://www.bostonglobe.com/opinion/2019/08/02/why -anyone-surprised-reagan-racism/wVSXLxvnSXV2WlUJ3rbcQL/story.html.

47. Monica Rhor, "George H. W. Bush Leaves Mixed Record on Race, Civil Rights," *USA Today*, December 4, 2018, https://www.usatoday.com/story /news/2018/12/03/george-h-w-bush-race-civil-rights-war-drugs /2197675002/.

48. Elliott, "Reagan's Embrace."

49. Milton Coleman and Kenneth E. John, "Reagan Rating Falls in Poll of Blacks," *Washington Post*, January 18, 1986, https://www.washingtonpost.com/archive /politics/1986/01/18/reagan-rating-falls-in-poll-of-blacks/b452138c-46ba-4353 -b6d7-eb895d650bdc/.

50. Tiffanie Darke, "The 1990s: When Technology Upended Our World," History .com, January 31, 2019, https://www.history.com/news/90s-technology-changed -culture-internet-cellphones?li_source=LI&li_medium=m2m-rcw-history.

51. Marcia A. Smith, *Black America: A Photographic Journey* (New York: Fall River Press, 2009), 346–47.

52. "The Reagan Years: 1980s: Apex of Black Political Power in the Age of Reagan," Picture This: California Perspectives on American History, http://picturethis .museumca.org/timeline/reagan-years-1980s/african-american-culture/info.

53. Terkel, *Race*, 95–96.

54. "A Tribute to 41 and His 'Kinder, Gentler' Legacy," *PBS News Hour*, December 1, 2018, https://www.pbs.org/newshour/show/a-tribute-to-41-and-his-kinder -gentler-legacy.

55. McPherson, *"To the Best of My Ability,"* 302–6.

56. Erin Haines, "What Was George H. W. Bush's Record on Race?," PBS: News Hour, December 4, 2018, https://www.pbs.org/newshour/politics/what-was -george-h-w-bushs-record-on-race.

57. Haines, "What Was George."

58. Wayne Dawkins, "George H. W. Bush's Complicated History with Blacks," *Washington Informer*, December 5, 2018, https://www.washingtoninformer.com/dawkins -george-h-w-bushs-complicated-history-with-blacks/.

59. Haines, "What Was George."

60. Haines, "What Was George."

61. Rhor, "George H. W. Bush."

62. Ann Devroy, "Bush Vetoes Civil Rights Bill," *Washington Post*, October 23, 1990, https://www.washingtonpost.com/archive/politics/1990/10/23/bush-vetoes -civil-rights-bill/cd68a6c4-8529-471a-b4f7-08c26cf65ac0/.

63. Devroy, "Bush Vetoes Civil Rights Bill."

64. Michelle Alexander, *The New Jim Crow: Mass Incarceration in the Age of Colorblindness* (New York: The New Press, 2012), 54.

65. Peter Baker, "Bush Made Willie Horton an Issue in 1988, and the Racial Scars Are Still Fresh," *New York Times*, December 3, 2018, https://www.nytimes.com /2018/12/03/us/politics/bush-willie-horton.html.

66. Smith, *Black America*, 345–79.

67. Smith, 345.

68. "Social and Economic Issues," https://www.amistadresource.org/the_future_in _the_present/social_and_economic_issues.html.

69. Smith, *Black America*, 344.

70. Clarence Page,"The '80s Have Been a Mixed Bag for Black Americans," *Chicago Tribune*, November 29, 1989, https://www.chicagotribune.com/news/ct-xpm -1989-11-29-8903130755-story.html.

71. Jonathan Peterson, "Clinton Tells Tuskegee Survivors: 'I Am Sorry,'" *Los Angeles Times*, May 17, 1997, https://www.latimes.com/archives/la-xpm-1997-05-17 -mn-59624-story.html.

72. "Donald Trump Fast Facts," CNN, October 4, 2020, https://www.cnn.com/ 2013/07/04/us/donald-trump-fast-facts/index.html.

73. Sheeri Mitchell, "Black History from the Pages of *Ebony*: The African-Americans of the 1990s," *Ebony*, February 21, 2020, https://www.ebony.com/exclusive /bhm-ebony-1990s/.

74. Danielle Kurtzleben, "Understanding the Clintons' Popularity with Black Voters," NPR, March 1, 2016, https://www.npr.org/2016/03/01/468185698 /understanding-the-clintons-popularity-with-black-voters.

75. "George W. Bush, the NAACP, and the Persistent Damage to Black Higher Education," *Journal of Blacks in Higher Education*, https://www.jbhe.com/features /51_specialreport.html.

76. Kurtzleben, "Understanding the Clintons' Popularity."

77. Alexander, *The New Jim Crow*, 55–58.

78. Donna Murch, "The Clintons' War on Drugs: When Black Lives Didn't Matter," *New Republic*, February 9, 2016, https://newrepublic.com/article/129433 /clintons-war-drugs-black-lives-didnt-matter.

79. Murch, "The Clintons' War on Drugs."

80. "Rebirth," Spotify, track 2 on Public Enemy, *Apocalypse 91 . . . The Enemy Strikes Back*, Def Jam, 1991; lyrics available at https://genius.com/Public-enemy -rebirth-lyrics.

81. Graham C. Kinlock, "Black America in the 1980s: Theoretical And Practical Implications," *Humboldt Journal of Social Relations* 14, no. 1/2 (1987), https://www .jstor.org/stable/23262550.

82. DeWayne Wickham, *Bill Clinton and Black America* (New York: Ballantine Books, 2002), 1.

83. Marc Mauer, "Bill Clinton, 'Black Lives' and the Myths of the 1994 Crime Bill," *The Marshall Project*, April 11, 2016, https://www.themarshallproject.org /2016/04/11/bill-clinton-black-lives-and-the-myths-of-the-1994-crime-bill.

84. Reniqua Allen, *It Was All a Dream: A New Generation Confronts the Broken Promise to Black America* (New York: Nation Books, 2019).

85. Allen, "The Missing Black Millennial."

86. Allen, "The Missing Black Millennial."

87. Allen, "The Missing Black Millennial."

88. Jessica Bailey, "Zendaya: 'Criticisms to Black Women Are Still Happening,'" *Grazia Magazine*, https://graziamagazine.com/articles/zendaya-guest-edit -opinion-piece/.

89. Akin Bruce, "Generational Differences among African Americans in Their Per- ceptions of Economic Opportunity," *Urban Edge*, Rice University Kinder Institute for Urban Research, July 4, 2018, https://kinder.rice.edu/2018/07/04 /generational-differences-among-african-americans-their-perceptions-economic -opportunity.

90. Terkel, *Race*, 294.

91. Ellis Cose, "The Black Generation Gap," *The Root*, June 1, 2011, https://www .theroot.com/the-black-generation-gap-1790864171.

92. Mia Scott, "Nielsen 2016 Report: Black Millennials Close the Digital Divide," Nielsen, October 17, 2016, https://www.nielsen.com/us/en/press-releases/2016 /nielsen-2016-report-black-millennials-close-the-digital-divide/.

93. Jack Loechner, "African American Millennials 1/4 of Black Population," Media- Post, October 27, 2016, https://www.mediapost.com/publications/article /287429/african-american-millennials-14-of-black-populati.html.

94. "Save Our Cities: Powering the Digital Revolution Annual Report 2018," National Urban League, https://nul.org/sites/default/files/2019-10/NUL _AR2018.pdf.

95. Bobby Allyn, "Ousted Black Google Researcher: 'They Wanted To Have My Presence, But Not Me Exactly,'" NPR, December 17, 2020, https://www.npr .org/2020/12/17/947719354/ousted-black-google-researcher-they-wanted-to -have-my-presence-but-not-me-exactl.

96. DeNeen L. Brown, "In Ferguson, Young Demonstrators Are Finding It's Not Their Grandparents' Protest," *Washington Post*, August 21, 2014, https://www .washingtonpost.com/politics/in-ferguson-young-demonstrators-are-finding -its-not-their-grandparents-protest/2014/08/21/95110be0-28a0-11e4-86ca -6f03cbd15c1a_story.html.

97. Brown, "In Ferguson, Young Demonstrators."

98. Yoni Appelbaum, "A Single Photo from Baton Rouge That's Hard to Forget," *Atlantic*, July 10, 2016, https://www.theatlantic.com/notes/2016/07/a-single -photo-that-captures-race-and-policing-in-america/490664/.

99. Kim Parker, "Within the Black Community, Young and Old Differ on Police Searches, Discrimination," Pew Research Center, August 27, 2014, https://www .pewresearch.org/fact-tank/2014/08/27/within-the-black-community-young -and-old-differ-on-police-searches-discrimination/.

100. Scott Clement, "Millennials Are Just About as Racist as Their Parents," *Washing- ton Post*, April 7, 2015, https://www.washingtonpost.com/news/wonk/wp/2015 /04/07/white-millennials-are-just-about-as-racist-as-their-parents/.

101. Jonathan Capehart, "A New Survey Shows White Millennials Think a Lot More Like Whites than Millennials," *Washington Post*, October 31, 2017, https://www

.washingtonpost.com/blogs/post-partisan/wp/2017/10/31/a-new-survey-shows
-white-millennials-think-a-lot-more-like-whites-than-millennials/?utm_term=
.b72d6eeaaf5c.

102. Jessica Mendoza, "South Carolina Student Suspended for Racial Slur.
Are Millennials Racist?," *Christian Science Monitor*, https://www.csmonitor
.com/USA/USA-Update/2015/0404/South-Carolina-student-suspended
-for-racial-slur.-Are-millennials-racist.

103. Mychal Denzel Smith, "White Millennials Are Products of a Failed Lesson in
Colorblindness," *PBS News*, March 26, 2015, https://www.pbs.org/newshour
/nation/white-millennials-products-failed-lesson-colorblindness.

104. Smith, "White Millennials."

105. Smith, "White Millennials."

106. Smith, "White Millennials."

107. Perry Bacon Jr., "How Geography and Religion Drive America's Blue vs. Red
Divide," *Washington Post*, May 28, 2024, https://www.washingtonpost.com
/opinions/2024/05/28/political-identity-beyond-education-race/.

108. Amanda Barroso, Kim Parker, and Jesse Bennett, "As Millennials Near 40,
They're Approaching Family Life Differently Than Previous Generations," Pew
Research Center, May 27, 2020, https://www.pewresearch.org/social-trends
/2020/05/27/as-millennials-near-40-theyre-approaching-family-life-differently
-than-previous-generations/.

109. Jeff Diamant and Besheer Mohamed, "Black Millennials Are More Religious
Than Other Millennials," Pew Research Center, July 20, 2018, https://www
.pewresearch.org/fact-tank/2018/07/20/black-millennials-are-more-religious
-than-other-millennials/.

110. Besheer Mohamed, "10 New Findings about Faith among Black Americans,"
Pew Research Center, February 16, 2021, https://www.pewresearch.org/fact
-tank/2021/02/16/10-new-findings-about-faith-among-black-americans/.

Chapter 6: Obama Generation

1. Rodney J. Reynolds, *American Legacy: The Magazine of African-American History &
Culture*, Spring 2009, 2.

2. Christine Tamir, "The Growing Diversity of Black America," Pew Research Center, March 25, 2021, https://www.pewresearch.org/social-trends/2021/03/25
/the-growing-diversity-of-black-america/.

3. Barack Obama, "A More Perfect Union Speech Transcript—Barack Obama,"
Rev, March 18, 2008, https://www.rev.com/blog/transcripts/a-more-perfect
-union-speech-transcript-barack-obama.

4. William H. Frey, "The Nation Is Diversifying Even Faster Than Predicted,
according to New Census Data," Brookings, July 1, 2020, https://www
.brookings.edu/research/new-census-data-shows-the-nation-is-diversifying
-even-faster-than-predicted/.

5. "#BlackHealthFacts and Statistics: A Knowledge Movement," Everyday Health,
https://www.everydayhealth.com/black-health-facts/statistics/.

6. Christine Tamir, "Key Findings about Black America in 2019," Pew Research
Center, March 25, 2021, https://www.pewresearch.org/fact-tank/2021/03/25
/key-findings-about-black-america/.

7. Richard Fry and Kim Parker, "Early Benchmarks Show 'Post-Millennials' on
Track to Be Most Diverse, Best-Educated Generation Yet," Pew Research
Center, November 15, 2018, www.pewsocialtrends.org/2018/11/15/early

-benchmarks-show-post-millennials-on-track-to-be-most-diverse-best-educated
-generation-yet/.

8. Fry and Parker, "Early Benchmarks."
9. Natasha Stoynoff, "Matthew McConaughey Is on a Mission to Heal America," *AARP*, June/July 2021, https://www.aarp.org/entertainment/celebrities/info -2021/matthew-mcconaughey.html.
10. William Frey, *Diversity Explosion: How New Racial Demographics Are Remaking America* (Washington, DC: Brookings Institute, 2018), 1.
11. Christine Tamir, Abby Budiman, Luis Noe-Bustamante, and Lauren Mora, "Facts about the U.S. Black Population," Pew Research Center, January 18, 2024, https://www.pewresearch.org/social-trends/fact-sheet/facts-about-the-us -black-population/.
12. Tim Craig and Aaron Williams, "A New Generation Challenges the Heartland," *Washington Post*, July 11, 2020, https://www.washingtonpost.com/nation /2020/07/11/midwest-changing-demographics-black-lives-matter-protests/.
13. Katherine Schaeffer, "In a Rising Number of U.S. Counties, Hispanic and Black Americans Are the Majority," Pew Research Center, November 20, 2019, https://www.pewresearch.org/fact-tank/2019/11/20/in-a-rising-number-of-u-s -counties-hispanic-and-black-americans-are-the-majority/.
14. Tamir et al., "Facts about the U.S. Black Population."
15. Tamir, "The Growing Diversity."
16. "Black/African American Health," U.S. Department of Health and Human Ser-vices Office of Minority Health, https://minorityhealth.hhs.gov/omh/browse .aspx?lvl=3&lvlid=61.
17. Sheeri Mitchell, "Black History from the Pages of *Ebony*: African-Americans in the Era of Black Lives Matter," *Ebony*, February 18, 2020, https://www.ebony .com/black-history/black-history-month-from-pages-ebony-african-americans -era-black-lives-matter/.
18. "Rep. King Reflects on King, Obama," *All Things Considered*, August 28, 2008, NPR, https://www.npr.org/2008/08/28/94076303/rep-lewis-reflects-on-king-obama.
19. Melinda D. Anderson, "Obama and the Kids: What Has Having a Black Presi-dent Meant to America's Preteens?," *Atlantic*, March 21, 2016, https://www .theatlantic.com/education/archive/2016/03/obama-and-the-kids/474462/.
20. Anderson, "Obama and the Kids."
21. Kanyakrit Vongkiatkajorn, Marian Liu, Rachel Hatzipanagos, and Linah Mohammad, "Voices of Protest," *Washington Post*, June 4, 2020, https://www .washingtonpost.com/graphics/2020/national/protesters-george-floyd.
22. Abigall Thernstrom and Stephan Thernstrom, "Black Progress: How Far We've Come, and How Far We Have to Go," Brookings, March 1, 1998, https://www .brookings.edu/articles/black-progress-how-far-weve-come-and-how-far-we -have-to-go/.
23. Michele Lerner, "One Home, A Lifetime of Impact," *Washington Post*, July 23, 2020, https://www.washingtonpost.com/business/2020/07/23/black -homeownership-gap/?arc404=true.
24. Mohamad Moslimani, Christine Tamir, Abby Budiman, Luis Noe-Bustamante, and Lauren Mora, "Facts about the U.S. Black Population," Pew Research Cen-ter, January 18, 2024, https://www.pewresearch.org/social-trends/fact-sheet /facts-about-the-us-black-population/.
25. Mark Hugo Lopez and Mohamad Moslimani, "Key Facts about the Nation's 47.9 Million Black Americans," Pew Research Center, January 18, 2024, https:// www.pewresearch.org/short-reads/2024/01/18/key-facts-about-black-americans/.

26. Kristen Bialik, "5 Facts about Blacks in the U.S.," Pew Research Center, February 22, 2018, https://www.pewresearch.org/fact-tank/2018/02/22/5-facts-about -blacks-in-the-u-s/.

27. Abby Budiman, "Key Facts about Black Eligible Voters in 2020 Battleground States," Pew Research Center, October 21, 2020, https://www.pewresearch.org /fact-tank/2020/10/21/key-facts-about-black-eligible-voters-in-2020 -battleground-states/.

28. Aaron Williams and Armand Emamdjomeh, "America Is More Diverse Than Ever—But Still Segregated," *Washington Post*, May 10, 2018, https://www .washingtonpost.com/graphics/2018/national/segregation-us-cities/.

29. "School Desegregation," Encyclopedia.com, October 3, 2020, https://www .encyclopedia.com/social-sciences-and-law/law/law/school-integration.

30. Sylvia Allegretto, Emma Garcia, and Elaine Weiss, "Public Education Funding in the U.S. Needs an Overhaul," Economic Policy Institute, July 12, 2022, https:// www.epi.org/publication/public-education-funding-in-the-us-needs-an-overhaul/.

31. Dan Keating and John Mintz, "Florida Black Ballots Affected Most in 2000," *Washington Post*, November 13, 2001, https://www.washingtonpost.com/archive /politics/2001/11/13/florida-black-ballots-affected-most-in-2000/16784e7d -439a-4b96-9653-1b7362312d2a/.

32. Hanes Walton Jr., "The Disenfranchisement of the African American Voter in the 2000 Presidential Election: The Silence of the Winner and Loser," *Black Scholar*, Summer 2001, https://www.jstor.org/stable/41068932.

33. Ari Berman, "Florida GOP Takes Voter Suppression to a Brazen New Extreme," *Rolling Stone*, May 30, 2021, https://www.rollingstone.com/politics/politics-news /florida-gop-takes-voter-suppression-to-a-brazen-new-extreme-184830/.

34. Wendy W. Simmons, "Black Americans Feel 'Cheated' by Election 2000," Gallup, December 20, 2000, https://news.gallup.com/poll/2188/black-americans-feel -cheated-election-2000.aspx.

35. "George W. Bush, the NAACP, and the Persistent Damage to Black Higher Edu- cation," *Journal of Blacks in Higher Education*, https://www.jbhe.com /features/51_specialreport.html.

36. "Text: George W. Bush's Speech to the NAACP," *Washington Post*, July 10, 2000, https://www.washingtonpost.com/wp-srv/onpolitics/elections/bushtext071000.htm.

37. "George W. Bush."

38. "Redefining Rights in America: The Civil Rights Record of the George W. Bush Administration, 2001–2004," U.S. Commission on Civil Rights Office of Civil Rights Evaluation, September 2004, available at Yumpu.com, https://www .yumpu.com/en/document/read/48622227/the-civil-rights-record-of-the -george-w-bush-administration.

39. "Reaction to 9/11," History.com, September 6, 2019, https://www.history.com /topics/21st-century/reaction-to-9-11#section_6.

40. Michael J. Klarman, *Unfinished Business: Racial Equality in American History* (Oxford: Oxford University Press, 2007), 184–85.

41. Klarman, 184–85.

42. Kenneth T. Walsh, "The Undoing of George W. Bush," *U.S. News & World Report*, August 28, 2015, https://www.usnews.com/news/the-report/articles/2015 /08/28/hurricane-katrina-was-the-beginning-of-the-end-for-george-w-bush.

43. Karen DeYoung, "Falling on His Sword: Colin Powell's Most Significant Moment Turned Out to Be His Lowest," *Washington Post*, September 30, 2006, https://www.washingtonpost.com/archive/lifestyle/magazine/2006/10/01 /falling-on-his-sword-span-classbankheadcolin-powells-most-significant

-moment-turned-out-to-be-his-lowestspan/0574eff4-0137-4c0a-8e6b-f8bf75
    75f389/.

44. Juan Williams, "True Black Power—Colin Powell," *Washington Post*, January 15,
    1989, https://www.washingtonpost.com/archive/opinions/1989/01/15/true
    -black-power-colin-powell/07061cff-ecc8-48e1-967e-7fc6316020a9/.

45. DeYoung, "Falling on His Sword."

46. DeYoung, "Falling on His Sword."

47. Henry Louis Gates Jr., "Powell and the Black Elite," *New Yorker*, September 25,
    1995, 65.

48. Caitlin Oprysko, "George W. Bush Laments 'Shocking Failure' in the Treatment
    of Black Americans," Politico, June 2, 2020, https://www.politico.com/news
    /2020/06/02/george-w-bush-protest-297133.

49. Reynolds, *American Legacy*, 26.

50. Klarman, *Unfinished Business*, 184.

51. Budiman, "Key Facts."

52. Chuck Todd, *The Stranger: Barack Obama in the White House* (New York: Little,
    Brown and Company, 2014), 16.

53. Jason Rodrigues, "The Obama Years: Timeline of a Presidency," *Guardian*,
    January 4, 2017, https://www.theguardian.com/us-news/2017/jan/03/the
    -obama-years-timeline-of-a-presidency.

54. Rashawn Ray and Keon L. Gilbert, "Has Trump Failed Black Americans?,"
    Brookings, October 15, 2020, https://www.brookings.edu/blog/how-we-rise
    /2020/10/15/has-trump-failed-black-americans/.

55. Ta-Nehisi Coates, "My President Was Black: A History of the First African
    American White House—and of What Came Next," *Atlantic*, January
    /February 2017, https://www.theatlantic.com/magazine/archive/2017/01
    /my-president-was-black/508793/.

56. Stephanie Stamm and Scott Clement, "How the First Black President Reshaped
    the Voting Public," *Washington Post*, April 22, 2016, https://www.washingtonpost
    .com/graphics/national/obama-legacy/2008-2012-election-voter-turnout.html.

57. "Rep. Wilson Shouts, 'You Lie!' to Obama during Speech," CNN, November 13,
    2013, https://www.cnn.com/2009/POLITICS/09/09/joe.wilson/.

58. Charles M. Blow, "Disrespect, Race, and Obama," *New York Times*, November 15,
    2013, https://www.nytimes.com/2013/11/16/opinion/blow-disrespect
    -race-and-obama.html.

59. Michael Eric Dyson, "The Ghost of Cornel West: What Happened to America's
    Most Exciting Black Scholar?," *New Republic*, April 19, 2015, https://new
    republic.com/article/121550/cornel-wests-rise-fall-our-most-exciting-black
    -scholar-ghost.

60. LZ Granderson, "What's Motivating Some of Obama's Black Critics?," CNN,
    July 26, 2013, https://www.cnn.com/2013/07/23/opinion/granderson-tavis
    -smiley/index.html.

61. Keeanga-Yamahtta Taylor, "Barack Obama's Original Sin: America's Post-Racial
    Illusion," *Guardian*, January 13, 2017, https://www.theguardian.com/us
    -news/2017/jan/13/barack-obama-legacy-racism-criminal-justice-system.

62. Coates, "My President Was Black."

63. Frank Newport, "Blacks' Approval of President Obama Remains High," Gallup,
    December 15, 2014, https://news.gallup.com/poll/180176/blacks-approval
    -president-obama-remains-high.aspx.

64. Stamm and Clement, "How the First Black President."

65. "Leave the US, Trump Tells Democratic Congresswomen of Color," *Sentinel*, July 14, 2019, https://sentinelcolorado.com/orecent-headlines/leave-the-us -trump-tells-democratic-congresswomen-of-color/.

66. Brooke Auxier, "Social Media Continue to Be Important Political Outlets for Black Americans," Pew Research Center, December 11, 2020, https://www .pewresearch.org/fact-tank/2020/12/11/social-media-continue-to-be-important -political-outlets-for-black-americans/.

67. Andrew Perrin, "23% of Users in U.S. Say Social Media Led Them to Change Views on an Issues; Some Cite Black Lives Matter," Pew Research Center, October 15, 2020, https://www.pewresearch.org/fact-tank/2020/10/15/23-of-users-in-us -say-social-media-led-them-to-change-views-on-issue-some-cite-black-lives-matter/.

68. John Eligon, Audra D. S. Burch, Dionne Searcey, and Richard A. Oppel Jr., "Black Americans Face Alarming Rates of Coronavirus Infection in Some States," *New York Times*, April 7, 2020, https://www.nytimes.com/2020/04/07 /us/coronavirus-race.html.

69. Tamir, "The Growing Diversity."

70. Rakesh Kochhar, "Unemployment Rose Higher in Three Months of COVID-19 Than It Did in Two Years of the Great Recession," Pew Research Center, June 11, 2020, https://www.pewresearch.org/fact-tank/2020/06/11/unemployment-rose -higher-in-three-months-of-covid-19-than-it-did-in-two-years-of-the-great-recession/.

71. Khadijah Edwards and Mark Hugo Lopez, "Black Americans Say Coronavirus Has Hit Hard Financially, but Impact Varies by Educational Level, Age," Pew Research Center, May 12, 2021, https://www.pewresearch.org/fact-tank/2021 /05/12/black-americans-say-coronavirus-has-hit-hard-financially-but-impact -varies-by-education-level-age/.

72. Heather Long and Andrew Van Dam, "The Black-White Economic Divide Is as Wide as It Was in 1968," *Washington Post*, June 4, 2020, https://www.washington post.com/business/2020/06/04/economic-divide-black-households/.

73. Tracy Jan, "A New Gentrification Crisis," *Washington Post*, July 31, 2020, https:// www.washingtonpost.com/business/2020/07/31/ethnic-enclaves-gentrification -coronavirus/.

74. Adrian Florida, "Black, Latino Two-Parent Families Have Half the Wealth of White Single Parents," NPR: Code Switch, February 8, 2017, https://www.npr .org/sections/codeswitch/2017/02/08/514105689/black-latino-two-parent -families-have-half-the-wealth-of-white-single-parents.

75. Long and Van Dam, "The Black-White Economic Divide."

76. Tracy Jan, "1 in 7 White Families Are Now Millionaires. For Black Families, It's 1 in 50," *Washington Post*, October 3, 2017, https://www.washingtonpost.com /news/wonk/wp/2017/10/03/white-families-are-twice-as-likely-to-be -millionaires-as-a-generation-ago/.

77. Florida, "Black, Latino Two-Parent Families."

78. Long and Van Dam, "The Black-White Economic Divide."

79. Michelle Singletary, "Systemic Racism, Not $200 Air Jordans, Suppress Black Wealth," *Washington Post*, November 6, 2020, https://www.washingtonpost.com /business/2020/11/06/black-net-worth-wealth-gap/.

80. Ray and Gilbert, "Has Trump Failed."

81. Ashraf Khalil, "HUD Revokes Obama-Era Rule Designed to Diversity the Sub-urbs," *Washington Post*, July 23, 2020, https://www.washingtonpost.com/politics /hud-revokes-obama-era-rule-designed-to-diversify-the-suburbs/2020/07/23 /b04bb6b2-cd18-11ea-99b0-8426e26d203b_story.html.

82. Valerie Strauss, "Why Republican Efforts to Ban the 1619 Project from Classrooms Are So Misguided," *Washington Post*, April 7, 2019, https://www.washingtonpost.com/education/2021/04/07/why-republican-efforts-to-ban-1619-project-classrooms-are-so-misguided/.

83. Meredith Conroy and Perry Bacon Jr., "The Partisan, Gender and Generational Differences among Black Voters Heading into Election Day," ABC News: FiveThirtyEight, September 23, 2020,https://fivethirtyeight.com/features/the-partisan-gender-and-generational-differences-among-black-voters-heading-into-election-day/.

84. Tamir, "The Growing Diversity."

85. Tiffany Dorris, "American's Black Gen Z: Proud, Driven, and Changing the Narrative," Paramount Insights, October 22, 2020, https://insights.viacomcbs.com/post/americas-black-gen-z-proud-driven-and-changing-the-narrative/.

86. Meredith Cash, "Simone Biles Opens Up about Competing in a Sport with Few Black Athletes: 'I Have Instilled Confidence in Little African Americans All Over the World,'" *Business Insider*, March 5, 2020, https://www.insider.com/simone-biles-on-black-gymnasts-and-inspiring-young-african-americans-2020-3.

87. Chloe Malle, "Yara Shahidi Has a Simple Goal: Empower a Generation of Activists," *Town & Country*, May 8, 2019, https://www.townandcountrymag.com/society/a27310620/yara-shahidi-activism-cover-interview/.

88. "Interview: Coco Jones Talks Independent Career, Leaving Disney & New Music," YouKnowIGotSoul.com, April 24, 2015, https://youknowigotsoul.com/interview-coco-jones-independent-career-leaving-disney-new-music.

89. Eric Gonzales, "Malia and Sasha Obama Give a Rare Interview in Netflix's Michelle Obama Documentary," *Harper's Bazaar*, May 4, 2020, https://www.harpersbazaar.com/culture/film-tv/a32369383/malia-sasha-obama-interview-becoming-documentary/.

90. Dorris, "American's Black Gen Z."

91. Craig and Williams, "A New Generation."

92. Mark Fainaru-Wada, "The Revival of Mahmoud Abdul-Rauf," ESPN, February 14, 2017, https://www.espn.com/espn/otl/story/_/id/18686629/before-colin-kaepernick-protested-national-anthem-nba-star-mahmoud-abdul-rauf-did-same-own-way.

93. Vongkiatkajorn et al., "Voices of Protest."

94. "Study: Black Millennials, Gen-Zers Believe in the American Dream," *Louisiana Weekly*, October 26, 2020, http://www.louisianaweekly.com/study-black-millennials-gen-zers-believe-in-the-american-dream/.

95. Conroy and Bacon, "The Partisan, Gender and Generational Differences."

96. Richard Fry, Jeffrey S. Passel, and D'Vera Cohn, "A Majority of Young Adults in the U.S. Live with Their Parents for the First Time since the Great Depression," Pew Research Center, September 4, 2020, https://www.pewresearch.org/short-reads/2020/09/04/a-majority-of-young-adults-in-the-u-s-live-with-their-parents-for-the-first-time-since-the-great-depression/.

97. Rheeda Walker, "Black Kids and Suicide: Why Are Rates So High, and So Ignored?," *The Conversation*, January 17, 2020, https://theconversation.com/black-kids-and-suicide-why-are-rates-so-high-and-so-ignored-127066.

98. *A Day in the Life of America*, directed by Jared Leto, PBS, January 11, 2021, https://www.pbs.org/independentlens/documentaries/a-day-in-the-life-of-america/.

99. Tiffany Dorris, "America's Black Gen Z."

100. Dorris, "American's Black Gen Z."

101. Kate Shelnutt, "Black Millennials and Gen Z Becoming More Cynical toward Christian Identity," *Christianity Today*, April 15, 2021, https://www.christianity today.com/news/2021/april/black-gen-z-millennial-christian-church-trends -barna.html.
102. Dorris, "American's Black Gen Z."
103. Shelnutt, "Black Millennials."
104. "Juneteenth Is the New Federal Holiday," Associated Press, *Frederick News-Post*, June 18, 2021.

Selected Bibliography

Allen, Reniqua. *It Was All a Dream: A New Generation Confronts the Broken Promise to Black America*. New York: Nation Books, 2019.

Alexander, Michelle. *The New Jim Crow: Mass Incarceration in the Age of Colorblindness*. New York: New Press, 2012.

Asante, M. K., Jr. *It's Bigger Than Hip Hop*. New York: St. Martin's Griffin, 2008.

Ashe, Arthur, and Arnold Rampersad. *Days of Grace: A Memoir*. New York: Alfred A. Knopf, 1993.

Bennett, Lerone, Jr. *Before the Mayflower: A History of Black America*. New York: Penguin Books, 1982.

Black, Kerrigan. "Afro-American Personal Naming Traditions." *Names: A Journal of Onomastics* 44, no. 2 (1996).

Brown, Teresa L. Fry. *Can a Sistah Get a Little Help? Encouragement for Black Women in Ministry*. Cleveland: Pilgrim Press, 2008.

Cone, James. *Malcolm and Martin and America: A Dream or a Nightmare*. Maryknoll, NY: Orbis Books, 1991.

Cose, Ellis. *The End of Anger*. New York: HarperCollins, 2011.

Delany, Sarah L., and A. Elizabeth Delany with Amy Hill Hearth. *Having Our Say: The Delany Sisters' First 100 Years*. New York: Dell Books, 1994.

Driskell, David, David Levering Lewis, and Deborah Willis Ryan. *Harlem Renaissance: Art of Black America*. New York: Harry N. Abrams, 1987.

Dunning, Jennifer. *Alvin Ailey: A Life in Dance*. Reading, MA: Addison-Wesley Publishing Company, Inc., 1996.

Ebony: Pictorial History of Black America, Volume III: Civil Rights Movement to Black Revolution. Nashville: The Southwestern Company, 1971.

Franklin, John Hope. *From Slavery to Freedom: A History of Negro Americans*. New York: Vintage Books, 1969.

Frey, William. *Diversity Explosion: How New Racial Demographics Are Remaking America*. Washington, DC: The Brookings Institution, 2018.

George, Nelson. *Buppies, B-Boys, Baps, and Bohos: Notes on Post-Soul Black Culture*. Cambridge, MA: Da Capo Press, 1992.

Haizlip, Shirlee Taylor. *The Sweeter the Juice: A Family Memoir in Black and White*. New York: Simon & Schuster, 1994.

Hakim, Joy. *An Age of Extremes*. Oxford: Oxford University Press, 1994.

Hannah-Jones, Nickole. *The 1619 Project*. New York: One World, 2021.

Harley, Sharon. *The Timetables of African-American History*. New York: One World, 1995.

Hitsville: The Making of Motown. Directed by Ben and Gabe Turner. Los Angeles: Capitol Music Group, 2019.

Hobbs, Allyson. *A Chosen Exile: A History of Racial Passing in American Life*. Cambridge, MA: Harvard University Press, 2014.

Iton, Richard. *In Search of the Black Fantastic: Politics and Popular Culture in the Post-Civil Rights Era*. Oxford: Oxford University Press, 2010.

Keeling, Ida, with Anita Diggs. *Can't Nothing Bring Me Down: Chasing Myself in the Race against Time*. Grand Rapids: Zondervan, 2018.

Kendi, Ibram X., ed. *Four Hundred Souls: A Community History of African America, 1619–2019*. New York: One World, 2021.

Kitwana, Bakari. *The Hip-Hop Generation: Young Blacks and the Crisis in African-American Culture*. New York: Civitas Books, 2002.

Klarman, Michael J. *Unfinished Business: Racial Equality in American History*. Oxford: Oxford University Press, 2007.

Levingston, Steven. *Kennedy and King: The President, The Pastor, and the Battle over Civil Rights*. New York: Hachette Books, 2017.

Lincoln, C. Eric, and Lawrence H. Mamiya. *The Black Church in the African American Experience*. Durham, NC: Duke University Press, 1990.

Locke, Alain. *Voices of the Harlem Renaissance*, originally published as *The New Negro: An Interpretation*. Old Saybrook, CT: Konecky & Konecky, 2019.

McPherson, James M. *"To the Best of My Ability": The American Presidents*. New York: Dorling Kindersley, 2000.

McQuirter, Keith, dir. *By Any Means Necessary: The Times of the Godfather of Harlem*. Season 1, episode 1, "Mecca." Aired November 2020 on Epix.

Meier, August, and Elliott Rudwick. *From Plantation to Ghetto*. New York: Hill and Wang, 1976.

Miller, Nathan. *Star-Spangled Men: America's Ten Worst Presidents*. New York: Touchstone Book, 1998.

Morris, Edmund. *Theodore Rex*. New York: Modern Library Paperbacks, 2002.

Nichols, David A. *A Matter of Justice: Eisenhower and the Beginning of the Civil Rights Revolution*. New York: Simon & Schuster, 2007.

Penrice, Ronda Racha. *African American History for Dummies*. Hoboken, NJ: Wiley Publishing, 2007.

Pietrusza, David. *1920: The Year of the Six Presidents*. New York: Carroll & Graf Publishers, 2007.

Quarles, Benjamin. *The Negro in the Making of America*. New York: A Touchstone Book, 1969.

Robertson, David. *Denmark Vesey: The Buried Story of America's Largest Slave Rebellion and the Man Who Led It*. New York: Vintage Books, 1999.

Robnelt, Belinda. *How Long? How Long? African-American Women in the Struggle for Civil Rights*. New York: Oxford University Press, 2000.

Sernett, Milton C. *Afro-American Religious History: A Documentary Witness*. Durham, NC: Duke University Press, 1985.

Shogan, Robert. *Harry Truman and the Struggle for Racial Justice*. Lawrence: University Press of Kansas, 2013.

Smith, Marcia A. *Black America: A Photographic Journey*. New York: Fall River Press, 2009.

Talbert, Clifton L. *When We Were Colored*. New York: Penguin Books, 1989.

Terkel, Studs. *Race: How Blacks & Whites Think & Feel about the American Obsession*. New York: The New Press, 1992.

Thurston, Baratunde. *How to Be Black*. New York: HarperCollins, 2013.

Time-Life Books, eds. *African American Voices of Triumph: Perseverance*. New York: Time-Life Custom Publishing, 1993.

Tisby, Jemar. *The Color of Compromise: The Truth about the American Church's Complicity in Racism*. Grand Rapids: Zondervan, 2019.

Tolbert-Rouchaleau, James. *James Weldon Johnson*. New York: Chelsea House Publishers, 1988.

Wickham, DeWayne. *Bill Clinton and Black America*. New York: Ballantine Books, 2002.

Wilkerson, Isabel. *Caste: The Origins of Our Discontents*. New York: Random House, 2020.

———. *The Warmth of Other Suns: The Epic Story of America's Great Migration*. New York: Vintage Books, 2010.

Williams, Juan. *Thurgood Marshall: American Revolutionary*. New York: Random House Times Books, 1998.

Wilmore, Gayraud S. *Black Religion and Black Radicalism: An Interpretation of the Religious History of African Americans*. Maryknoll, NY: Orbis Books, 1998.

Wilson, Charles Reagan, and William Ferris, eds. *Encyclopedia of Southern Culture: Volume 1*. Chapel Hill: University of North Carolina Press, 1989.

Woodson, Carter G. *The Mis-Education of the Negro*. Washington, DC: The Associated Publishers, 1933.

Index